JOURNAL · OF M·O·R·A·L THEOLOGY

VOLUME 13, SPECIAL ISSUE 1
APRIL 2024

CATHOLICISM,
CHALLENGES TO DEMOCRACY,
AND THE
LEGACY *OF*
JACQUES MARITAIN

EDITED BY
LAURIE JOHNSTON
AND
GRÉGOIRE CATTA

JOURNAL · OF
M · O · R · A · L
THEOLOGY

Journal of Moral Theology is published semiannually, with regular issues in January and July. Our mission is to publish scholarly articles in the field of Catholic moral theology, as well as theological treatments of related topics in philosophy, economics, political philosophy, and psychology.

Articles published in the *Journal of Moral Theology* undergo at least two double blind peer reviews. To submit an article for the journal, please visit the "For Authors" page on our website at jmt.scholasticahq.com/for-authors.

Journal of Moral Theology is available full text in the *ATLA Religion Database with ATLASerials®* (RDB®), a product of the American Theological Library Association.
Email: atla@atla.com, www.atla.com.
ISSN 2166-2851 (print)
ISSN 2166-2118 (online)

Journal of Moral Theology is published by The Journal of Moral Theology, Inc.

Copyright © 2024 individual authors.

Pickwick Publications, An Imprint of Wipf and Stock Publishers, 199 W. 8th Ave., Suite 3, Eugene, OR 97401
www.wipfandstock.com. ISBN: 979-8-3852-3572-8

JOURNAL · OF
M · O · R · A · L
THEOLOGY

EDITOR EMERITUS
Jason King, *St. Mary's University, San Antonio, TX*

EDITOR
M. Therese Lysaught, *Loyola University Chicago Stritch School of Medicine*

SENIOR EDITOR
William J. Collinge, *Mount St. Mary's University*

ASSOCIATE EDITORS
Mari Rapela Heidt, *Notre Dame of Maryland University*
Alexandre A. Martins, *Marquette University*
Christopher McMahon, *Saint Vincent College*
Kate Ward, *Marquette University*

MANAGING EDITOR
Jean-Pierre Fortin, *St. Michael's College, University of Toronto*

EDITORIAL ASSISTANT
Aaron Weisel, *Ave Maria University*

EDITORIAL BOARD

Christina Astorga, *University of Portland*
Jana M. Bennett, *University of Dayton*
Mara Brecht, *Loyola University Chicago*
Jim Caccamo, *St. Joseph's University*
Carolyn A. Chau, *King's University College at Western University, Ontario, Canada*
Meghan Clark, *St. John's University*
David Cloutier, *The Catholic University of America*
Christopher Denny, *St. John's University*
Julia Fleming, *Creighton University*
Joseph Flipper, *University of Dayton*
Nichole M. Flores, *University of Virginia*
Craig Ford, *St. Norbert College*
Matthew J. Gaudet, *Santa Clara University*
Natalia Imperatori-Lee, *Manhattan College*
Kelly Johnson, *University of Dayton*
Andrew Kim, *Marquette University*
Warren Kinghorn, *Duke University*
Leocadie Lushombo, *Santa Clara University*
Ramon Luzarraga, *St. Martin's University*
William C. Mattison III, *University of Notre Dame*
Christina McRorie, *Creighton University*
Cory D. Mitchell, *PeaceHealth*
Suzane Mulligan, *Catholic Theological Ethics in the World Church Liaison, St. Patrick's Pontifical University, Maynooth, Ireland*
Anna Perkins, *University of the West Indies*
Matthew Shadle, *Window Light*
Joel Shuman, *King's College*
Christopher P. Vogt, *St. John's College*
Paul Wadell, *St. Norbert College*

JOURNAL OF MORAL THEOLOGY
VOLUME 13, SPECIAL ISSUE 1
APRIL 2024

CONTENTS

Introduction: Jacques Maritain and Contemporary Challenges to Democracy
   Laurie Johnston 1

Threading the Needle: Jacques Maritain's Defense of a Christian and Liberal Democracy
   Mary Doak 14

Jacques Maritain, "Pure" Nature, and the State's Teleological Crisis
   Gilbrian Stoy, CSC 37

Distinct But Not Separate: Rethinking Maritain's Distinction of Planes to Recover His Democratic Potential
   Travis Knoll 59

Rescuing Maritain from His Reception History: A Reappraisal of William T. Cavanaugh's Critique in *Torture and Eucharist*
   Brian J. A. Boyd 86

Revisiting Maritain in the Present Context—A Response to Gilbrian Stoy, Travis Knoll, and Brian Boyd
   William T. Cavanaugh 106

Partners in Forming the People: Jacques Maritain, Saul Alinsky, and the Project of Personalist Democracy
   Nicholas Hayes-Mota 121

Community Organizing for Democratic Renewal: The Significance of Jacques Maritain's Support for Saul Alinsky and His Methods
   Brian Stiltner 146

A Common World is Possible: Maritain, Pope Francis, and the
   Future of Global Governance
      Kevin Ahern 169

Catholic Social Teaching: Toward a Decolonial Praxis
      Alex Mikulich 194

Afterword
      John T. McGreevy 220

Introduction: Jacques Maritain and Contemporary Challenges to Democracy

Laurie Johnston

Abstract: Introducing the collection of articles regarding Jacques Maritain and his relevance for challenges to democracy today, this article describes the complexity and some of the main themes of his intellectual journey. Maritain played a major role in the development of Catholic social teaching on democracy, and can provide moral and spiritual grounding for a renewal of democracy now. He articulates the moral value of democracy as the form of politics that best allows Christians to live out love of neighbor and enemy in concrete ways, while still making an appropriate distinction between the spiritual and temporal spheres. Articles in this volume examine the implications of the friendship between Maritain and Saul Alinsky, William Cavanaugh's interpretation of Maritain's influence (with a response from Cavanaugh himself), and reflections upon how we can critically appropriate the thought of Maritain in the contemporary context, fifty years after his death. The introduction concludes with words Maritain addressed to US Catholics in 1939.

We cannot avoid noting with concern how today, and not only in Europe, we are witnessing a retreat from democracy. Democracy requires participation and involvement on the part of all; consequently, it demands hard work and patience. It is complex, whereas authoritarianism is peremptory and populism's easy answers appear attractive. In some societies, concerned for security and dulled by consumerism, weariness and malcontent can lead to a sort of skepticism about democracy. Yet universal participation is something essential; not simply to attain shared goals, but also because it corresponds to what we are: social beings, at once unique and interdependent.

At the same time, we are also witnessing a skepticism about democracy provoked by the distance of institutions, by fear of a loss of identity, by bureaucracy. The remedy is not to be found in an obsessive quest for popularity, in a thirst for visibility, in a flurry of unrealistic promises, or in adherence to forms of ideological colonization, but in good politics. For politics is, and ought to be in

practice, a good thing, as the supreme responsibility of citizens and as the art of the common good.
—Pope Francis, Presidential Palace Address, Athens, December 4, 2021[1]

It is easy to hear echoes of Jacques Maritain in this plaintive defense of democracy by Pope Francis, especially in the assertion that democratic participation befits humans as "social beings, at once unique and interdependent." Perhaps more than any other thinker, Maritain is responsible for the Catholic Church's remarkable journey in the twentieth century from deep hostility to strong endorsement of democracy and human rights.[2] In his books *Integral Humanism* (1936), *The Natural Law and Human Rights* (1942), *The Person and the Common Good* (1947), and *Man and the State* (1951), Maritain presented a democratic vision rooted in Thomism and personalism.[3] Together with other "fraternal modernists," as James Chappel has called them, Maritain laid a foundation for Christian democratic movements and political parties in many countries.[4] Charting a path between fascism, communism, capitalism, and the extremes of the Enlightenment and French republicanism, Maritain developed a thoroughly Catholic and pluralist vision of society with a limited government and a body politic constituted by many groupings, from the family to religious communities to "a multiplicity of other particular societies which proceed from the free initiative of citizens."[5] Along the way, he "made himself the premier interpreter of human rights among Catholics, and indeed almost singlehandedly reinvented

---

[1] Pope Francis, "Meeting with Authorities, Civil Society, and the Diplomatic Corps," December 4, 2021, www.vatican.va/content/francesco/en/speeches/2021/december/documents/20211204-grecia-autorita.html.
[2] John McGreevy (who has kindly authored the afterword for this issue) has helpfully described this journey in Chapter 3 of *Catholicism: A Global History from the French Revolution to Pope Francis* (New York: W. W. Norton, 2022).
[3] Jacques Maritain, *Humanisme intégral: Problèmes temporels et spirituels d'une nouvelle chrétienté* (Paris: Aubier, 1936), later published as *Integral Humanism: Temporal and Spiritual Problems of a New Christendom*, trans. Joseph Evans (South Bend, IN: University of Notre Dame Press, 1973); *The Natural Law and Human Rights* (Windsor: Christian Culture, 1942); *The Person and the Common Good* (New York: Charles Scribner's Sons, 1947); *Man and the State* (Chicago: The University of Chicago Press, 1951).
[4] James Chappell, *Catholic Modern* (Cambridge, MA: Harvard University Press, 2018).
[5] Maritain, *Man and the State*, 11.

them as a Christian tradition."⁶ Paul Valadier describes Maritain's subject matter as "Gospel inspiration of politics."⁷

Fifty years after Maritain's death, the themes he addressed continue to spark lively debate as Christians attempt to understand the relationship between their faith and political life. It is likely that Maritain would share many of Pope Francis's concerns about the challenges to democracy around the world today, as articulated in the speech above; Maritain might even note similarities with some of the worrying trends he observed in the 1930s. Economic inequality is undermining the social cohesion and solidarity required to sustain democratic governance. Populism, nationalism, and authoritarianism are on the rise, often accompanied by disregard for the human rights of minority groups and migrants. Political propaganda, social media, and viral disinformation contribute to splintering and polarization in societies, and political leaders attack the press, even in traditionally democratic countries. Authoritarian governments attempt to exert totalitarian control over the civic space. Civil society is also threatened by the overwhelming power of multinational corporations, especially through the colonization of public discourse by tech companies accountable to no one. The coronavirus pandemic provoked deep controversies over how to balance coercive public health measures with individual liberties. And whether contemporary democracies are even capable of responding effectively to the climate emergency remains to be seen. Meanwhile, support for democracy has declined to a striking degree among young people globally, as Yascha Mounk and others have documented.⁸ On an international level, there remains a "democratic deficit" in international institutions such as the UN, WTO, and World Bank. At the same time, growing empirical evidence would seem to justify Maritain's belief that human dignity is best served by democratic forms of government; from the work of Amartya Sen on famines⁹ to more recent work on the correlation between democracy and improved health,¹⁰ the benefits to human life and the common good can clearly be observed.

---

⁶ Samuel Moyn, "Personalism, Community, and the Origins of Human Rights," in *Human Rights in the Twentieth Century*, ed. Stefan-Ludwig Hoffmann (Cambridge: Cambridge University Press, 2011) 85–106.

⁷ Paul Valadier, *Maritain à contre-temps. Pour une démocratie vivante* (Paris: Desclée de Brouwer, 2007), 10. "A son sujet, nous pouvons utiliser l'expression provocatrice d'une 'inspiration évangélique du politique.'"

⁸ Roberto Stefan Foa and Yascha Mounk, "The Democratic Disconnect," *Journal of Democracy* 27, no. 3 (July 2016): 5–17, doi.org/10.1353/jod.2016.0049.

⁹ Amartya Sen, *Poverty and Famines: An Essay on Entitlement and Deprivation* (Oxford: Oxford University Press, 1981).

¹⁰ See, for example, Thomas J. Bollyky, Tara Templin, Matthew Cohen, Diana Schoder, Joseph L. Dieleman, and Simon Wigley, "The Relationships between

Why might Maritain be helpful now? The authors in this journal issue suggest a range of reasons. Among the most important is that Maritain has described the moral and spiritual grounding of democracy. He articulates the moral value of democracy as the form of politics that best allows Christians to live out love of neighbor and enemy in concrete ways. Because it requires making space for those with whom we disagree and limits our ability to coerce others, democratic politics preserves space for human dignity to flourish in community. Furthermore, the limited form of government Maritain envisions permits the flourishing of civic life by means of both subsidiarity and solidarity.

Mary Doak's article in this volume gives a helpful analysis of Maritain's relevance for contemporary debates about democracy. Doak responds to the surprising re-emergence of integralism, a stream of thought which argues that to promote the common good, a government must affirm a particular (religious) vision of the good, and therefore Christianity should be established as state religion (despite the fact that the Second Vatican Council taught otherwise in *Dignitatis Humanae*). If Catholics truly believe that what their church teaches is true (this line of thinking goes), they have a responsibility to ensure that temporal authorities are subject to spiritual authorities, since the spiritual is superior to the temporal. Contra the integralists, Doak affirms that Maritain offers "an intellectually coherent and thoroughly Catholic defense of the substantive good achievable through liberal democracy."[11] Maritain's contention was precisely that the truth about God and humans leads him to conclude that Catholics have a *religious* duty to promote democracy and religious liberty; that is how, *concretely*, they fulfill their obligation to obey the natural law and promote the common good of all. As Paul Valadier puts it when writing about Maritain's support for the UN Universal Declaration on Human Rights:

> The necessity of living together obliges us not to compromise on the truth (as some intransigent Thomists accused [Maritain]), but to admit, perhaps in a spirit of restraint when it comes to deeper ideas, that the good of humanity and peace depend on a shared agreement about concrete issues where the fate of everyone is at stake. It is therefore the truth that leads us to accept the merits of this common platform [of the UDHR] as a source of peace and harmony, but a truth

---

Democratic Experience, Adult Health, and Cause-Specific Mortality in 170 Countries between 1980 and 2016: An Observational Analysis," *The Lancet* 393, no. 10181 (April 20, 2019): 1628–1640, doi.org/10.1016/S0140-6736(19)30235-1.

[11] See Mary Doak, "Threading the Needle: Jacques Maritain's Defense of a Christian and Liberal Democracy," *Journal of Moral Theology* 13, special issue 1 (2024): 18.

that does not look down on, let alone scorn, the exigencies of our common life together as individuals and peoples.[12]

This "necessity of living together" requires more than mere agreement about concrete issues, though; Doak notes that Maritain saw *civic friendship* as vital for the healthy functioning of democracy, something urgently needed in this era of political polarization.

Doak's chapter is a reminder that in the face of temptations towards authoritarianism, integralism, or Christian nationalism, it is important to affirm democracy not just as a useful technique, but as something with real moral value. To be sure, democratic governments in the US and elsewhere have often failed to deliver on their promises in many ways, at great cost to the human dignity of their own citizens as well as the dignity of citizens of other countries. But the solution is more, not less, democracy. Anything in human life that consumes more than its fair share of power is both an affront to the sovereignty of God and a threat to the common good. As Maritain wrote in *Christianity and Democracy*, "How could the people be expected to obey those who govern unless it is because the latter have received from the people themselves the custody of the people's common good?"[13]

While Doak's retrieval of Maritain is timely and helpful, applying Maritain's ideas to today's challenges remains a complex task. For example, Maritain's language about creating a "New Christendom," with Christians as a vivifying (as opposed to ruling) force, sounds strange in a Euro-American context perhaps better described as post-Christian than post-Christendom. It is not unusual to find that the politicians who make the most explicit appeals to Christianity in public life are in fact the ones who are the least Christian. But the issue of Maritain's terminology is only a small part of the problem.

Drawing on Maritain's thought is complex because his intellectual journey was complex, taking him from the far-right Action Française in the 1920s to the left in the 1930s, to an eventual skepticism of all totalizing systems. His geographical journey was also complex, shaped by frequent international travel, then exile in the US with his

---

[12] Paul Valadier, *Maritain à contre-temps*, 31: "La nécessité d'une vie commune oblige non pas à transiger sur la vérité (comme le lui reprocheront des thomistes intransigeants), mais à admettre, peut-être dans la détresse par rapport à des ententes plus profondes, que le bien de l'humanité et la paix passent par l'accord commun sur des bases concrètes où se joue le sort de tous. C'est donc la vérité encore qui conduit à admettre le bien-fondé de cette plate-forme commune, source de paix et d'harmonie, mais une vérité qui ne regarde pas de haut, encore moins avec mépris, les exigences de la vie commune entre personnes et peuples."

[13] Jacques Maritain, *Christianity and Democracy*, trans. Doris C. Anson (London: Geoffrey Bles, 1945), 34.

wife Raïssa, then time in Rome as French ambassador to the Holy See. He was deeply affected by the rise of totalitarianism in Europe, the brutality of World War II, and the ugliness of anti-Semitism, but also moved by the hopefulness of the American democratic experiment and (short-lived) emergence of democratic leadership in Chile and elsewhere. Along the way, he engaged with a remarkable number of interlocutors on multiple continents—corresponding with everyone from the popes, Charles de Gaulle, and Thomas Merton to Saul Alinsky—as discussed in the articles that follow here. The very range of his thought, though, means that his readers risk merely confirming their own biases if they fail to understand the entire corpus of his thought; thus, Maritain's blessing has been claimed by political thinkers of many stripes. The story of Maritain's thought, therefore, must also be told as the story of its reception and effects—which were immense and varied. While it would be unfair to hold a thinker responsible for every problematic appropriation of her ideas, on the other hand, one should not ignore the consequences; Maritain himself was certainly sensitive to the consequences of ideas, including his own.

Maritain's recent reception, especially in the US, has been significantly affected by a work written twenty-five years after his death: William Cavanaugh's *Torture and Eucharist*.[14] Three of the authors here take up Cavanaugh's interpretation of Maritain, particularly with regard to the impact of Maritain's thought in Chile. In each case, the authors address questions about how to understand the relationship between the spiritual and temporal, church and state, and Christian discipleship and secular political engagement. Maritain was concerned about how to preserve the integrity of the temporal, political sphere of life against undue encroachment by religious authority, while also maintaining the importance of Christian responsibility to promote the common good, including via politics. His theological task was to help the church come to terms with a new post-Christendom understanding of itself and its mission in the temporal sphere. In so doing, he emphasized the distinction between spiritual and temporal authority to a degree Cavanaugh has found to be problematic. At certain points during the Pinochet regime in Chile, Cavanaugh argues, this stark distinction helped prevent the church from sufficiently playing its role as a moral judge of political realities—notably the practice of torture. Such a "ghostly" vision of the church's mission grants the state free rein in temporal affairs, and the state soon makes an idol of itself—as all nation-states are prone to doing, in Cavanaugh's account. Gilbrian Stoy points out that ironically,

---

[14] William Cavanaugh, *Torture and Eucharist: Theology, Politics, and the Body of Christ* (Malden, MA: Blackwell, 1998).

such a sacralization and expansion of the state to consume the body politic is precisely what Maritain also feared.[15]

Still, Stoy agrees with Cavanaugh that Maritain's "temporal plane" is too starkly distinguished from the spiritual realm, and therefore this presents an eschatological difficulty. It is important to maintain the real—but relative—importance of the temporal sphere as something which has a share in the salvation to come (transformed, but not destroyed, by grace). Christians acting in the temporal sphere do so with an aim that is not merely temporal but also referred to God (which is why Maritain attempts to introduce the notion of a third plane, overlapping between the temporal and spiritual—an attempt Stoy sees as misguided). Stoy suggests that by emphasizing a Thomistic understanding of human nature as endowed with openness—real, but imperfect—to God, we can more rightly understand the relationship of the political realm to the spiritual.

Travis Knoll firmly defends Maritain's legacy against Cavanaugh's criticisms, offering, as a counterpoint, historical evidence from Maritain's time in Argentina and Brazil.[16] There, Knoll shows Maritain's influence to have led Catholic intellectuals *away* from nationalism and authoritarianism—though with limited effect in Argentina. His audiences there did not necessarily share his opposition to Franco in Spain, an opposition which, for Maritain, was *necessitated* by the proper separation of the temporal and spiritual planes. In Brazil, Maritain's influence was somewhat more fruitful, helping Catholic thinkers like Alceu Lima and Helder Camara to take strong positions in favor of democracy and against authoritarianism. These different trajectories provide important context for understanding the missed opportunities in Chile Cavanaugh describes.

While Knoll engages Cavanaugh's argument about Maritain primarily with a historical lens, and Stoy a strictly theological lens, Brian Boyd's article addresses Cavanaugh's arguments from a theological perspective particularly attentive to our contemporary context.[17] Boyd seeks to push back against some of the skepticism Maritain has faced from political theologians (partly because of Cavanaugh) because, as he puts it, "Maritain remains a vital resource for theologians who seek to avoid both, on the right hand, a resurgent integralism and Christian nationalism and, on the left hand, a

---

[15] See Gilbrian Stoy, CSC, "Jacques Maritain, 'Pure' Nature, and the State's Teleological Crisis," *Journal of Moral Theology* 13, special issue 1 (2024): 37–58.

[16] See Travis Knoll, "Distinct but not Separate: Rethinking Maritain's Distinction of Planes to Recover his Democratic Potential," *Journal of Moral Theology* 13, special issue 1 (2024): 59–85.

[17] See Brian Boyd, "Rescuing Maritain from his Reception History: A Reappraisal of William T. Cavanaugh's Critique in *Torture and Eucharist*," *Journal of Moral Theology* 13, special issue 1 (2024): 86–105.

relativizing of the Gospel in what Maritain called 'kneeling before the world.'"[18]

Boyd acknowledges that Maritain was (understandably) naïve about the nature of the modern nation-state, whose claims to sovereignty will always undermine subsidiarity and lead inevitably to idolatry—that is, self-aggrandizement beyond the temporal realm into the realm of the absolute. Boyd goes on to suggest, however, that Cavanaugh has underestimated the degree to which Maritain *did* envision a role for the church in shaping the temporal realm, and emphasized the transformative power of the virtue of charity for Christians' activities in the "earthly city." These activities might require Christians to dirty their hands; as Maritain writes, "The fear of soiling ourselves by entering the context of history is a Pharisaical fear. We cannot touch the flesh of the human being without staining our fingers. To stain our fingers is not to stain our hearts. The Catholic Church has never feared to lose its purity in touching our impurities."[19] However, this does not mean abandoning sanctity, nor that charity ceases to shape Christian engagement; Boyd compares this statement to Pope Francis's admonition that good pastors ought to "smell like the sheep."

This comparison is unconvincing to Cavanaugh, who has written a detailed and gracious reply to Boyd's article.[20] Cavanaugh points out that this passage follows directly after a section in which Maritain treats the tragic necessity of political violence for the cause of justice. Claiming that "dirty hands" are unavoidable is precisely the type of argument utilized by political actors who draw too stark a distinction between their Christian vocation and their political role. Cavanaugh is sensitive to the ways this logic has been used in situations like Chile under Pinochet in order to sideline Christian ethics as irrelevant; he wants instead to emphasize that the call to Christian charity is something that must be lived out in *all* spheres of life.

Cavanaugh acknowledges that there is much more to Maritain's approach and appreciates the nuances Boyd brings to the fore by drawing upon some of Maritain's later writings. Still, Cavanaugh remains hesitant about Maritain's usefulness as a resource for political theology today, given the very disparate ways in which his influence seems to have led. After describing some of the many directions various Christian Democratic parties have taken in subsequent decades, Cavanaugh concludes: "The variety of positions associated

---

[18] Boyd, "Rescuing Maritain from his Reception History," 86.
[19] Maritain, *Integral Humanism*, 249.
[20] See William T. Cavanaugh, "Revisiting Maritain in the Present Context—A Response to Gilbrian Stoy, Travis Knoll, and Brian Boyd," *Journal of Moral Theology* 13, special issue 1 (2024): 106–120.

with Maritain's followers indicates to me that the political relevance of the Gospel remains underspecified in Maritain's thought."[21]

Perhaps the political relevance of the Gospel is clearer if we read Maritain alongside his friend Saul Alinsky, the dean of community organizing, as two of the authors in this journal suggest. Nicholas Hayes-Mota writes that such a reading illuminates "the practical implications of Maritain's democratic philosophy, as well as its inherent radicalism."[22] For many years, Maritain was a close friend and correspondent with Alinsky, and deeply admired the work of his Industrial Areas Foundation. In a complementary article, Brian Stiltner describes the friendship between the two men as a moving testimony of affection and collaboration across differences.[23] Such friendships are "both the form of the common good and the path to it," Stiltner writes.[24] Maritain reviewed Alinsky's 1946 book *Reveille for Radicals* in glowing terms, and then also cited it directly in *Man and the State*.[25] He explained that the accomplishments of Alinsky's movement "open a new road to real democracy, and show us the only way in which that deep need for communion which today stirs up men threatened by technocratic civilization, can be satisfied in freedom and through freedom, in and through genuine respect for the human person, in and through actual and living trust in the people."[26]

Hayes-Mota explains that Maritain and Alinksy shared a commitment to what might be called "democratic personalism."[27] Stiltner describes what the two men had in common as a practice of "humane regard."[28] What Maritain saw in Alinsky's approach was a means of engagement in the temporal sphere deeply compatible with the Gospel, notwithstanding the fact that Alinsky was an atheist and a Jew. Maritain acknowledged the irony, writing to Alinksy:

> You—being a Jew (whom I consider a Christian at heart, a better Christian perhaps than I am) committed to the quest of justice on

---

[21] Cavanaugh, "Revisiting Maritain," 118.
[22] See Nicholas Hayes-Mota, "Partners in Forming the People: Jacques Maritain, Saul Alinsky, and the Project of Personalist Democracy," *Journal of Moral Theology* 13, special issue 1 (2024): 123.
[23] See Brian Stiltner, "Community Organizing for Democratic Renewal: The Significance of Jacques Maritain's Support for Saul Alinsky and His Methods," *Journal of Moral Theology* 13, special issue 1 (2024): 146–168.
[24] Stiltner, "Community Organizing for Democratic Renewal," 152.
[25] Saul D. Alinsky, *Reveille for Radicals* (Chicago: The University of Chicago Press, 1946).
[26] Maritain's review is reproduced in *The Philosopher and the Provocateur: The Correspondence of Jacques Maritain and Saul Alinsky*, ed. Bernard Doering (Notre Dame, IN: University of Notre Dame Press, 1994), 18–20.
[27] Hayes-Mota, "Partners in Forming the People," 221.
[28] Stiltner, "Community Organizing for Democratic Renewal," 152.

earth—are giving priority to the first of love's requirements, and offering your life for the temporal salvation and emancipation of mankind.... You act and fight also... for the recovery by man of his inner, moral dignity—that is to say, finally, even if you do not have such a purpose in your mind, for his spiritual redemption.[29]

Here we see Maritain gesturing towards the porosity of the division between two planes, the spiritual and temporal. He is describing a social and political movement as a form of both temporal salvation *and* spiritual redemption. Democratic organizing that begins from relationships among a people and sees their concrete concerns as the beginning of a quest for the common good *is*, in fact, Christian love at work in the world. It is both a moral vision and a practical project.

Stiltner points out that in his book *Rules for Radicals*, Alinsky used a quote from Maritain's *Man and the State*: "The fear of soiling ourselves by entering the context of history is not virtue, but a way of escaping virtue."[30] It is striking to note how similar this quote is to the controversial one above about "staining our fingers" that provoked the debate between Boyd and Cavanaugh about the possible use of political violence. Alinsky's use of this quote about "soiling" casts a slightly different light on that debate. Despite the accusations of his critics, Alinsky never advocated violence. It would be more accurate to say that he (and also Maritain) are referring instead to the use of power, force, or coercion when they describe "soiling" or "staining." Catholic social teaching has rarely discussed power in clear ways (including colonial power, as Alex Mikulich points out in his article here).[31] But without frank discussions about power, including the immense disparities of power that exist in the world today, there is little hope for democratic renewal. As Stiltner puts it, "Elites left to their own devices have little interest in practicing a politics of the common good. Community organizations carry the promise of forcing them to do so."[32] Both democracy and community organizing are based on the recognition that shared power is more *just* than power concentrated in the hands of a few. Stiltner concludes with a case study of an interfaith community organization in Connecticut whose recent political victories show that what Alinsky called "democratic faith" is not misplaced.

Even though Alinsky's approach to organizing is focused on local issues and begins from direct personal relationships, both he and

---

[29] Maritain to Alinsky, 5 November 1962, in Doering, *The Philosopher and the Provocateur*, 94.
[30] Alinsky, *Rules for Radicals: A Practical Primer for Realistic Radicals* (New York: Random House, 1971), 25–26; see Maritain, *Man and the State*, 63.
[31] See Alex Mikulich, "Catholic Social Teaching: Toward a Decolonial Praxis," *Journal of Moral Theology* 13, special issue 1 (2024): 194–219.
[32] Stiltner, "Community Organizing for Democratic Renewal," 148.

Maritain see implications for larger scale social and political change. Hayes-Mota points out that, when reviewing Alinksy's *Reveille for Radicals*, Maritain wrote that grassroots participatory democratic movements can awaken an awareness of the common good that becomes much larger in scope. In Maritain's words, "A small community, thus organized from within as a living whole, becomes definitely aware of its power of initiative and its common good, [and] naturally develops into concrete awareness of the common good of the nation and the common good of the international community."[33]

Promoting "the common good of the international community" is no small challenge, and Kevin Ahern's article takes up the problem of global governance today, asking what insights Maritain and Pope Francis offer. Acknowledging that Maritain's utopian vision of a world state has its limitations, Ahern nevertheless calls attention to Maritain's vision of a world political *society*. Maritain sees a pluralist and democratic global society as an important counterweight to Machiavellian notions of state sovereignty that, today, are ill-suited to dealing with our many transnational challenges. Pope Francis agrees, but emphasizes the need for organizing *from below* in order to counteract the many forces threatening the climate and vulnerable peoples (perhaps he too has read Alinsky). This is connected to an appeal for global siblinghood across the boundaries of the nation-state.

Finally, Alex Mikulich asks us to step back and consider the very nature of the conversation about Catholic social teaching in general, including Maritain's thought.[34] Drawing on Frantz Fanon among others, Mikulich argues that theology has been deeply malformed by the "colonial matrix of power," which means that a decolonial approach is an absolute necessity; there is little point in writing about justice, human rights, or the common good so long as a Eurocentric, white supremacist approach goes unacknowledged and uncorrected. Mikulich points to a critical review James Baldwin wrote of Maritain's *The Person and the Common Good* in which he complained that it is "unhelpful to be assured of future angels when mysteries of the present flesh are so far from being solved."[35] Maritain may in fact have agreed with Baldwin in many ways; he wrote in *True Humanism* that "It is vain to assert the dignity and vocation of human personality if we do not strive to transform the conditions that oppress man."[36] But while

---

[33] Doering, *The Philosopher and the Provocateur*, 19.
[34] Mikulich, "Catholic Social Teaching," 195.
[35] James Baldwin, "*The Person and the Common Good* by Jacques Maritain," in *The Cross of Redemption: Uncollected Writings,* ed. Randall Kenan (New York: Pantheon, 2010, originally published as "Present and Future," *New Leader*, March 13, 1948), 264–266, cited in Mikulich, "Catholic Social Teaching," 202.
[36] Jacques Maritain, *True Humanism* (New York: Scribner's, 1938), 87.

acknowledging the ways in which Maritain moved the church beyond a feudal paradigm, Mikulich is calling for a truly radical reckoning with the paradigms that continue to shape Catholic social teaching. We must, he says, "shift from applying abstract universals and philosophical idealism to the priority of geopolitical praxis with and for *les damnés*," and "shift from anthropocentrism to a primary focus on land and earth democracy."[37] Indeed, Catholic social teaching today must move beyond Maritain's integral humanism or Christian personalism and find its way towards integral *ecology*.

This year marks an election year in the United States, so it is appropriate to conclude this introduction with some of Maritain's words to Americans in particular. During his time in the US, Maritain found much to admire in American democracy; what he observed in the United States helped shape his influence on the Catholic Church as a whole. He was also a friendly critic, never failing to challenge as well. In 1939, the editors of *Commonweal* published an interview with Maritain, which included the following interchange:

> **CW:** What do you think of the position of Catholics in the United States?
> **JM:** I think that much is expected of Catholics in America and that at the moment they have an incomparable opportunity to serve the common good. May it please God that they do not miss this opportunity!
> **CW:** Perhaps you could be a little more precise on this subject?
> **JM:** One always wishes many good things for those whom one loves. I should prefer that you make your own self-criticisms. From my conversations I gather the impression that the hopes of many Catholics among you are principally concerned, it seems, with the following: to intensify the intellectual, metaphysical, and theological life of Catholics . . . to affirm more and more an apostolic rather than a political conception of religion, that is to say a conception which is truly Catholic (which before being "anti-communist" and, to the same extent, "anti-fascist" and "anti-racist," is the calling of everyone to eternal life).[38]

The interviewers also asked a question which must have been very acutely felt in 1939, but remains sadly relevant today:

> **CW:** Many of us today are troubled by the question of how we can prevent the domination of the world by force and the fear of force. By what means can this be done?

Maritain replied with just two words:

---

[37] Mikulich, "Catholic Social Teaching," 216.
[38] Editors, "An Interview with Jacques Maritain," *Commonweal*, February 3, 1939, www.commonwealmagazine.org/interview-jacques-maritain.

JM: "By sanctity." M

Laurie Johnston, PhD, is Professor of Theology and Religious Studies at Emmanuel College in Boston. She also serves as Executive Vice President of the Sant'Egidio Foundation for Peace and Dialogue. A social ethicist, she has written and edited works on just war theory, peacebuilding, reconciliation, and political theology.

Gregoire Catta, SJ, is Assistant Professor of Theology at the Facultés Loyola Paris (formerly Centre Sèvres). He has served as the Director of the Service National Famille et Société at the Conference of Catholic Bishops of France, and is the author of numerous works, including *Catholic Social Teaching as Theology* (New York: Paulist, 2019).

Threading the Needle: Jacques Maritain's Defense of a Christian and Liberal Democracy

Mary Doak

Abstract: Some of the key oppositions tearing apart American public life in the early twenty-first century are related to issues explored in the mid-twentieth century political philosophy of Jacques Maritain. Supporters of liberal democracy, then and now, insist it is a political system that privatizes religion and all concepts of a common good. Supporters of an integralist alternative demand official state support for religion as the vision underlying political goals. And, of course, arrayed against both are authoritarian movements that threaten democracy altogether. In this context, Maritain's nuanced political philosophy is far from outdated. He thoughtfully defends liberal democracy's protection of human rights, while also demonstrating that democracy is strengthened by a Catholic vision of the ultimate human good. His political wisdom provides a way through our current impasses and points to a path that will support the survival of this fragile experiment in democracy and the even more fragile hope that democratic processes could be a means to create a more just world.

According to US President Woodrow Wilson, the First World War was fought because "the world must be made safe for democracy."[1] A mere century later, democracy is again under attack. The International Institute for Democracy and Electoral Assistance (IDEA) recently concluded that "half of the democratic governments around the world are in decline while authoritarian regimes are deepening their repression."[2] Political movements that espouse fascist authoritarian nationalism are moving from the far right margins to the political mainstream across the globe. While at times appearing to work within a democratic framework, many are willing to undermine elections to achieve their ends via tactics such as gerrymandering, voter suppression, and denying the

---

[1] Woodrow Wilson, "April 2, 1917: Address to Congress," University of Virginia Miller Center Presidential Speeches, millercenter.org/the-presidency/presidential-speeches/april-2-1917-address-congress-requesting-declaration-war.
[2] International Institute for Democracy and Electoral Assistance, "Global Democracy Weakens in 2022," www.idea.int/news-media/news/global-democracy-weakens-2022.

validity of elections their party does not win.³ A good deal of this anti-democratic activity is no doubt motivated by bigotry as well as by the ubiquitous jockeying for political power. In this time of massive global migration, along with demands for greater equality, the active resentment of those called to share their power with "others" of different ethnicity, class, language, race, or religion should not be surprising to any student of human history.⁴

There is, however, a deeper and disturbingly religious rationale for the contemporary rejection of liberal democracy. Emerging Christian nationalist movements in the United States maintain that the laws of the United States should support their particular version of Christian beliefs, regardless of the will of the majority, and quite contrary to the US Constitution's proclamation that "Congress shall make no law respecting an establishment of religion."⁵ Similarly, Catholic neo-integralists proffer a more philosophical argument that the political order ought not to be agnostic about the ultimate purpose of human life because the temporal order is intended to serve the higher, spiritual, good of the person. Political power, they maintain, must be subservient to the proper religious authority, as was commonly held by official Catholic teachings prior to the Second Vatican Council.⁶

Many of these post-liberal positions are explicitly concerned with the putative soullessness of a politics based on maximizing the self-interests of the greatest number of atomized individuals.⁷ Faced with the choice between either a merely procedural democracy agnostic about values or a value-based politics oriented by a religious account of human life and purpose, neo-integralists decisively choose the latter. They contend that to do otherwise would be a self-contradiction

---

³ See especially "Lessons for Our Elections from the January 6 Hearings," Brennan Center for Justice, www.brennancenter.org/our-work/research-reports/lessons-our-elections-january-6-hearings; and "New Polling Data Confirms the Negative Effects of Election Denial on Republican Voters," electioninnovation.org/press/new-polling-data-confirms-the-negative-effects-of-election-denial-on-republican-voters.

⁴ For current data on the scope of global migration, see especially the statistics available from the Migration Data Portal, www.migrationdataportal.org/resource/key-global-migration-figures.

⁵ One variant of Christian nationalism is Dominionism. See Keri Ladner, "The Quiet Rise of Christian Dominionism," *Christian Century*, November 2022, www.christiancentury.org/article/features/quiet-rise-christian-dominionism. See also "All Amendments to the United States Constitution," University of Minnesota Human Rights Library, hrlibrary.umn.edu/education/all_amendments_usconst.htm.

⁶ Edmund Waldstein, OCist, "Integalism in Three Sentences," *The Josias*, thejosias.com/2016/10/17/integralism-in-three-sentences.

⁷ Edmund Waldstein, OCist, "What is Integralism Today?," *Church Life Journal*, October 31, 2018, churchlifejournal.nd.edu/articles/what-is-integralism-today; and Thomas Pink, "Integralism, Public Philosophy, and the State," *Public Discourse,* May 9, 2020, www.thepublicdiscourse.com/2020/05/63226.

for people who fully believe their religion is true. To endorse a political system that denies humanity's ultimate goal would contradict their most fundamental beliefs.

While religious establishmentarianism is likely to remain a minority perspective in the West for the near future, neo-integralism nevertheless raises serious questions about the adequacy of a merely procedural democracy. Leaving these questions unaddressed weakens commitment to liberal democracy, by which I mean governments elected by popular franchise which include structural protections so that personal rights cannot be infringed by majority vote.[8] Defenders as well as critics of liberal democracy often share the assumption that this regime's promise of personal freedom requires bracketing questions about the goods we ought to pursue.[9] When discernment of public goals is banished from politics, the function of the state is narrowed to safeguarding the private interests of individuals rather than the enrichment of the common life. To the extent that political activities are in fact oriented to some common good or public purpose, this political goal will not be identified or subject to debate by a public (or by politicians) who lack the language for engaging in such deliberations. As David Tracy has warned, "If our society applied only 'intuitions' to the technoeconomic realm, society would wreck the technoeconomic structure itself with more than deliberate speed. The application of instrumental reason alone to ethical questions . . . is similarly destructive."[10]

The neo-integralist challengers are also right to suggest that a procedural liberal democracy eschewing any public responsibility to achieve greater equality and justice, or to otherwise enrich the common life, will fail to generate deep loyalty and commitment.[11] If democratic self-governance is to persist and flourish in the coming decades, we need a more robust account of liberal democracy's value and purpose, an account that does not limit democracy to policing conflicts between individual rights. Without a concept of liberal democracy connected to hopes for a more just society, hopes that can motivate religious as well as non-religious citizens, it is unlikely that people will support democratic procedures when other political processes promise to increase their personal well-being more easily and more successfully.

---

[8] "Liberal Democracy," *European Center for Populism Studies,* www.populismstudies.org/Vocabulary/liberal-democracy.
[9] See especially the concise discussion of a debate between representatives of liberalism and integralism in Waldstein, "What is Integralism?"
[10] David Tracy, *The Analogical Imagination: Christian Theology and the Culture of Pluralism* (New York: Crossroad, 1981), 10.
[11] See especially Pink, "Integralism."

In the face of these many contemporary challenges to democracy, there is considerable insight to be gained from the political philosophy of Jacques Maritain, who grapples deeply with issues that are again (or perhaps still) major problems in our time. Maritain began thinking on these topics in an era where fascism was not only a live option but a strong and growing political force. He developed a vigorous defense of liberal democracy, including the right to religious freedom, even though official Catholic teaching took a decidedly dim view of both democracy and religious freedom at that time.[12] Moreover, he rejected the claim that liberal democracy is unconcerned with a common good and agnostic about the purposes of human life. This approach, he argued, was the mistaken assumption of the truncated form of democracy dominant in nineteenth century Europe he critiques as "bourgeois democracy."[13] A vital liberal democracy, Maritain maintained, is instead one that pursues a common good, is energized by worthwhile goals, and widely supported as a political system appropriate to human dignity and consistent with our deepest understandings of human life. In other words, Maritain staunchly refuses the false choice between either the religious (and other) freedoms of liberal democracy or a politics oriented to a higher, shared human good. In his view, we can and must have both.

While contemporary supporters of a secular state will thus find an ally in Maritain's espousal of the freedoms protected by liberal democracy, contemporary neo-integralists will discover that Maritain agrees with their insistence that true politics must be based on the ultimate (religious) truth of the human person. Maritain develops a defense of democracy thoroughly grounded in his Catholic faith, yet one he believes will also be acceptable to non-Christians and even non-theists. He understands—and fully endorses—the view that one cannot bracket the question of the ultimate truth of human life as one discerns the purposes of the temporal order. I maintain that he would also agree with those who argue today that a merely procedural liberal democratic system (understood as implying that there is no true goal to human life) is not religiously neutral, but instead incompatible with religious belief in an ultimate human good. In sum, Maritain envisions a society that, as paraphrased by John Cooper, would be "'religiously inspired and vitally Christian' while at the same time 'secular in nature.'"[14]

---

[12] See especially Jude P. Dougherty, *Jacques Maritain: An Intellectual Profile* (Washington, DC: The Catholic University of America Press, 2003).

[13] Jacques Maritain, *Man and the State* (Chicago: The University of Chicago Press, 1951), 109–110.

[14] John W. Cooper, *The Theology of Freedom* (Macon, GA: Mercer University Press, 1985), 85.

But can a political philosophy be both vitally Christian and also secular? Is it possible to support both religious freedom and a religious basis for democracy? Or is Maritain's philosophy finally incoherent, falling into self-contradiction as it tries to defend liberal democracy on the basis of a Catholic account of the good of humanity?

I will argue here that Maritain did, on the whole, manage to thread this narrow needle by providing an intellectually coherent and thoroughly Catholic defense of the substantive good achievable through liberal democracy. Maritain's thought remains an important resource for efforts to overcome the current impasse between religious commitment and secular government in the United States. Furthermore, Maritain's diagnosis of the dangers of a liberal polity without a common purpose challenges our contemporary tendency to focus on democratic procedures without attention to any greater goals democracy might achieve. A reader of Maritain would not be surprised that there is today so little evident enthusiasm for procedural democracy or patience for the political debate and disagreement that are the lifeblood of democracy. Maritain's work provides a strong foundation for any effort to affirm a liberal democracy committed to substantive goods, while also reminding us that such an account is essential to the defense of this fragile political ideal.

MARITAIN'S CHRISTIAN DEFENSE OF PLURALISTIC DEMOCRACY

Jacques Maritain's developed thinking on democracy emerges in his *Christianity and Democracy*, written during WWII. Though it was published in 1944, Maritain notes that he wrote the book in 1942 when the outcome of the war was not certain.[15] Yet his concern here is not so much winning the war as winning the peace, which requires healing the underlying sickness that led to war.[16] According to Maritain's astute diagnosis, this sickness was due to the lack of spiritual inspiration, grounded in truth, for a liberal democracy committed to seeking greater social justice. He considers it a great tragedy of history that European democratic movements rejected Christianity and placed their confidence solely in human efforts bound to disappoint, while the church rejected these irreligious democratic movements and opposed working class efforts to attain greater justice.[17] "If the democracies are to win the peace after having won the war," Maritain argues, "it will be on condition that the Christian inspiration and the democratic inspiration recognize each other and become reconciled."[18] Thus his

---

[15] Jacques Maritain, *Christianity and Democracy*, trans. Doris C. Anson (New York: Charles Scribner's Sons, 1944), 9.
[16] Maritain, *Christianity and Democracy*, 9–16.
[17] Maritain, *Christianity and Democracy*, 21.
[18] Maritain, *Christianity and Democracy*, 29.

project, set forth in *Christianity and Democracy* and further nuanced in his later political writings, especially *Man and the State* (1951), was to facilitate this mutual reconciliation by demonstrating that Christianity has socio-political implications which support the democratic goals of liberty, justice, and equality, while liberal democracy is properly grounded in a spiritual vision of the ultimate truth of humanity consistent with Christianity.[19]

Maritain's Christian defense of democracy is based primarily on the dignity of the human person, an argument echoed in the 1965 Vatican II document *Dignitatis Humanae*, which similarly affirms (decades later!) a personal right to religious freedom due to the dignity of the person. Maritain seeks to remind Christians that there are political implications inherent in the Christian belief that all people have equal dignity before God and have been blessed with a spiritual vocation and responsibility that transcends this world and is ultimately fulfilled in participation in the divine life.[20] At the same time, he intends to clarify the religious inspiration that led to the emergence of secular ideals of political equality. Though Maritain is careful to note that Christianity is not inherently yoked to any particular political regime, he holds that commitment to the dignity of the person ought to compel Christians to support whatever political regime is most consistent with human dignity in their context.[21] Maritain further contends that, at this point in human history, the political system most in accord with human dignity is democracy or, in the quotation he borrows from Abraham Lincoln, "government of the people, by the people, and for the people."[22] Political institutions have developed to the point that the Thomistic insistence that political authority is rooted in the consent of the governed can now be clearly embodied in democratic politics as the "normal state" for people who have "come of age in political life."[23]

While the equal dignity of all before God thus supports democratic self-governance, this dignity also sets limits to political authority. Human rights, including the right to religious freedom, must be safeguarded because the person's ultimate good transcends the

---

[19] Our contemporary version of this dichotomy is the exaggerated tendency to oppose conservative Christians and liberal secularists, though there are many notable conservative non-believers as well as important voices arguing for religious commitment to social justice.

[20] Maritain, *Christianity and Democracy*, 47. See also Maritain, *Man and the State*, 148–150.

[21] Maritain, *Christianity and Democracy*, 37.

[22] Maritain, *Christianity and Democracy*, 71. Maritain is of course quoting Abraham Lincoln's Gettysburg Address, November 19, 1863, www.abrahamlincolnonline.org/lincoln/speeches/gettysburg.htm.

[23] Maritain, *Christianity and Democracy*, 52, 46–50.

temporal good—and the expertise—of the state. Moreover, if people are to participate in political life, the rights essential to such participation must be protected by a "juridically formulated constitution."[24] As Maritain further clarifies in *Man and the State*, recognition of the equal dignity of all persons entails that the members of the political community must be equal before the law regardless of their religious affiliation. Given that religious faith cannot be coerced and consciences must be respected for the good of the community and of the person, it would be detrimental to society and a fundamental abridgment of political equality to deny full rights to citizens on the basis of their religion.[25]

Maritain defends a liberal democracy that protects human rights but is by no means to be identified with the atomized liberal democracy solely concerned with maximizing individual freedom. Maritain is quite scathing in his critique of individualistic nineteenth century bourgeois democracy: "Just as it had no real *common good*, it had no real *common thought* . . . it had become a society without any idea of itself, without any *common faith* which could enable it to resist disintegration."[26] In contrast, the liberal democracy Maritain advocates has the limited but significant task of serving the common good of the community so that life can become more fully human and society more just.[27]

It is important to note that the common good here is not a least common denominator reflecting a personal good each person happens to want for themselves. Instead, the Catholic understanding of the common good is the good of the community, and thereby the good of all who are formed by and in that community.[28] Or, to put it another way, to the extent that humans are relational beings who flourish only in community, what ensures the healthy functioning and development ("the good") of that community also benefits all community members, even if it comes at some personal cost. Because we are relational as well as physical (embodied) beings, the common good of the community contributes to our personal growth as we strive toward what Maritain refers to as our "supra-temporal" or spiritual good.[29]

The temporal good of politics thus serves but must never be equated with our ultimate destiny, a destiny that grows but cannot be completed within history. While Maritain agrees with Augustine that

---

[24] Maritain, *Christianity and Democracy*, 69–70.
[25] Maritain, *Man and the State*, 161.
[26] Maritain, *Man and the State*, 110.
[27] Maritain, *Christianity and Democracy*, 47, 51–52.
[28] See especially Jon Tveit, "A Brief Introduction to the Common Good," *The Josias*, thejosias.com/2023/03/27/a-brief-introduction-to-the-common-good. See also Jacques Maritain, *The Person and the Common Good*, trans. John J. Fitzgerald (New York: Charles Scribner's Sons, 1947), esp. 37–79.
[29] Maritain, *Man and the State*, 158–160.

the members of the City of God do not find their final home in this world, Maritain hopes for more from the City of Man (or secular government) than simply civic order and peace.[30] In Maritain's view, "The kingdom of God is not meant for earthly history, but . . . it must be enigmatically prepared in the midst of the pains of earthly history."[31] For Maritain, political life is an important part of that painful preparation for God's kingdom.

Notwithstanding his commitment to highlighting this connection between Christian faith and this-worldly politics, Maritain thus maintains a strong eschatological proviso. Christian political activity seeks to make the world more just, more consistent with human dignity, and more in harmony with the ideal of the reign of God, even while recognizing that the fullness of God's reign will never be achieved in history. His thought agrees on this, as on many other points, with that of his American friend Reinhold Niebuhr, who similarly argued that the perfect harmony of the reign of God will not and cannot be achieved in history, even while Niebuhr also acknowledged that there is no established limit to how close society might get to that harmony.[32]

As John Cooper astutely observes, the differences between Maritain and Niebuhr are less substantive than matters of emphasis and tone appropriate to the focus of their particular contexts and arguments.[33] Maritain is largely concerned with clarifying the connections between the Gospel and democracy so as to motivate Christian political action and provide religious inspiration for democratic politics. Niebuhr, on the other hand, seeks to chasten an overly enthusiastic Social Gospel Movement that became at times too confident in its ability to bring about God's reign in twentieth century America.

In addition to maintaining this eschatological proviso and defending juridically protected rights, Maritain further develops his thought on the limits of democratic politics with his attention to the important role of intermediate groups and his distinction between the body politic and the state. Maintaining a variety of community and social (or "intermediate") groups preserves the healthy pluralism that enriches society while also preventing totalitarianism in which the state assumes and controls all aspects of society. A full assessment of Maritain's defense of intermediate groups is beyond the scope of this article, but it should be noted that, as Robert Putman more recently argued,

---

[30] See especially the discussion of Maritain's relation to Augustine's two cities in Cooper, *The Theology of Freedom*, 72–74.

[31] Maritain, *Christianity and Democracy*, 44.

[32] Reinhold Niebuhr, *The Nature and Destiny of Man: A Christian Interpretation*, vol. 2, *Human Destiny* (New York: Scribner, 1943), 244, 286.

[33] Cooper, *The Theology of Freedom*, esp. 3–28.

decreasing membership in clubs, organizations, and churches has diminished the social capital necessary to hold US society together.[34] Other studies have also noted that political polarization increases when political parties take over the social functions of securing identity and belonging that social clubs and churches have fulfilled in the past.[35]

More central to our analysis of Maritain's political philosophy, however, is his specification of the difference between the body politic and the state. The body politic is the people as a whole sharing a common good, whereas the state is the part of the body politic with authority to maintain order and act to promote the common good of the body politic.[36] With its coercive laws and administrative procedures, the state is thus only one instrument through which the body politic achieves its goals. For example, many cultural and economic activities are supported by and contribute to the common good of the body politic without being directly under the administration of the state.

This distinction between body politic and state is an especially salutary reminder for public life in the United States. As people from different cultures, races, languages, and religions, Americans tend to consider the law a force for unity amid this diversity.[37] This leads to equating the state with the body politic, with people seeking to resolve through legislation issues that would be more appropriately handled through other social institutions or functions of the body politic.

Maritain further warns that collapsing the distinction between the body politic and the state is a perversion destructive of democracy.[38] Totalitarian state control of the functions of the body politic stifles the legitimate plurality of society, suppresses its proper subsidiarity, and impedes the various contributions social groups and institutions would otherwise make to the enrichment of the common life. As we will see below, maintaining Maritain's differentiation between body politic and state is especially helpful in efforts to discern a public role for religion consistent with religious disestablishment because this distinction reminds us that not all public expressions or actions need

---

[34] Robert D. Putnam, *Bowling Alone: The Collapse and Revival of American Community* (New York: Simon and Schuster, 2000).
[35] Paige Holloway, "Losing Faith: The Decline of Religion and Rise of Political Polarization in America," *Medium*, medium.com/illumination/losing-faith-the-decline-of-religion-and-rise-of-political-polarization-in-america-703602c78682.
[36] Maritain, *Man and the State*, 10, 12.
[37] I will follow common practice here and use the term "American" to describe the people, history, culture, and ideas pertaining to the United States of America, as there is no good alternative to that commonly used but problematic adjective. There is no intent here to equate the United States with the entirety of the North and South American continents, which could also be properly called "American."
[38] Maritain, *Man and the State*, 20–21.

be those of the state. Religion can then be brought into the public square without being inserted there by governmental authority.[39]

A final point about the body politic that must be discussed here is the role the body politic plays in constituting, and being constituted by, the civic friendship that, along with a passion for justice, commitment to democracy, and virtuous habits, is essential to democracy. Maritain defines civic friendship as the desire to live together, a desire without which, he says, the body politic cannot be maintained.[40] This insight is especially pertinent in the United States today with political polarization becoming one of the most obvious threats to the health of our democracy. It is not at all clear that Americans have sufficient desire to live together to sustain our political system: political opponents view each other as enemies to be vanquished if not humiliated, and there is little willingness to compromise for the greater good of all. The civic friendship Maritain recognizes as crucial to democracy can no longer be taken for granted, and divisions threaten to rip apart the social fabric. However critical this civic friendship is, though, the will to live together cannot be legislated, just as the other politically indispensable virtues of justice, respect for truth, and self-sacrifice cannot be legislated. Again, we see why Maritain considers it disastrous to replace the body politic with the state, as these key attitudes and virtues cannot be legislated by the state but must be developed by other aspects of the body politic.

In setting forth Maritain's nuanced understanding of Christian reasons for supporting a liberal, or limited, democratic regime, our discussion has led us already into the second part of his project: the need of democracy for just such religious support. The essential democratic virtues of self-sacrifice, respect for truth, and openness to others essential to civic friendship are, Maritain contends, fostered by religion, especially Christianity. But this is not all that religion provides to democracy. Maritain also maintains that belief in the ultimate dignity of the person (which transcends and limits the power of the state), commitment to justice, and hope for history are all Christian ideals essential to democracy, even if people may find other reasons for supporting these ethical ideals.[41]

More than these particular "democratic" principles and virtues, however, Maritain further insists that democracy needs to be

---

[39] The possibility and indeed the reality of much public religion not directly sponsored by the state is overlooked in many arguments suggesting that state neutrality has left us without public religion. For a classic example, see Richard John Neuhaus, *The Naked Public Square: Religion and Democracy in America* (Grand Rapids, MI: Eerdmans, 1988).

[40] Maritain, *Man and the State*, 207–209.

[41] Maritain, *Christianity and Democracy*, 47–49.

supported by a coherent account of the good of this political system in relation to the true purpose of human life.[42] If democracy is merely a preference, then we are not likely to find strong support for it when it becomes difficult, inconvenient, or does not achieve the desired results. Maritain thus devotes much of his intellectual work to articulating of the relationship between democratic politics and the ultimate or eternal good humanity not only to clarify Christian reasons for supporting democracy, but also to underscore the democratic need for Christianity (and, as he occasionally concedes, other religions).

Not all people will find Maritain's thoroughly Catholic defense of democracy persuasive or even palatable, a point Maritain acknowledges. For this reason, he encourages arguments in defense of democracy based on whatever other religious or metaphysical perspectives people hold to be true. What is crucial, he argues, is that the body politic's commitment to democracy be grounded in an understanding not only of what democracy is and how it functions but also how democratic regimes may serve the ultimate good of humanity. To this end, Maritain exercises some creativity in envisioning how schools could possibly carry out this task of teaching the truth of democracy's goodness from various religious perspectives.[43]

It is not likely that teaching a religious defense of democracy as true would be acceptable in American public education systems, even if a variety of religious and philosophical systems were presented. Nevertheless, Maritain raises an important point here. Secondary education in the United States usually includes some (arguably scant) attention to civics and government, but these courses are likely to focus on the structure and processes of American democracy rather than the goodness, let alone the truth, of the democratic system. When, if at all, are children taught to value democracy? Have American youth been exposed to inspiring accounts of the noble adventure democracy can be? Perhaps some part of the shallowness of commitment to democracy today is rooted in a national failure to provide our young with an appropriate appreciation of the strengths of democratic regimes.

A more common, and modest, American defense of democracy is Reinhold Niebuhr's rather practical approach in which he describes democracy as necessary because people are evil and inclined to self-interest (so their power must be checked by the power of others) but also as possible because people are good and able to overcome their self-interest.[44] This is not far from the common adage that democracy

---

[42] See especially Maritain, *Man and the State*, 77, 80, 121.
[43] Maritain, *Man and the State*, 119–126.
[44] Reinhold Niebuhr, *The Children of Light and the Children of Darkness: A Vindication of Democracy and a Critique of Its Traditional Defense* (New York: Charles Scribner's Sons, 1944), xiii, 9–15.

is the worst possible political system—except for all the others.⁴⁵ There is some wisdom here: democratic political processes are messy and often ineffective, but they do provide protections against the abuse of power other political systems lack. Niebuhr reminds his readers that no one (and he does mean no one!) is so virtuous that they can be trusted with unchecked power. Yet he also notes that democracy depends on some people striving to be virtuous enough to put the common good above their own immediate self-interests at least some of the time.⁴⁶ This helpfully realistic account of democracy does not, however, attempt to provide what Maritain has persuasively argued is also needed: an inspiring vision of the goal of democracy in relation to humanity's ultimate good (which, of course, can never be fully realized in this world).

Even though Maritain devotes considerable effort to proffering such a religiously informed vision of the good of democracy, it is important to keep in mind that Maritain has no intention of sacralizing politics. As he points out, any identification of the temporal and supra-temporal goals will distort both politics and religion.⁴⁷ Erasing the distinction between these two realms results not only in an overly politicized religion but also the idolatrous absolutization of politics limiting human hopes to what little can be achieved in this world and turning every political dispute into an ultimate or religious conflict. As utterly opposed as Maritain is to this kind of political theology, he is nevertheless keenly supportive of the *théologie politique* that discerns a connection between the temporal and supra-temporal good such that religion judges the state but without being collapsed into the state.⁴⁸

However allergic the contemporary pluralistic, post-modern moment may be to the idea of a political good rooted in an accurate understanding of the purpose of human life, Maritain's critique of purposeless "bourgeois" democracy remains valid. On this point, Maritain agrees with the neo-integralists of today insofar as they call attention to the dangers of an individualistic, self-centered politics that recognizes no common good or higher value than personal whims and desires. Such a political system will not only fail to increase justice and ennoble the community; it will also be unable to withstand the inevitable pressures, whether from within or without the polis, that can destroy democratic political systems.

---

⁴⁵ Winston Churchill popularized this saying in a speech on November 11, 1947, but apparently the adage was not original to him. See the International Churchill Society discussion of February 25, 2016, available online at winstonchurchill.org/resources/quotes/the-worst-form-of-government/.
⁴⁶ Niebuhr, *Children*, esp. 59–79.
⁴⁷ Maritain, *Man and the State*, 148–150.
⁴⁸ This point is developed in Cooper, *The Theology of Freedom*, 165, 5–6.

THE CHALLENGE OF RELIGIOUS FREEDOM

I have argued here that Maritain avoids the unpalatable extremes of both individualistic liberalism and religious nationalism, as he defends religious pluralism while also maintaining an integral connection between the temporal goals of democracy and a religious account of the ultimate goal of human life. The question remains, though, whether Maritain's position is coherent. Has he genuinely threaded this needle, or has he fallen into self-contradictions? Is it truly possible to have a society that is both secular and vitally religious?

On the one hand, there can be no doubt that Maritain fully endorses religious freedom in a pluralistic society. The state has no expertise in discerning the true religion and, in any case, faith cannot be coerced. The dignity of the person oriented to an eternal destiny endows all people with freedoms the state must recognize, and these include freedom of religion and the right to be included in the processes by which the people consent to government. It follows, then, that no one ought to be considered less of a citizen or hampered in their political participation due to their religious beliefs.[49] This, Maritain argues, is so thoroughly grounded in Catholicism that he approvingly quotes Cardinal Manning's reply to Gladstone that "'if Catholics were in power tomorrow in England, not a penal law would be proposed, not the shadow of a constraint put upon the faith of any man.'"[50] Maritain further adds that "even if one single citizen dissented from the religious faith of all the people, his right to dissent could by no means be infringed upon by the State in a Christianly inspired modern democracy."[51]

Yet Maritain also maintains that democracy depends on a Christian (or at least theistic) foundation. He can certainly sound like a neo-integralist when he argues that democracy depends on Christianity not only historically, in the sense that modern democracy developed in a Christian culture, but also philosophically, in that democratic systems require the intellectual support of Christian beliefs in the equal dignity of all and the possibility of greater justice in society.[52] He even accepts that "a political society really and vitally Christian . . . would express this faith publicly."[53]

It might seem, then, that Maritain's position allows only the religious tolerance consistent with religious establishment. In such a scenario, no one would be coerced to be Christian, but Christianity (or at least Western monotheism) would be the publicly acknowledged

---

[49] Maritain, *Man and the State*, 161.
[50] Maritain, *Man and the State*, 181.
[51] Maritain, *Man and the State*, 181.
[52] Maritain, *Christianity and Democracy*, 27, 37, 47, 59–60.
[53] Maritain, *Man and the State*, 172.

foundation for understanding the temporal good politics pursues. If Maritain is read in this way, then his position is very difficult to reconcile with the religious disestablishment required by the United States Constitution, and Maritain would contribute little to the current impasse between Christian nationalists and those who insist on a strict separation between religion and politics. What is at stake in these debates is not whether people will be coerced to belong to a religion but what the public role of religion will be, and especially whether the state should endorse a religious position. If interpreted as advocating state endorsement of the religion upon which it depends, Maritain's political philosophy would lend considerable support to the neo-integralist argument that Catholics must embrace the pre-Vatican II position that the ideal to be achieved whenever possible is the political establishment of Catholicism, as though the Vatican II document *Dignitatis Humanae* added nothing of substance to Catholic teaching.

This interpretation of Maritain is, however, in conflict with his claim that no one should be a lesser citizen on account of their religious beliefs. If American democracy necessarily pursues a temporal good defined by Christian beliefs (or, in a more modest position Maritain at times suggests, a temporal good based on the monotheistic beliefs shared by Jews, Christians, and Muslims), then those who do not adhere to these beliefs would be hindered in their citizenship. They could participate in this democracy without performatively contradicting their own ultimate beliefs, whether religious, atheistic, or agnostic. In other words, those who are not monotheists would be compelled in their political participation to act as if they were. Moreover, one might then wonder whether there is any real point to the Constitutional disestablishment of religion, if the prohibition on legal establishment of religion is no more than a ban on rendering explicit the implicit religious foundation of the US system of democracy.

A more careful and nuanced reading of Maritain, however, clarifies a major difference between his position and that of neo-integralists of today. In his more developed *Man and the State,* Maritain elaborates on the possibility of differing religious and metaphysical systems providing diverse views of democracy's relation to the ultimate purpose of human life (even if these accounts are not in his judgment equally true).[54] From his experience of the United Nations Declaration of Human Rights, Maritain learned that unity in political values is possible amid a diversity of philosophical and religious perspectives. While the signatories of the Declaration of Human Rights could not agree on the rationale supporting these rights, they could nevertheless

---

[54] Maritain, *Man and the State,* 122–123.

agree on the rights.⁵⁵ Maritain argues that the same is true of pluralistic democracies: democracy depends on citizens committed to human dignity, equality, and justice, but the citizenry do not need to agree on the reasons these values are important—though democracy fares best when people do have such reasons.

In my judgment, then, Maritain is best understood as recognizing that many religious and even non-theistic philosophies provide more-or-less adequate intellectual foundations for democracy, while also explicating his deep commitment to Catholicism as the basis for democracy most in accord with the truth of humanity. The tradition of Thomistic natural law makes sense of this consensus about democracy because, as Maritain says, all people have an "inclination" that enables them to recognize their temporal good even if they lack the full understanding provided by Christian revelation.⁵⁶ There can thus be sufficient agreement on democratic values among the plural differing perspectives on the meaning of human life. Cooperation for the temporal good does not then require that religious and philosophical differences about the ultimate good of humanity be fully resolved. In light of this mature thought, Maritain's statements about democracy requiring a Christian foundation are best understood as meaning that democracy requires citizens to have some religious or philosophical foundation for the temporal good of the polis, and that in his view Catholic Christianity provides the best such foundation.

The careful reader will recognize that even this more nuanced version of Maritain's political philosophy does not entirely resolve the problem of religious freedom. After all, this view still maintains not only that democracy is based on shared values but also that political activity ought to direct the state to act through its laws and procedures in accord with people's concepts of the ultimate good. Since the activities of the state are then not neutral regarding concepts of the good, is the state not implicitly establishing religion when it legislates in accordance with this supposed consensus about political values? To be sure, no single particular religion would be established, but why not explicitly establish the shared set of religious/philosophical values that provide the basis for democracy as a sort of composite or least common denominator religious foundation?

Of course, we might also question whether there is in fact such a consensus on political values today—or at least whether that consensus is sufficient to unite a contemporary pluralistic polity. Even if Americans generally agree on the equal dignity of all in theory, and more-or-less support democratic procedures and human rights as set forth in the US Constitution, what happens when there are disagreements

---

⁵⁵ Maritain, *Man and the State*, 77–78. See also Cooper, *The Theology of Freedom*, 108–110.
⁵⁶ Maritain, *Man and the State*, 90–93.

over actual laws because of different religious understandings of the ultimate good of humanity?

Many of the political issues that divide Americans today are based in fundamentally religious disagreements about the good of humanity. To give just one of several possible examples, is same-sex marriage to be condemned because it is inconsistent with the procreative, complementarian, monogamous sexuality some maintain is integral to a biblical view of true human flourishing? Or should same-sex marriage be endorsed as consistent with a gospel informed inclusion of the marginalized, who seek in freedom to realize the good of committed sexual companionship as they experience it? Since the laws of the state will either recognize or deny recognition to same-sex unions, it follows that some "religious" views will be supported by law while others will not. Has our detour here through the complexities of Maritain's political thought simply brought us back to our starting point in the impasse between those who argue for an individualistic privatizing of the good and those who contend that the government should support the shared human good their religion teaches?

A classic expression of the dilemma of religious freedom has been set forth by Franklin I. Gamwell in his 1986 essay "Religion and Reason in American Politics."[57] As Gamwell describes the conundrum that continues to roil American public life today, those who advocate for laws informed by their religious beliefs have not explained how such laws avoid establishing religion, while those who insist that religion must not influence political decisions have not explained how this privatization avoids prohibiting the free exercise of those who believe their religion must inform their political activity.[58] It would seem that the two clauses of the Constitution are inherently in conflict, and religious freedom is an impossibility.

Stanley Fish is among those who have concluded that legally protected religious freedom is impossible for this reason.[59] In his

---

[57] Franklin I. Gamwell, "Religion and Reason in American Politics," in Robin W. Lovin, ed., *Religion and American Public Life: Interpretations and Explorations* (New York: Paulist, 1986), 88–112. See also Franklin I. Gamwell, "Reason and the Public Purpose," *Journal of Religion* 62, no. 3 (1982): 277–288, doi.org/10.1086/486945; and Franklin I. Gamwell, *The Meaning of Religious Freedom: Modern Politics and the Democratic Resolution* (Albany, NY: State University of New York Press, 1995).
[58] Gamwell, "Religion and Reason," 88–89.
[59] Among his many writings on this topic, see especially Stanley Fish, "Mission Impossible: Settling the Just Bounds between Church and State," *Columbia Law Review* 97, no. 8 (1997): 2255–2333, doi.org/10.2307/1123373. See also the similar arguments in Stanley Hauerwas and Michael Baxter, CSC, "The Kingship of Christ: Why Freedom of 'Belief' is Not Enough," *DePaul Law Review* 42, no. 1 (1992): 107–127, via.library.depaul.edu/law-review/vol42/iss1/9; and Winnifred Fallers Sullivan, *The Impossibility of Religious Freedom* (Princeton, NJ: Princeton University Press,

reading, the disestablishment clause of the First Amendment requires a privatization of religion, so that no political activity can be informed by the religious views of citizens. He contends that this privatization prohibits the free exercise of those who (in my judgment correctly) understand their religion as requiring that they seek laws consistent with their account of the ultimate human good. Moreover, as Fish further argues, the privatization of religion is itself based on a particular liberal philosophy in which religion only concerns matters of private life. He concludes that even this disestablishment of religion in effect establishes a liberal or Enlightenment perspective on religion. Thus, the First Amendment manages both to establish a certain form of religion and prohibit the free exercise of other forms of religion. Religion, it seems, cannot be removed from politics, and religious freedom is nonsensical.

If we cannot resolve this dilemma, then it follows that not only is the US Constitution's First Amendment guarantee of religious freedom incoherent but so too is Maritain's project as well as the official Catholic teaching as set forth in *The Declaration on Religious Freedom (Dignitatis Humanae)*. The Catholic Church has never accepted the privatization of religion, which is why Catholic teaching had a difficult time accepting religious disestablishment as anything other than a concession to those countries in which Catholicism is not the dominant religion. The Catholic Church was only able officially to endorse a robust civic religious freedom due to the thought of Catholic scholars such as Maritain and especially John Courtney Murray and Pietro Pavan, as their work outlined the possibility of a religious disestablishment that did not privatize religion.[60]

The neo-integralists are then partly right to point to *Dignitatis Humanae's* insistence that it "leaves untouched traditional Catholic doctrine on the moral duty of men (sic) and societies" (no. 1). *Dignitatis Humanae* provides an even clearer rejection of religious privatization in a later section, where the document specifies that "religious communities should not be prohibited from freely undertaking to show the special value of their doctrine in what concerns the organization of society" (no. 4).

Yet the neo-integralists are quite wrong to present their religious establishmentarianism as consistent with official Catholic teaching today, as doing so ignores *Dignitatis Humanae's* insistence that "government is to see to it that equality of citizens before the law ...

2005). Regarding Sullivan's argument, I concur that there are significant problems with the various state Religious Freedom Restoration Acts, but I do not agree that she has adequately demonstrated that the First Amendment to the Constitution is unworkable.

[60] See especially the discussion in Hermínio Rico, *John Paul II and the Legacy of Dignitatis Humanae* (Washington, DC: Georgetown University Press, 2002), 27–91.

is never violated, whether openly or covertly, for religious reasons" (no. 6). As noted above, equality is surely violated if citizens are required to confine their political agendas to temporal goods consistent with religious accounts of an ultimate good that they reject. We should further ask how someone could in good conscience accept a political or military office that requires them to swear to uphold a Constitution that supports a religion they believe is untrue.[61] Surely such religious establishment involves at least implicitly denying the equality of citizens.

Yet *Dignitatis Humanae* goes further in clarifying its distance from the establishment of religion former Catholic teaching supported. The document describes civic recognition (not establishment) of a particular religion as no longer the norm but rather a "peculiar circumstance" and one in which the government must take care to ensure that the rights of all other religious communities as well as citizens are fully protected (no. 6). Either *Dignitatis Humanae*'s defense of religious freedom is incoherent, or religious freedom must in fact be possible.

Gamwell has developed a cogent solution to the problem. The first step is to recognize that religion cannot be removed from public life or walled off from the realm of politics. Insofar as religion answers the question of the ultimate or, in Gamwell's term, "comprehensive" purpose or goal of human life, religious people strive to avoid acting in ways that impede their attainment of that comprehensive (religious) goal as they understand it.[62] So, even though political activities do not aim to achieve the ultimate good, they should, as Maritain similarly argues, contribute to rather than contradict its achievement. The second step is to recognize that political activities, like all activities, implicitly embody values consistent with some accounts of the ultimate good and not with others.[63] These two steps clarify that religion and politics are distinct but not separable. Religion concerns one's ultimate good or final telos, while the activities of the state, as Maritain also emphasizes, are limited to the temporal good of the body politic—but that temporal good is always envisioned in ways consistent with some and not with other accounts of the ultimate or comprehensive good.

As long as the state stays in its proper zone and regulates behavior as appropriate to the common good and public order, while refraining

---

[61] This example was suggested to me in a conversation with Franklin I. Gamwell in the early 1990s.
[62] Gamwell, "Religion and Reason," 90. See also Gamwell, "Religion and Public," 280–281.
[63] Gamwell, "Religion and Reason," 104–105. See also, Gamwell, "Religion and Public," 280–281.

from explicitly teaching or promoting any particular account of the ultimate or all-encompassing good, Gamwell contends that the state has not established a religion. This remains the case even though political activities cannot avoid implicitly embodying values consistent with some and not with other possible accounts of the ultimate goal of human life.[64] According to this analysis, Fish is wrong to think that religious disestablishment requires the privatization of religion. Laws may—in fact, must—be informed by some concept(s) of the ultimate good, as long as that ultimate good remains implicit and is not explicitly promoted by the state.

To clarify this further, we should note that what is gained by religious disestablishment is not religious privatization, but that the state leaves the question of the ultimate good officially open to ongoing debate. To the extent that a majority of citizens are persuaded of the same ultimate good (or, more likely, of versions of the ultimate good relevantly similar insofar as temporal goods are concerned), they will then support the policies in accord with their agreed upon values.[65] Assuming that the democratic regime is so structured that legislation is consistent with the will of the majority, the laws and state activities will change as the majority's beliefs about the ultimate or comprehensive purpose change. Religious people are as free as all others to enter public debate arguing for laws and procedures consistent with their understanding of the ultimate good and arguing against laws inconsistent with that understanding. Moreover, Gamwell encourages people to debate publicly and freely what that ultimate good is as well as how politics relates to it.[66]

Some may object to being required to abide by laws that reflect values other than their own, but that is inevitable in any form of government. All remain free to argue not only against the laws but also against the values implied therein, and to seek to persuade others to change their minds—politically and religiously—so that they support revising or rescinding the laws accordingly. Yet one must generally abide by laws one disagrees with or suffer the consequences. As *Dignitatis Humanae* affirms, religious freedom is not and cannot be an absolute right that justifies impeding the common good or disrupting the public order.[67]

The first two clauses of the First Amendment are not, then, inherently in contradiction. Laws may not prohibit the free expression of religion, as long as that expression does not violate others' rights or the common good. This means that people are free to advocate for

---

[64] Gamwell, "Religion and Reason," 98–100.
[65] Gamwell, "Religion and Reason," 107–109.
[66] Gamwell, "Religion and Reason," 104–109.
[67] See especially the discussion of the proper qualification of rights in *Dignitatis Humanae*, no. 7.

laws and public policies consistent with their religious beliefs and even to defend the truth of those religious beliefs and their importance for public life—provided that the laws and policies concern behavior appropriately regulated by the government and do not employ the power of the state to teach or promote religious beliefs. There is no establishment of religion when laws are passed on the basis of religiously informed arguments, so long as the understanding of the ultimate human good remains open to debate free from interference by the state—something religious establishment does not allow.

One might yet wonder whether contemporary pluralistic societies will be able to achieve sufficient agreement in order to govern, given our very different opinions about the ultimate good of humanity. It seems unlikely that society today would achieve much religious agreement, however lengthy the debate. This is, of course, why some form of religious establishment has been common in history: people have long recognized the need for a unifying basis of social and political values.

Fortunately, as Maritain has argued, there is considerable consensus among different religious (and non-religious) positions about what generally constitutes the public order and the common good. This is exemplified not only by the United Nations Declaration of Human Rights but also by the Global Ethic of the Parliament of the World's Religions, which explicates five major socio-political principles held in common by many of the world's religions and philosophies.[68] It may not be possible to achieve religious agreement, but it seems that even in today's radically pluralistic societies we can achieve considerable consensus about the values to be embodied in law, culture, and society.

Perhaps, then, as Richard McBrien has argued, religious freedom means focusing public debates on these commonly shared socio-political values rather than on the underlying—and differing—religious accounts of the ultimate or comprehensive good.[69] Doing so would have the benefit of recognizing, and building on, the considerable consensus already achieved, while focusing debate on the practical issues at stake rather than on practically irresolvable religious disagreements.

Despite the benefits of such a common values approach, I am not persuaded that only those agreed-upon values belong in public life;

---

[68] See United Nations, "The Universal Declaration of Human Rights," www.un.org/en/about-us/universal-declaration-of-human-rights; and The Parliament of the World's Religions, "Towards a Global Ethic: An Initial Declaration," parliamentofreligions.org/global-ethic/towards-a-global-ethic-an-initial-declaration.
[69] Richard P. McBrien, *Caesar's Coin: Religion and Politics in America* (New York: Macmillan, 1987).

nor do I think that specifically religious arguments can or should be barred from political debate. As explained above, barring religious arguments would impede the religious freedom of those who appropriately refuse to separate their ultimate (religious) good from their understanding of the political good. It can also be argued that so policing the public debate privileges secular discourse, requiring that religious views be translated into non-religious language, while the non-religious are not similarly required to translate their values into religious language. Of course, there is some wisdom in expressing one's religious values in common language in order to be more politically effective, as many argue. Yet there are also good reasons to support specifically religious expressions of public values in order to elevate and inspire, as Martin Luther King, Jr.'s civil rights speeches demonstrate.[70] Indeed, as discussed above, Jacques Maritain is concerned with demonstrating the Christian roots of democratic values in order to increase the depth of public support for democracy. Regardless of these practical considerations, however, from the perspective of the First Amendment's guarantees of religious freedom as well as freedom of speech, religious views on the ultimate good cannot and should not be barred from the public debate.

I would further argue that religious views must be part of the public debate especially when they differ from the shared consensus. If the public understanding of the good of politics is to develop and grow, then minority positions must be allowed to challenge the public to rethink its consensus. After all, the point of religious disestablishment is to encourage continued debate about the comprehensive purpose and its relation to the public good.

To return to our earlier example of opposing positions on same sex marriage based on differing understandings of the ultimate good of humanity, a few observations on this debate may help clarify the issues we face regarding religion in public. First, those who oppose legal recognition of same-sex marriage remain as free to argue against the current status quo as others are free to defend it. Second, all citizens have the right to discuss their concept of the ultimate good (whether rooted in traditional religion or secular philosophy) and to demonstrate the relation between their ultimate good and the legal recognition of same sex marriage. There is no violation of religious freedom as long as the government does not explicitly endorse the ultimate good(s) implicit in its marriage laws and there are sound reasons to consider marriage a matter that is appropriately legislated for the common good

---

[70] See especially the deep discussion of the positive and negative aspects of these divergent positions on the appropriateness of religious language in political debate in the still timely David Hollenbach, ed., "Theology and Philosophy in Public: A Symposium on John Courtney Murray's Unfinished Agenda," *Theological Studies* 40, no. 4 (1979): 700–715, doi.org/10.1177/004056397904000403.

and the public order. (As Maritain reminds us, some goods are more appropriately sought not through the state but through other institutions of the body politic.)

If the above discussion has been successful in its defense of religious freedom, then it follows that Maritain's argument for a religiously vital yet secular society is an internally coherent position when presented with care and nuance. His argument that the temporal good sought by the activities of the state ought to be informed by our best understanding of humanity's ultimate good is consistent with contemporary Catholic social teaching and the meaning of religious freedom properly undertsood. His focus on appreciating the good of democracy is also consistent with Gamwell's emphasis on religious disestablishment's role in preserving the conditions for ongoing debate about the meaning of our public life.

One part of Maritain's approach that does not easily fit the account of religious freedom defended above is his argument for having schools teach various religious and philosophical rationales for the good of democracy. In the American public school system, such an arrangement would surely raise questions about whether the state was thereby teaching or promoting a particular set of religious positions (and not others) in violation of religious disestablishment. However, Maritain's attention to the breadth of the body politic is an important resource that can resolve this tension between the need for such education and the prohibition on government establishment of religion. We do indeed need more attention to instructing youth about the concepts of the ultimate good that justify and enliven support for democracy, but such instruction can and should be undertaken over by other parts of the body politic, including not only the family but also civic organizations and other intermediate groups so that the state is not directly involved.

Conclusion

Jacques Maritain is a source of nuanced, complex thinking on precisely the issues of public life that most need nuanced and complex thought today. Maritain confirms that today's neo-integralists are right about our public need for a vision that orients political life toward the ultimate good of humanity. Moreover, as Maritain argues, such a vision of democracy's service of the good is indispensable to engender the support and even sacrifice necessary to the survival of fragile democracy. Yet Maritain is at the same time a staunch defender of liberal democracy, arguing at length in defense of limiting the government so that people are able to direct their lives to their ultimate good in freedom—and freely contribute to the enrichment of the body politic as well. While thus clarifying the truth on both sides, Maritain also points out their errors: he rejects the neo-integralist ideal of religious establishment and excoriates the hyper-individualist liberal democracy that refuses any shared political purpose beyond securing individual freedoms. Maritain thus demonstrates that, properly understood, liberal democracy is thoroughly consistent with the deepest understandings of Christianity in ways neither of these two commonly opposed alternatives are.

Perhaps even more important than Maritain's substantive contribution to overcoming the impasse between these two incomplete views of democracy is his embodiment of a deep and nuanced argumen-tation lacking today even, or perhaps especially, in academic thought. Maritain consistently refuses simplistic alternatives, including the common academic tendency to label a difficult issue—like religious freedom—as irresolvable when it is merely complex. If our fragile experiment in democracy is to survive, nuanced and careful thought of the type Maritain exemplifies will have to become more rather than less common. If instead our democracy is overthrown by one of the forms of authoritarianism growing today, we will seriously regret that we did not join Maritain in thinking carefully and deeply about the sources of the meaning, value, and survival of liberal democracy. M

Mary Doak, PhD, is Professor in the Department of Theology and Religious Studies at the University of San Diego. She holds a doctorate in Christian Theology from the Divinity School of the University of Chicago and has published in the areas of public theology, ecclesiology, and religious freedom.

Jacques Maritain, "Pure" Nature, and the State's Teleological Crisis

Gilbrian Stoy, CSC

Abstract: In response to increased threats of totalitarianism in the twentieth century, Jacques Maritain proposed a separation of the spiritual and temporal planes which purported to limit State power and resist the totalitarian and absolutist claims found in rising political movements. I argue, however, that the very distinction Maritain attempts to establish pushes the temporal plane into a teleological crisis which results in the totalitarianism Maritain sought to resist. By granting that temporal powers pursue ultimate ends autonomous from humanity's absolute ultimate end, Maritain's schema yields an unstable temporal plane which requires supernatural claims to make itself intelligible as ultimate end. Whereas William Cavanaugh criticizes Maritain for mistakenly relying upon a scholastic understanding of "pure nature," I propose that a recovery of Thomas Aquinas's understanding of the openness of nature to supernatural ends can better justify Maritain's proposed limited and prevent the teleological instability at the root of Maritain's political theory.

Jacques Maritain sets the distinction between the temporal and spiritual planes as a foundational feature of his political philosophy. Maritain thought that such a distinction could resist the totalitarian State which claims that no human goods exist outside of the State's domain. Furthermore, he saw Christ's command to "give what is Caesar's to Caesar, and that which is God's to God" as the evangelical justification which separated the temporal and spiritual planes and purified the pagan world from the perpetual temptation to collapse the supernatural into the natural for its own worldly purposes. However, the fundamental separation upon which Maritain grounds his proposal is significantly more unstable than Maritain recognizes. In fact, it is inherently so.

By distinguishing the temporal from the spiritual and establishing "ultimate ends" within each plane, Maritain deviates from what Thomas Aquinas considered a single chain of ends. I argue that this separation causes intrinsic instability in the temporal plane and pushes that plane into a teleological crisis, resolved only through temporal powers claiming to supply even supernatural goods—precisely what Maritain sought to prevent. By drawing on recent scholarship on the hypothetical state of "pure nature," I argue that the temporal plane must be understood as an intermediary end within a single teleological chain which finds its ultimate end in God alone. While William Cavanaugh's critique in *Torture and Eucharist* accuses Maritain of relying too heavily on the concept of "pure nature," I argue that rightly understood "pure nature" provides the necessary metaphysical foundation for the limited State Maritain seeks to establish. Furthermore, while Cavanaugh's criticism emphasizes the State's desire for ever greater power, attention to this teleological account provides a metaphysical explanation for why temporal powers seemingly inevitably claim to be repositories of ultimate identity and sacred value and become the idols against which he so forcefully argues.

To do so, I will first present Maritain's political schema and the metaphysical distinction he draws on his own terms. Second, I will turn to Cavanaugh's critique to show how the nature-grace debate informs political theology. Finally, I will turn to Thomas Joseph White's recovery of the usefulness of the concept of "pure nature" to show how, when properly understood, human nature situates all human goods within a single chain of ends. This provides an anthropological and ontological explanation of political absolutism and the sacralization of the State.

Ironically, both Maritain and Cavanaugh describe their work as arguments against these absolutist temporal powers. By properly situating human nature's relationship to supernatural ends, I offer a metaphysical description that both critiques and potentially reconciles these two influential Catholic thinkers.

Maritain's Teleological Politics

While appealing to metaphysics and teleology may seem at first to be an unnecessary and useless philosophical attempt to define and prescribe political structures, Maritain makes teleology essential and fundamental to his political scheme. It is not merely metaphysical window dressing to what might otherwise belong only to practical reasoning, but rather the foundational rock upon which he builds his political vision, to which he appeals throughout his political treatises.[1]

---

[1] For example, in the preface to the 1939 English edition of *The Things That Are Not Caesar's*, Maritain notes that while the first chapter, devoted to articulating and applying Bellarmine's notion of indirect power, received the most critique and commentary, it is rather the third chapter that is "the most important" for his project. See Jacques Maritain, *The Things That Are Not Caesar's*, trans. J. F. Scanlan (London: Sheed & Ward, 1939), xxi. This chapter begins with a direct appeal to Thomas Aquinas's doctrine of nature and grace, and especially to the relation between the natural and supernatural ends, and continues with repeated appeals to the significance of Thomistic thought for his philosophical project (78ff.). In *The Peasant of the Garonne*, near the end of his laudable and impressive life, Maritain once again places teleology at the center of his thinking as he examines the lay vocation and

Maritain seeks to distinguish the natural, temporal goods of the human person from her supernatural, spiritual goods. Drawing on Thomistic teleology, he separates the temporal and spiritual into two autonomous planes, protecting the autonomy of both political and ecclesial authorities from threatening the goods of the other. He makes this distinction while still subordinating the temporal plane to the "absolute, ultimate end" of the spiritual. However, he modifies Thomas's understanding of the ultimate end in order to better protect the autonomy of each plane by introducing two distinct ultimate ends. Such a claim contradicts Thomas's argument for a single chain of ends and introduces instability into the temporal plane.

It would be a mistake to see Maritain's project as merely theoretical; the threats he saw to the church's freedom were not imagined bogeymen but real political developments. Maritain's early work *The Things That Are Not Caesar's* was written in 1927 in defense of Pope Pius XI's condemnation of Action Française, a self-proclaimed integralist and royalist political movement that explicitly desired to use the spiritual goods of the church as a means towards civil unity and political power.[2] Action Française's atheist leader Charles Maurras saw the church as a useful instrument that could provide stability and identity to France and thereby unify the State. While at first some Catholic voices saw a useful ally in Maurras, eventually the hierarchy would reject his co-opting of spiritual goods for the sake of political and temporal ends.[3] But it was not simply political movements in 1920s France which sought to use the spiritual for their own benefit. Beyond Maritain's France, Mussolini in Italy likewise deployed religious rhetoric for the benefit of political gain.[4]

Christian mission with respect to the temporal plane (*The Peasant of the Garonne: An Old Layman Questions Himself about the Present Time*, trans. Michael Cuddihy and Elizabeth Hughes [New York: Holt, Rinehart, and Winston, 1968], 40–43, 199–212). In this article, I intentionally refer to "the State" and capitalize it to designate the post-Westphalian modern nation-state. This is to align my terms with how William T. Cavanaugh deploys the difference, as seen in his "A Fire Strong Enough to Consume the House: The Wars of Religion and the Rise of the State," *Modern Theology* 11, no. 4 (1995): 397–420.

[2] Maritain, *The Things That Are Not Caesar's*, xxiv.

[3] For an overview of the political context in early Twentieth century France, with particular attention to Charles Maurras's influence, see Michael Sutton, "Conservatives and Conservatism: Early Catholic Controversy about the Politics of Charles Maurras," *Journal of Contemporary History* 14, no. 4 (1979): 649–676, dx.doi.org/10.1177/002200947901400405.

[4] Emilio Gentile describes how Mussolini made mythic thought and religious claims fundamental to his political imagination. These categories served to provide a transcendent purpose and identity to his political project. See Emilio Gentile, "Fascistese: The Religious Dimensions of Political Language in Fascist Italy," in *Political Languages in the Age of Extremes*, ed. Willibald Steinmetz and German Historical Institute in London, Studies of the German Historical Institute London

In fact, Maritain begins his critique of Maurras by describing how ancient pagan society claimed authority over the whole human being, and "absorbed the spiritual in the temporal power and at the same time apotheosized the State."[5] The temptation for temporal power to appropriate supernatural claims and sacralize itself is a constant presence in human history. As we will see later, it is not simply a temptation but the inevitable result of teleological instability.

The very first pages of Maritain's response to Maurras reveal the divine command upon which Maritain will ground his political philosophy, to which he returns throughout his later political writings: Christ's command to "render to Caesar the things that are Caesar's, and to God, the things that are God's" (Matt 22:21). Maritain considers this declaration by Christ to have instituted the perpetual distinction of the temporal plane from the spiritual plane and looks to Thomas Aquinas to provide a metaphysical explanation for this distinction.[6] Thomas recognizes the reality of both natural and supernatural desires, which arise from nature and grace. There is a real human nature, which desires ends proportionate and connatural to itself; there also are real supernatural desires which, because the goods desired transcend human nature, can only be moved by God.[7] Maritain sees in this distinction an elaboration of Christ's distinction of Caesar and God. What pertains to humanity's natural end relates to the temporal plane, and what pertains to humanity's supernatural end relates to the spiritual plane. While not always apparent, Maritain treats as synonymous the terms temporal, earthly, and natural.[8] Similarly, the eternal, spiritual, and supernatural are synonyms for the transcendent end in which grace elevates human nature to God. Each

---

(New York: Oxford University Press, 2011), 69–82. Maritain explicitly condemns Mussolini's fascist project as an example of the totalitarian State which claims to be the end of all human activities, outside of which no human or spiritual goods exist. See Jacques Maritain, *Integral Humanism, Freedom in the Modern World, and A Letter on Independence*, trans. Otto A. Bird, Collected Works of Jacques Maritain, vol. 11 (Notre Dame, IN: University of Notre Dame Press, 1996), 237, n. 5.

[5] Maritain, *The Things That Are Not Caesar's*, 1.

[6] "[The primacy of the spiritual] presents itself to us under three different aspects which the Doctrine of St. Thomas, better than any other after the Gospel and St. Paul, enables us to understand. . . . By his doctrine concerning nature and grace and the subordination of ends, he makes us understand the primacy of spiritual over political ends and of the universal domain of grace over all the particular divisions of nature" (Maritain, *The Things That Are Not Caesar's*, 78).

[7] For a survey of the debate regarding natural powers and supernatural ends within the Thomistic tradition, see "PaleoThomism? The Continuing Debate over the Natural Desire for the Vision of God," in Reinhard Hütter, *Dust Bound for Heaven: Explorations in the Theology of Thomas Aquinas* (Grand Rapids, MI: Eerdmans, 2012), 129–183.

[8] Maritain likewise uses the terms "plane," "sphere," and "order" synonymously to refer to the distinct ontological categories of the natural and supernatural. For consistency and clarity, I will only use the term "plane."

plane has its own proper end as well as powers and authorities ordered to the attainment of that end.

On Thomas's account, humanity has only one ultimate end (ST I-II, q. 1, aa. 4–8), which is the beatific vision and participation in divine life (ST I-II, q. 3, a. 8).[9] Furthermore, everything a person wills, they will either directly or as an intermediary for the sake of this single, ultimate end, whose attainment results in beatitude, or perfect happiness.[10] Therefore, the intermediate and ultimate ends desired by an individual belong to a single chain of ends, in which either imperfect goods (intermediate ends) are desired as "tending towards a perfect good" or the perfect good is desired as ultimate end, "since the beginning of something is always ordered toward its consummation."[11] Each intermediary good is desired explicitly or implicitly for the sake of attaining a higher, more ultimate good until at last one comes to rest in one's ultimate good, which cannot be anything except "seeing God's essence" (ST I-II, q. 3, a. 8). However, this end can only be attained by God's grace, because human nature and its powers can only attain ends proportionate to itself. Since God transcends all nature, human nature requires grace in order for its rational powers to be proportionate to God as its ultimate end.[12]

Maritain's proposal hinges upon a distinction between human ends appropriate to each plane and the proper autonomy derived from this distinction. In order to justify each plane's autonomy, Maritain attributes "ultimate ends" proper to each specific plane. He provides

---

[9] All translations of Thomas's *Summa Theologiae*, unless otherwise stated, are from Alfred Freddoso, www3.nd.edu/~afreddos/summa-translation/TOC.htm.

[10] For critiques of Thomas's argument for a singular ultimate end, see Peter F. Ryan, "Must the Acting Person Have a Single Ultimate End?," *Gregorianum* 82, no. 2 (2001): 325–356. See also Germain Grisez, "The True Ultimate End of Human Beings: The Kingdom, Not God Alone," *Theological Studies* 69, no. 1 (2008): 38–61, doi.org/10.1177/004056390806900102. For a defense of a singular last end, and an articulation of the different ways in which an action can be referred to the last end, see Thomas Osborne, "The Threefold Referral of Acts to the Ultimate End in Thomas Aquinas and His Commentators," *Angelicum* 85, no. 3 (2008): 715–736. See also William Mattison, "A New Look at the Last End: Noun and Verb, Determinate Yet Capable of Growth," *Journal of Moral Theology* 8, special issue no. 2 (2019): 95–113, jmt.scholasticahq.com/article/11427-a-new-look-at-the-last-end-noun-and-verb-determinate-yet-capable-of-growth. For a defense of Thomas against Grisez's critique, see Reinhard Hütter, *Bound for Beatitude: A Thomistic Study in Eschatology and Ethics* (Washington, DC: The Catholic University of America Press, 2022), 416–426.

[11] "What is not desired as a perfect good must be desired as tending toward a perfect good, i.e., an ultimate end, since the beginning of something is always ordered toward its consummation" (ST I-II, q. 1, a. 6).

[12] "Seeing God through his essence lies not only beyond human nature, but also beyond every creature's nature. . . . Hence, neither man nor any other creature can attain ultimate beatitude through his own natural power" (ST I-II q. 5, a. 5).

the clearest description in his later and perhaps most known work, *Man and the State*:

> For human life has two ultimate ends, the one subordinate to the other: an ultimate end *in a given order*, which is the terrestrial common good, or the *bonum vitae civilis*; and an *absolute* ultimate end, which is the transcendent, eternal common good. And individual ethics takes into account the subordinate ultimate end, but directly aims at the absolute ultimate one; whereas political ethics takes into account the absolute ultimate end, but its direct aim is the subordinate ultimate end, the good of the rational nature in its temporal achievement.[13]

In the temporal plane, a person seeks those ends proportionate to human nature as such. These ends include goods such as organizing society, agriculture, and raising a family, and can be achieved without supernatural graces and insight. All proximate ends within the temporal plane are ordered to the ultimate temporal end: the common good of civic life, even if the individual "takes into account" their absolute ultimate end. The temporal powers that order temporal goods to the ultimate temporal end have exclusive and legitimate autonomy within this plane. This both gives the State autonomy in its own plane but also strictly limits its concerns to the "the temporal life of men and their temporal good."[14] Or at the very least, it limits the State in theory.

While he makes a clear distinction between these planes, Maritain rejects an absolute distinction which sees each plane as equal and parallel. The temporal plane must always be understood as subordinate to the higher spiritual plane.[15] Humanity's supernatural end transcends the natural, and likewise the spiritual plane is superior to and higher than the temporal. The spiritual plane alone is ordered to the singular, absolute, ultimate end of the person, beatific vision and participation in divine life. The authority on the supernatural plane is the church, and in so far as this plane is superior to the temporal plane, the church also wields certain authority in the temporal plane, as when the papacy denounces a temporal group such as Action Française and forbids Catholics from participating in it.

In order to protect each authority's autonomy, Maritain deviates from a strictly Thomistic metaphysics and makes the surprising decision to refer to the ends of each plane as "ultimate" ends, where the temporal ultimate end is nevertheless subordinate to the spiritual ultimate end. This deviation from Thomas is absolutely essential to

---

[13] Jacques Maritain, *Man and the State* (Washington, DC: The Catholic University of America Press, 1998), 62, emphasis in original.

[14] Maritain, *Man and the State*, 153.

[15] Maritain is clear that things which are not Caesar's belong to a supernatural end transcending the temporal plane and having "higher place" and "higher dignity." See Maritain, *Man and the State*, 148–154.

Maritain's distinction of powers in each given plane. By avoiding the association of the temporal plane with a proximate end, Maritain can legitimize its proper autonomy. Within its proper plane, each authority acts as the highest power and directly towards its proper ultimate end. In order to clearly establish this autonomy, Maritain introduces two independent chains of ends, one temporal and one spiritual, each culminating in an ultimate end.

As Maritain develops his articulation of the distinct planes, we notice a change in language with regards to types of ends. In his 1936 work *Integral Humanism*, he explicitly describes the temporal common good as an "*intermediate end*," or what he coins as an "*infravalent end*."[16] Yet he elaborates that more precisely, the temporal common good can be recognized as an "ultimate end" in a given plane, yet subordinate to the absolute ultimate end. Nearly fifteen years later in *Man and the State*, Maritain drops any use of "intermediate" or "infravalent," maintaining that the temporal is subordinate to the spiritual, and establishing each as proper ultimate ends. Maritain offers two different notions of what the ultimate end of the natural plane may be. As seen above, he explicitly describes the temporal ultimate end as the temporal common good. Later in the same work, however, he describes how the end of the temporal common good is relativized, even in its own plane. While the temporal common good is an ultimate end, it "is an ultimate end in a relative sense and in a certain order, not the absolute ultimate end."[17] Maritain refers to a more traditional Aristotelian understanding, which subordinates even temporal goods to the higher natural end of contemplation.[18] He notes that even the common good is not the absolute ultimate end within the natural plane. There is hierarchy even here, so that the goods of society are subordinate to what Maritain terms "supra-temporal natural goods," such as justice, love of fellow persons, the transcendentals of truth and beauty, and the natural beginnings of contemplation.[19] These supra-temporal goods are found and pursued in the temporal plane yet transcend what Maritain has so far described as the ultimate temporal end. As he notes, "even in the natural order, the common good of the body politic implies an intrinsic

---

[16] Maritain, *Integral Humanism*, 237.

[17] Maritain, *Man and the State*, 149.

[18] Maritain even more explicitly ties the natural end of humanity to contemplation in *An Introduction to the Basic Problems of Moral Philosophy*, where he states that in the natural order humanity is ordered to the contemplation of God in God's effects, which nevertheless cannot perfectly satisfy the human desire to know God. In this work, Maritain anticipates our later discussion on the hypothetical state of "pure nature." See *An Introduction to the Basic Problems of Moral Philosophy*, trans. Cornelia N. Borgerhoff (Albany, NY: Magi, 1990), 90–110.

[19] Maritain, *Man and the State*, 148.

though indirect ordination to something which transcends it."[20] Even within the temporal plane, human nature points to a good beyond the common good, towards a natural good proportionate to a person's highest power: the actualization of the intellect in contemplating universal truths.[21] However, this cannot be considered an "absolute" ultimate natural end. For Maritain, there is only one absolute ultimate end, the supernatural end of life in God: "God is man's beatitude in the supernatural order, but not in the natural order, because man has no beatitude in the natural order."[22]

Relativizing the temporal common good serves a crucial function for Maritain: it delineates the powers and limitations of the State in the temporal plane. By clearly delineating the ends over which powers have authority, Maritain not only protects the freedom of the church but also describes a surprisingly limited State. The State is only a part of the body politic, the larger communal reality tending towards the common good and encompassing within itself all human temporal goods and relations.[23] Nevertheless, the State is the highest power of the body politic concerned with "the maintenance of law, the promotion of the common welfare and public order, and the administration of public affairs."[24] Even though it is the highest temporal power, Maritain expects the State to play only the limited role of the "central agency" of the body politic, working for the sake of the temporal good and allowing the body politic and its constitutive guilds, organizations, groups, and individuals to pursue their proper activity and ends.[25]

---

[20] Maritain, *Man and the State*, 149.
[21] For Maritain's most clear subordination of the temporal common good to the spiritual common good and the individual's contemplation, see Jacques Maritain, *The Person and the Common Good*, trans. John J. Fitzgerald (Notre Dame, IN: University of Notre Dame Press, 1947). Denis Bradley has argued that an intrinsic tension arises from Aristotle between the highest form of *eudaimonia*, found in pure contemplation, and Aristotle's claim that humanity is by nature social and the highest form of certain virtues must be exercised in and for the *polis*. See Denis J. M. Bradley, *Aquinas on the Twofold Human Good: Reason and Human Happiness in Aquinas's Moral Science* (Washington, DC: The Catholic University of America Press, 1997), 390–396. Kevin Flannery provides a history of this debate, especially recounting Maritain's and Charles De Koninck's influential contributions, and advocates for a relative understanding of the political common good in which the whole of political life is directed towards the good of contemplation. See Kevin Flannery, "The Common Good in Aristotle and Aquinas," in *Self-Transcendence and Virtue: Perspectives from Philosophy, Psychology, and Theology*, ed. Jennifer A. Frey and Candace A. Vogler, Routledge Studies in Ethics and Moral Theory (New York: Routledge, Taylor & Francis, 2019), 160.
[22] Maritain, *Basic Problems of Moral Philosophy*, 110.
[23] Maritain, *Man and the State*, 10.
[24] Maritain, *Man and the State*, 12.
[25] Bradley Lewis describes how Maritain's Thomistic personalism frames his political theory and situates the temporal common good as "a good precisely for persons" and

The State, therefore, has only an instrumental role. Maritain explains the limitations intrinsic to the body politic and temporal plane, stating: "Political society is essentially destined, by reason of the earthly end itself which specifies it, to the development of those environmental conditions which will so raise men in general to a level of material, intellectual, and moral life in accord with the good and peace of the whole, that each person will be positively aided in the progressive conquest of his full life as a person and of his spiritual freedom."[26] This need not be understood as some radically libertarian vision of the State. Robust healthcare systems, social safety nets, and any number of contemporary civil institutions are perfectly compatible with Maritain's vision of the State. What we are left with, however, if Maritain's vision were to be successfully implemented, would be an instrumental State whose function is to facilitate the conditions necessary for other associations and individuals to have the possibility of attaining their own ends while itself remaining subordinate to those ends. In fact, Maritain asserts that if human society attempted to liberate itself from this subordination to higher ends, "and to proclaim itself the supreme good, in the very same measure it perverts its own nature and that of the political common good."[27]

This limited and functional understanding has a surprising resemblance to what Alasdair MacIntyre refers to when he compares the State to a telephone company. MacIntyre famously described how the nation-state is capable of furnishing certain temporal goods and services so long as it is appropriately small enough for real civic deliberation. In this way, it functions as a "bureaucratic supplier of goods and services," which only seeks to provide the conditions by which citizens might pursue their true ends.[28] Such a State would allow the freedom not only for the church and religious believer to be most fully themselves, and various other public non-State organizations to pursue their own ends, but would also restrain itself and resist claiming higher ends than appropriate to its plane. MacIntyre contrasts this limited State with the totalitarian nation-state,

---

the development of individual personality and flourishing. This personalist political theory was meant to oppose and resist the totalitarianisms of the mid-twentieth century but was itself attacked by Thomists in part for situating individual good in opposition to the common good. See V. Bradley Lewis, "Thomism, Personalism, and Politics: The Case of Jacques Maritain," *Quaestiones Disputatae* 9, no. 2 (2019): 151–173, dx.doi.org/10.5840/qd2019929.

[26] Maritain, *Integral Humanism*, 237.
[27] Maritain, *Man and the State*, 149.
[28] Alasdair MacIntyre, "A Partial Response to My Critics," in *After MacIntyre: Critical Perspectives on the Work of Alasdair MacIntyre*, ed. John Horton and Susan Mendus (Notre Dame, IN: University of Notre Dame Press, 1994), 303.

which presents itself as a "repository of sacred values."[29] This sort of nation-state, which claims to supply identity and purpose while also purporting to be the supreme vehicle to achieve meaning, progress, and temporal happiness, has already collapsed into the perversion Maritain described by proclaiming itself a supreme good.

By uniting Thomistic philosophy and Christ's distinction, Maritain gave the twentieth century a means by which a diverse populace could nevertheless unite to pursue temporal goods, while still subordinating these goods to human nature's ultimate supernatural end. However, we shall see that by cleaving these two planes to two separate chains of ends, Maritain unwittingly built his distinction upon a fundamentally unstable foundation. We can see the cracks in the distinction by examining how Maritain understands Christian action in the temporal plane.

CHRISTIAN ACTION AND THE BLURRING OF SEPARATION

How might a Christian, who knows that her ultimate, absolute end transcends the temporal common good, function in the temporal plane? According to Maritain's vision, a Christian operates in the world according to the acquired virtues and seeks natural ends appropriate to the temporal plane. Maritain distinguishes between the action of a Christian and that of a Christian *qua* Christian.[30] The Christian is formed by the teachings of the Gospel and the church; she is directed to care for the poor according to Christ's command, but nevertheless participates in the temporal plane as a citizen, not essentially *qua* Christian. The action of a Christian could be anything she does in the temporal plane: organizing a political campaign, cooking a meal, founding a business, etc. These acts are done by a Christian, no doubt. Yet these acts are properly temporal, they make use of natural powers and virtues, and do not directly have as their object supernatural ends.

The acting person, therefore, becomes the uniting reality which integrates otherwise separate planes. The person alone is "simultaneously a member of that society which is the Church," as well as a member of the body politic, and therefore "an absolute division between those two societies would mean that the human person must be cut in two."[31] Maritain sees that the Christian acts in the temporal plane for the sake of natural goods, but properly refers them to God indirectly. Even while pursuing such temporal goods as nutrition, the Christian can perform these actions with God in mind. Maritain thereby unites the two separate chains of ends, one

---

[29] MacIntyre, "A Partial Response to My Critics," 303.
[30] Maritain, *Integral Humanism*, 338.
[31] Maritain, *Man and the State*, 153.

subordinate to the other, not as one single chain as proposed by Thomas but as united only in the person herself. The result is that all actions are done by the singular human person, but according to the distinct planes and intelligible within their specific plane. For example, the fortitude of a Christian prosecutor seeking justice against organized crime utilizes the same powers and goods as that of the unbaptized fellow prosecutor in the same office. However, the purpose for the Christian prosecutor's actions may be indirectly referred to God, such that she pursues natural goods but does so for the sake of a supernatural end. Nevertheless, Maritain considers these to be acquired virtues, performed by both Christians and non-Christians for authentically temporal ends. This distinction protects the reality of the natural goods while still allowing the Christian to refer these goods to God.

Despite his persistent efforts to maintain a complete distinction between the two planes, Maritain himself must introduce qualifying statements which shows the instability of this division. A 'direct' and 'indirect' distinction cannot adequately describe all the actions that take place within the proper planes. In *Integral Humanism,* he introduces a third plane, partially uniting the separated two ends of human nature, which attends to those matters that do not fit exclusively within only one plane.[32] This intermediary plane contains spiritual matters interwoven into the temporal plane and "differs from the purely spiritual plane only by accidental distinction; the intermediary plane is the plane of the spiritual itself as inflected on the side of the temporal and joining the later."[33] These include realities such as marriage, education, certain civic activities, and all temporal activity nevertheless directed toward a supernatural end.[34] In this third plane, a Christian is not merely acting in the temporal plane and indirectly referring their temporal ends to God. They pursue truly temporal realities with a direct reference to God. This plane is the realm of Catholic Action, where Christians act in the temporal plane for the sake of temporal goods, and do so *as Christians.*[35] These goods defy the absolute distinction between temporal and spiritual, and "while concerning the earthly city, they concern also, directly or indirectly, the good of souls and eternal life" and therefore "the Christian, as a member of the Mystical Body, has to consider them primarily and above all not according as they concern the temporal

---

[32] See Maritain, *Integral Humanism*, 339–342.
[33] Maritain, *Integral Humanism*, 339.
[34] Maritain, *Integral Humanism*, 340–342.
[35] Maritain, *Integral Humanism*, 340.

order . . . but according to as they concern the supratemporal goods of the human person and the common good of the Church of Christ."[36]

Maritain recognizes that supratemporal goods seem to reside in a gray area between the temporal and spiritual planes. There is something even within the temporal plane which does not seem restricted merely to that plane. Even certain temporal goods belong to a single chain of ends, not two independent ends as suggested by the distinction of the two planes. Maritain's attempt to find stability by introducing an "intermediate" third plane only serves to crack the wall of separation Maritain constructs throughout his corpus.

CAVANAUGH, DE LUBAC, AND HUMANITY'S SINGULAR END

Maritain's argument depends upon a clear distinction between two legitimate, independent, though unequal, human ends. While Maritain primarily seeks to liberate the church from being co-opted by worldly powers, William Cavanaugh has accused Maritain's distinction of preventing the church from speaking forcefully against temporal injustices. In his book *Torture and Eucharist,* Cavanaugh targets Maritain as the source of the deficient ecclesiology that silenced ecclesial authorities in the face of Pinochet's regime of torture and terror against the Chilean people.[37] Cavanaugh argues that Maritain's distinct planes reduced the church to an invisible reality, responsible only for the immaterial soul, and therefore ceded all temporal concerns to the authority of the State. While Cavanaugh's primary concern is to show that the church must recognize itself as a real, material body with authority and concerns regarding temporal goods, Cavanaugh criticizes Maritain precisely because of the metaphysical distinction discussed above. His critique reveals that properly understanding the relationship between human ends is essential to political theology. However, despite Cavanaugh's insightful critiques of Maritain and his insistence upon a single chain of ends, his own proposal is detrimental to properly understanding the relationship between humanity's natural and supernatural ends.

---

[36] Maritain, *Integral Humanism*, 340.
[37] William T. Cavanaugh, *Torture and Eucharist: Theology, Politics, and the Body of Christ*, Challenges in Contemporary Theology (Oxford: Blackwell, 1998). Cavanaugh shows the influence Maritain had on the South American Church, and most especially Chile. He argues that Maritain's distinction gave the state responsibility over Chilean bodies and the church responsibility over Chilean souls (*Torture and Eucharist*, 16). Because Pinochet's torture regime targeted supposed enemies of the political body, the State alone had power over what occurred to these Chilean bodies. Cavanaugh argues that only by recovering a theology of the church as Christ's *corpus verum* can the church properly understand itself as a real political body, instituted by Christ against the violent order of the world. See *Torture and Eucharist*, 15–18.

Cavanaugh critiques the foundational distinction Maritain attempts to forge between temporal and spiritual ends. He sees in Maritain the general failure of neo-Thomism, and accuses him of relying on the Thomistic commentaries of Cajetan, Suarez, and John of St. Thomas and their Thomistic school, which claims to find in Thomas a justification for a "pure nature," an aspect of the human person wholly autonomous from humanity's spiritual end.[38] Neither fallen due to sin nor elevated by grace, this "pure nature" gives the metaphysical justification for truly autonomous and independent natural ends. In this reading, while temporal ends are subordinate to spiritual ends, the temporal is nevertheless protected from any "permeation" of the spiritual into the temporal.[39]

The result, according to Cavanaugh, is a temporal plane sealed off from supernatural ends. However, a State in such a plane rarely limits itself to the restricted temporal goods over which Maritain grants it responsibility. Cavanaugh claims that the State, in order to direct a society to a common good, must accrue to itself the absolute power Maritain himself wishes to limit. As Cavanaugh retorts, "The State cannot be expected to limit itself to the body; it will colonize the soul as well. A secular faith will not stay long confined to some temporal sphere; the secular god is a jealous god."[40] Even though Maritain notes time and time again that the temporal is subordinate to the supernatural, in reality what results is a "pure temporal plane" only subordinated to the supernatural by an interior disposition of the acting Christian, not by any metaphysical reality stitched into the created order.

Cavanaugh seeks to emphasize the complete transformation grace brings about in the life of the Christian, and rejects the idea that a Christian can seek "purely" temporal goods with only a minimal indirect reference to supernatural ends. Cavanaugh accuses Maritain of believing that Christian truth "is not directly applicable to concrete problems in the political and prudential sphere."[41] At its most extreme, this distinct separation allows for practical and prudential natural reasoning which at times necessitates Christians in the world to "soil ourselves" through the toleration of lesser evils such as the use of police methods which "cannot help being rough" while securing peace and order.[42] By separating the two planes and claiming two

---

[38] Cavanaugh, *Torture and Eucharist*, 183.
[39] Cavanaugh, *Torture and Eucharist*, 184.
[40] Cavanaugh, *Torture and Eucharist*, 196.
[41] Cavanaugh, *Torture and Eucharist*, 169.
[42] Cavanaugh cites at length the complete passages that follow Maritain's distinction between the ultimate temporal end and the absolute ultimate end. He brings attention to the dangerous way in which Maritain's distinction gives direct support to violent though "necessary" police action for the sake of securing the temporal common good.

autonomous ultimate ends, Maritain allows for a temporal plane subordinate to the spiritual in name only. Instead, "the very distinction of planes" eliminates any interference the church may have had against the State and erases the church as the material body of Christ on earth, with the result that "only the State is left to impersonate God."[43] As Cavanaugh describes throughout his historical account of the Pinochet regime, this leads the State to insist that the church remain in its own plane, speaking only to matters of conscience, not matters of temporal concern such as what is to be done to the bodies of those "enemies of the State."

Uncharacteristically for the adamant pacifist, Cavanaugh enters into the fierce nature-grace debate not as a peacemaker but with a sword. Drawing upon De Lubac, Cavanaugh considers Maritain's position to be a gross distortion of Thomas's theology of grace and the infused virtues. Christian action in the temporal plane must do more than merely 'take into account' the absolute ultimate end of God. For Thomas, rather, "The supernatural virtues *transform* the natural virtues to direct them to their proper end."[44] According to Cavanaugh, when Aquinas says that charity is the form of the virtues, he does not mean that charity merely should be "'taken into account' while acting in history."[45] Rather, Cavanaugh claims that supernatural virtues "transform" the acquired virtues and direct them towards their "proper end."[46]

Cavanaugh critiques a two-tiered understanding of the human person by appealing to Henri De Lubac's *Surnaturel*.[47] This work, Cavanagh claims, "showed that the Dominican's understanding of a hypothetical state of 'pure nature' and the resultant dual finality of human nature was nowhere to be found in Thomas."[48] Following De Lubac, Cavanaugh claims that grace elevates and directs nature so that it might serve a new end which informs and touches all aspects of human life. Against Maritain, who considered it possible for a Christian to go about the world seeking temporal goods and entering into temporal projects properly speaking, Cavanaugh assumes that

---

Cavanaugh shows how Pinochet's Chile appealed to this distinction to justify police action against dissidents, police action which clandestinely included sophisticated kidnapping and torture. See Cavanaugh, *Torture and Eucharist*, 182; Maritain, *Man and the State*, 62–63.

[43] Cavanaugh, *Torture and Eucharist*, 193.
[44] Cavanaugh, *Torture and Eucharist*, 182, emphasis original.
[45] Cavanaugh, *Torture and Eucharist*, 182.
[46] Cavanaugh, *Torture and Eucharist*, 182.
[47] Cavanaugh reads De Lubac in no small way through John Milbank. For a critique of Milbank and a presentation of the wide agreement and remaining disagreement between the De Lubac school and various contemporary Thomists, see Nicholas Healy, Jr., "Henri de Lubac on Nature and Grace: A Note on Some Recent Contributions to the Debate," *Communio* 35, no. 4 (2008): 535–564.
[48] Cavanaugh, *Torture and Eucharist*, 184.

grace in general, and charity in particular, ought to inform and transform all actions and virtues such that they are all now directed towards God.[49] The whole of the Christian has been shaped and elevated by grace, such that they might actually be able to obey Paul's command: "whether you eat, or drink, or whatsoever else you do, do all for the Glory of God" (1 Cor 10:31). The Christian cannot remain unaffected, because where the waters of baptism reach, they elevate and sanctify, and there is no aspect of human life they do not reach.

Cavanaugh is right to criticize Maritain's absolute distinction between the temporal and supernatural planes. While Maritain makes this distinction with laudable intention, the consequences are dire: by relegating the church to a mere mystical body, he cedes the material body to the power of the State. While Maritain wishes to see the State as a limited institution functioning only to allow other real temporal associations to flourish, instead his scheme tends towards the absolutist State he himself condemns. As Cavanaugh notes, this failure is actually unavoidable in Maritain's schema. However, Cavanaugh's emphasis on grace also leads him into dangerous waters regarding the good of human nature itself. By claiming that the supernatural virtues not only elevate human nature, but "transform" the acquired virtues and direct them towards their "proper" ends, Cavanaugh erases any possibility of natural human goods *qua* nature. Human nature is not merely elevated, but destroyed and replaced by something new when grace introduces a new end. But such violence can be avoided, as can Maritain's State slipping into totalitarianism. We must navigate a different approach, which can unite Maritain's two planes without destroying the reality and goodness of human nature.

NATURAL OPENNESS, NATURAL INSTABILITY, AND THE TELEOLOGICAL CRISIS

While Cavanaugh and De Lubac are right to be critical of an absolutely separate and autonomous "pure" human nature, we can look beyond the late scholastic commentaries and recover Thomas's own understanding of "pure nature" to discover a more secure metaphysical description of human ends. The concept of "pure nature" ought to be understood simply as a hypothetical through which Thomas can describe human teleology. By examining "pure nature" as a hypothetical

---

[49] "In Aquinas, however, the supernatural virtues *transform* the natural virtues to direct them to their proper end.... Charity transforms both the status and the *content* of the natural virtues, which is precisely the importance in Aquinas's account of *infused natural virtues,* which are essentially different from acquired natural virtues because of the end to which they are directed" (Cavanaugh, *Torture and Eucharist*, 182, emphasis in original).

state, we can come to appreciate that while ordered to real natural ends, human nature is also inherently open to supernatural ends. Such an openness relativizes the happiness that comes from attaining natural ends as "imperfect happiness" and reserves perfect *eudaimonia* for the single ultimate end of participation in the Divine Life. This reading reunites human ends within a single chain of ends. It also reveals inherent instability in natural ends when considered in themselves. This natural instability provides a metaphysical explanation for the State's collapse into authoritarian absolutism: when the State claims to be, or is forced to become, an ultimate end, it enters into a teleological crisis it seeks to resolve through the stability found only in supernatural claims.

The concept of "pure nature" is not meant to suggest that at any point in creation there actually existed an ungraced, unfallen nature capable of perfect and complete happiness. Rather, "pure nature" is a hypothetical necessary for rationally describing what and how grace elevates. In order to understand what grace does to the redeemed person, we must postulate what the rational creature is capable of on its own. According to Thomas Aquinas, the human person is a strange composite. The human person is a union of material, sensible animality with the immaterial, rational soul capable of understanding and contemplating universals (ST I, q. 75, a. 4; ST I, q. 76, aa. 1, 5). Perhaps part of the trouble with which Maritain's work wrestles is the problem that nowhere else in creation except humanity are material body and rational soul brought together in this way. This union complicates our understanding of humanity's natural end. Human nature is capable of goods appropriate to its natural ends: it is capable of reproducing and raising children, proportionate to its animality. It is capable of living in society, and most importantly, of contemplation according to its rational soul. Because the rational powers of the soul are the highest and most noble powers, the ends to which they are ordered are appropriately understood as the highest human ends.

However, as Thomas argues through appeal to Aristotle, this natural end is itself unstable.[50] The highest good the human can achieve, the contemplation of the First Mover in its effects, is exceptionally difficult to reach, and even the rare few who do achieve it in this life do so only momentarily. Maritain himself recognizes this in *The Basic Problems of Moral Philosophy*.[51] There, he sympathizes with the lament of the Book of Ecclesiastes, which bemoans that no

---

[50] Aristotle notes that human contemplation cannot attain its perfection perpetually, but only intermittently, interrupted by exhaustion or death. Thomas reframes Aristotle's argument in a Christian metaphysics, seeing that the imperfect happiness attainable by reason alone is properly understood as incomplete, but that the potential for perfect, perpetual happiness is found only in participating in the divine essence, which transcends the capabilities of human reason. See Bradley, *Aquinas on the Twofold Human Good*, 396–408.

[51] Maritain, *Basic Problems of Moral Philosophy*, 89–110.

real happiness can be found in this life.⁵² As Maritain notes, "If we had a purely terrestrial existence, Ecclesiastes would be right" in his existential lament.⁵³ The knowledge of the First Mover attained naturally only is of God's effects, never of God directly. And so, the highest achievable good by natural means cannot satisfy; the ends of the temporal plane cannot provide the perfect happiness that ought to constitute an ultimate end.⁵⁴

Nevertheless, humanity is not and has never been confined to a "purely terrestrial" State. That idea is simply a logical tool necessary to understand how grace perfects human nature without destroying it.⁵⁵ As Maritain's fellow Thomist Thomas Joseph White has argued, "There must be at least *some concept of natural teleological ends* in human beings based upon *what* human beings are that can be identified rationally as a precondition for any narrative of human teleology, *theological or otherwise*."⁵⁶ Only by attending to the hierarchy of humanity's natural ends can we understand that grace elevates human nature without doing violence to it.⁵⁷ For White, this means recognizing that the individual's natural desire to contemplate God through the rational powers is the necessary prerequisite to the

---

⁵² "The highest act I am capable of concerning God in the order of nature, is to know Him by his effects, an act of philosophical contemplation which, even if it is experiential like the wordless contemplation of natural mysticism, will always remain knowledge seen as in mirror, enigmatic, incapable of uniting me really and directly with the divine object which yet must be my ultimate end" (Maritain, *Basic Problems of Moral Philosophy*, 108).

⁵³ Maritain, *Basic Problems of Moral Philosophy*, 96.

⁵⁴ "Thus, God is indeed the end I am turned toward; but from the point of view where I am placed, from the point of view simply of nature, it is an end which–even when I have quit the present life–does not fulfill me, does not satisfy all my capacity for desire. The philosopher is left facing a paradox: the absolute Good, the subsisting Good, is not existentially what it should be, namely my *total good*" (Maritain, *Basic Problems of Moral Philosophy*, 108. emphasis in original).

⁵⁵ David Grumet has argued that De Lubac himself recognized this theoretical role of hypothetical "pure nature," but also saw how after the hypothesis was introduced, it slowly reified into a real category. See David Grumett, "De Lubac, Grace, and the Pure Nature Debate," *Modern Theology* 31, no. 1 (January 2015): 123–146, doi.org/10.1111/moth.12116.

⁵⁶ Thomas Joseph White, "The 'Pure Nature' of Christology: Human Nature and *Gaudium et Spes* 22," *Nova et Vetera* 8, no. 2 (Spring 2010): 313, emphasis in original.

⁵⁷ This, for Thomas, is the meaning of *capax dei*, that human nature is naturally capable of God. If this were not the case, the elevation of nature's end to God would make of the person something new. It would be violence upon the person, instead of perfection. As Hütter notes, "Because the human being, qua intellect and will, has been made capable for this end (*capax Dei*) by God such that human nature indeed is characterized by a genuine openness to and capacity for God. For this very reason, human nature is in no way transmuted into something else by being elevated to such a surpassing end" (Hütter, *Dust Bound for Heaven*, 141).

claim that grace elevates human nature such that it can now proportionately attain God as such. Human nature, therefore, is ordered to contemplating God in God's effects, but intrinsically open to this higher end.

What does this openness entail? As we have noted, the final end of human nature according to Thomas and Maritain is not the temporal common good. Rather, it is the natural contemplation of the first mover, God. This can be achieved by the natural powers of rational intellect alone. However, despite being humanity's natural end, humanity also seems unable to perfectly attain it. Aquinas develops Aristotle's notion of natural happiness, showing how the happiness of contemplation lacks the necessary characteristic of stability. As White explains, such a contemplation is "frail and can only be exercised periodically, rather than in an enduring way."[58] Because it is frail and incomplete, and knowledge is attained only indirectly through sensible realities, "the happiness it procures, while real, is also fundamentally incomplete."[59] Thomas terms it "imperfect happiness." It lacks the permanence that perfect, immediate knowledge of God and beatitude requires. Nevertheless, the human intellect "stirs up in us a desire for knowledge of something we cannot attain perfectly," the knowledge of God, a desire that only grace can fulfill.[60] By virtue of its ordering to the knowledge of God despite its inability to perfectly attain that knowledge, human nature is intrinsically open to this higher end.[61] White can summarize, therefore, that human nature has a natural capacity and desire to see God, while the human soul nevertheless "is in no way naturally inclined to the supernatural object of faith as such."[62] The instability of human nature's proper natural end is an essential reality pointing beyond itself to the only end which can actually satisfy that same nature. Only by carefully attending to this balance can we maintain a natural orientation to God while still preserving real but imperfect natural beatitude.

Although such a reflection has much to say to the nature-grace debate in general, it also provides a path to reconcile some aspects of

---

[58] Thomas Joseph White, "Imperfect Happiness and the Final End of Man: Thomas Aquinas and the Paradigm of Nature-Grace Orthodoxy," *The Thomist* 78, no. 2 (2014): 275, dx.doi.org/10.1353/tho.2014.0015.
[59] White, "Imperfect Happiness and the Final End of Man," 264.
[60] White, "Imperfect Happiness and the Final End of Man," 275.
[61] White argues that Thomas cautiously balances his distinction between natural and supernatural ends on a razor's edge: "If we affirm too one-sidedly a merely natural end that is not constituted by the immediate knowledge of God, . . . we lose sight of the intrinsic orientation of the human spirit toward God himself. If we emphasize the latter inclination exclusively . . . then we will be obliged to deny that indirect philosophical contemplation of God is a truly teleological form of beatitude (White, "Imperfect Happiness and the Final End of Man," 277).
[62] White, "Imperfect Happiness and the Final End of Man," 282.

the otherwise divergent approaches of Maritain and Cavanaugh. Maritain and Cavanaugh both lament that the State seems to continually appropriate the supernatural for its own purposes. This happens in empires like pagan Rome, and also in modern nation-states such as Maurras's France and Pinochet's Chile. Yet by recovering Thomas's carefully balanced distinction we can understand the metaphysical explanation as to why temporal powers continually seize upon the spiritual. Natural ends are not stable when isolated and siloed into their own plane. Human reason cannot attain its perfect beatitude by natural means, and to make a proximate end such as the temporal common good an ultimate end asks a lesser good to give more than it can provide. By attempting to build a clear division between the temporal and spiritual, Maritain actually allows for the unstable conditions that lead the State to grasp for a transcendent anchor.

It is not simply a historical reality that nation-states have established themselves as keepers of supernatural identity. This is a metaphysical necessity. Thomas claims that an individual can have only one ultimate end towards which all actions are directed and ordered. To have two ultimate ends renders human action unintelligible (ST I-II, q. 1, aa. 5–6). By making temporal goods into ultimate ends, Maritain throws the temporal plane into a teleological crisis. When the temporal attempts to justify itself as an ultimate end, when natural ends are seen not only as distinct but also separate from supernatural ends, they become susceptible to the same intrinsic instability found in humanity's natural end. It must then justify and make itself intelligible as an ultimate end, which for Thomas means that it must "fulfill the whole of man's appetite in such a way that nothing is outside of it that is left to be desired" (ST I-II, q.1, a. 5). In order to render itself intelligible and stable, the State must implicitly or explicitly propose an account of human nature and desire which finds its fulfillment in what the State claims to provide. It must become totalizing, and totalitarian.

This becomes evident most clearly in the ways the State violates the boundaries Maritain establishes and instead becomes a pseudo-religious institution and keeper of ultimate identity and meaning. The result is what Emilio Gentile describes as a "sacralization of politics" which "comes about every time any political entity, such as nation, state, race, class, or party, assumes the characteristics of a sacred entity, that is to say, a supreme power that is indisputable and intangible, and that becomes the object of faith, reverence, worship, loyalty, and dedication of citizens to the point where they are prepared to sacrifice their own lives."[63] Durkheim famously describes the

---

[63] Gentile, "Fascistese," 75.

functional way in which religion operates in society, acting as a binding agent which unites societies and provides transcendental purpose and direction.[64] This was precisely how Maurras sought to use Catholicism. Recent scholarship has also analyzed the way in which nationalism operates as a "politicization of religion" and "messianisation of politics."[65] The State begins not only to provide the conditions for human flourishing, but the sole and ultimate means to accomplish that flourishing. It seeks to make what can only be an imperfect end into an ultimate end, crashing the distinct planes together once again, but underneath the absolute State.

If such is the case, it seems any natural end can devolve into an absolutist institution. Why is it that nation-states become sacralized, and yet telephone companies rarely do? Based on the metaphysics of human nature presented by Thomas, it appears to occur only when natural ends are made to be ultimate ends and claim the authority to bring about that end. Were a corporation to do so, it would likewise enter a teleological crisis and need to bolster itself with supernatural meaning. But rarely, if ever, do corporations see themselves as anything more than instrumental realties seeking intermediate goods. Corporations therefore seldom enter into teleological crisis. Similarly, limited temporal powers such as cities are understood to be instrumental goods and therefore cities such as Paris or Chicago do not claim to be the keeper of the temporal ultimate end.

The temporal plane is unstable not because nature itself is unstable, but because humanity cannot attain perfection in nature. Any imperfect human end is intrinsically unstable. Any attempt to claim a natural good as an ultimate end necessarily puts that end on a path towards absolutism. While Maritain and Cavanaugh have attributed this to a desire for power, Thomas's metaphysics suggests there is also an intrinsic metaphysical failure at the root of this teleological crisis. We find in Thomas that all conflicts do not inevitably boil down to base power games. The nation-state does not merely claim the soul because it can. It seizes the supernatural like a drowning person seizes a tree branch: it is the only thing that can save it from its inherent unintelligibility.

Here, we can deepen Cavanaugh's own description of the rise of nationalism and provide a metaphysical description for the State's temptation towards idolatry. Cavanaugh has outlined the historical developments that led to the nation-state as we know it, and the

---

[64] See Émile Durkheim, *The Elementary Forms of Religious Life*, trans. Carol Cosman (Oxford: Oxford University Press, 2001).

[65] For an overview of diverse approaches to the relationship between nationalism and religion, see Anthony D. Smith, "The 'Sacred' Dimension of Nationalism," *Millennium* 29, no. 3 (December 1, 2000): 791–814, dx.doi.org/10.1177/03058298000290030301.

secularism that elevated the State into a pseudo-religious cult.[66] He has also provided an analysis of the way nationalisms elevate the nation-state into a sacred institution, mirroring religious devotion and practice.[67] Most recently, he has described Nationalism as a form of idolatry, in which devotion is directed towards the wrong end and treats the political community as an end in itself.[68] The argument I propose does not undermine his claims, but rather suggests an intrinsic explanation as to why temporal powers, isolated into their own independent plane, seem to inevitably unite in themselves the temporal and spiritual to become an idol.

CONCLUSION

A proper understanding of "pure human nature" reveals that human nature is open to goods beyond what its powers can attain. If this reality is not properly situated within a singular chain of human ends which relegates temporal ends to intermediate status, it will create a situation in which the temporal must claim to satisfy even supernatural desires.

This analysis suggests that there is a proper role for temporal powers and authentically natural ends. Maritain is correct to name the ways in which civil powers can foster the attainment of true human ends. However, by making so stark a separation between the temporal and spiritual planes and granting temporal powers ultimate ends, Maritain creates a teleological crisis in which the State, to secure its intelligibility and resolve its intrinsic instability, must accrue to itself the myths and grammar which signify it as an ultimate good. Cavanaugh sought to resolve this intrinsic instability by transforming all human ends into supernatural ends. However, by recognizing that human nature is itself open to supernatural fulfillment we can begin to construct a properly Christian understanding of civil society allowing for real natural ends. Such an understanding necessarily introduces limits into the purview and authority of the State, but does so in order

---

[66] Cavanaugh describes the transformation of the State into the nation-state in the nineteenth century, which was only possible because of the increased influence temporal powers accrued over citizens' identity. State-sponsored education, standardized language, and national identity united disparate peoples and inculcated a common vision and common original mythos of the nation and claimed a citizen's highest allegiance and deepest identity. See William T. Cavanaugh, *Migrations of the Holy: God, State, and the Political Meaning of the Church* (Grand Rapids, MI: Eerdmans, 2011), 12–24, 34–37.
[67] William T. Cavanaugh, *The Myth of Religious Violence: Secular Ideology and the Roots of Modern Conflict* (Oxford: Oxford University Press, 2009), 57–122.
[68] William T. Cavanaugh, "The Splendid Idolatry of Nationalism," *Pro Publico Bono–Magyar Kozigazgatas*, no. 2 (2021): 20, doi.org/10.32575/ppb.2021.2.1.

to keep an institution from swimming in waters in which it should not find itself in the first place. The result is not a further subjection of temporal powers to the supernatural, but merely the necessary recognition that the temporal is ordered to intermediate ends, that there are higher ends, and that the State lacks the power to attain those ends. Furthermore, it maintains this limitation by properly placing temporal ends within the single chain of ends Thomas Aquinas grounds in human teleology. Such an approach points to a resolution of the teleological crisis and provides a foundation for a humble yet effective State buffered against the threat of idolatry.

Gilbrian Stoy, CSC is a priest in the Congregation of Holy Cross and doctoral student at the Catholic University of America. He is particularly interested in political theology and economic ethics.

Distinct But Not Separate: Rethinking Maritain's Distinction of Planes to Recover His Democratic Potential

Travis Knoll

Abstract: Few Catholic theologians wielded as much influence over the Twentieth-Century Catholic Church as Jacques Maritain. Furthermore, few have stirred as much global controversy in the realm of theological politics (especially in the area of global affairs). Considered treasonous by Latin American conservatives and impractical by those arguing for a politically active church, Maritain's work touts a contemplative moderation that frustrates all political sides. Maritain's canon daunts even the best readers and often breeds practical misinterpretation of his own philosophy. Using primary sources from Argentina and Brazil, this article reexamines Maritain's distinction of the spiritual and worldly planes and its application to Maritain's political thought during both the Spanish Civil War period and Brazil's twenty-one-year dictatorship (1964–1985). It thereby pushes back on longstanding theological critiques of this distinction. Far from advocating a church aloof from the political sphere, Maritain advocated for vigorous engagement with it while maintaining the church's spiritual integrity.

INTRODUCTION: MISREADING MARITAIN

"From Jacques Maritain, bishops had learned to distinguish the spiritual and the temporal planes and expected that the Church as a body would *only act to form individuals* on the spiritual plane."[1] With those words, theologian William T. Cavanaugh summed up why Jacques Maritain, a proponent of center-left politics and community organizing, and vehement critic of both Catholic and secular fascism, has been dismissed as an unwitting aid and comfort to authoritarians. While Maritain never fully separated spiritual from earthly affairs, distinguishing the two gave earthly matters precedence and allegedly prevented concrete responses to oppressive governments. Cavanaugh advanced this reading as a central theme of

---

[1] William T. Cavanaugh, "The Church in the Streets: Eucharist and Politics," *Modern Theology* 30, no. 2 (2014): 389, dx.doi.org/10.1111/moth.12103, emphasis added.

his dissertation and subsequent book based upon it, *Torture and Eucharist*, to explain the reticence of the Chilean Church to speak out against the horrific abuses of the Pinochet regime.

In this telling, social Catholics like Maritain, from the time of Benito Mussolini and Adolf Hitler through Augusto Pinochet, had sought to separate the mystical body of Christ from politics in favor of civil society participation through groups such as Catholic Action. They had failed. Figures such as Pius XI had been outsmarted by states constantly breaking their agreements and demanding more and more loyalty to the state.[2]

Cavanaugh's dissertation and the book do an exemplary job of detailing how Christian Democrats in Brazil and Chile picked up Maritain's work, which began as a reaction to Falangists' sacralization of Francisco Franco's efforts in the Spanish Civil War. He details the tensions Maritain caused in Argentina, and Maritain's skepticism over some reforms at the Second Vatican Council. Cavanaugh glosses several iterations of the spiritual/temporal (worldly) distinction and cites many of the Argentine and Brazilian intellectual debates I deal with here.[3] Cavanaugh uses a quote from Maritain's *Integral Humanism* (1936) on the participation of Christians in war to drive Maritain's complacency home: "To stain our fingers is not to stain our hearts."[4]

Cavanaugh takes special umbrage at Maritain's view of rights and the role of the state. Maritain's political vision, in Cavanaugh's reading, did not allow Christians to involve themselves *as Christians* in social actions, including human rights. Human rights themselves were too vague to provide sustenance to concrete communities outside of the state, and human rights were inseparable from the anti-clerical historical context that gave rise to them. This ahistorical reading of rights led naïve political philosophers such as Hernan Montealegre Klenner to aggrandize the state and paved the way for Pinochet's ideologues such as Jaime Guzman to enshrine Maritain's view of man and the state into the junta's founding documents and the Chilean Constitution. In an ironic twist, and again due to the supposed influence of Maritain, Christian Democratic parties would continue Pinochet's neoliberal policies, earning praise from Pinochet's former officials.[5]

Cavanaugh does not see Maritain's use in Chile as an aberration. While there may have been "difficulty with translating Maritain's ideas" from Europe, Cavanaugh does not claim Pinochet's right-hand

---

[2] William T. Cavanaugh, *Torture and Eucharist: Theology, Politics, and the Body of Christ* (Malden, MA: Wiley-Blackwell, 1998), 124, 132–135, 140–141.
[3] Cavanaugh, *Torture and Eucharist*, 155–160.
[4] Cavanaugh citing Maritain, *Integral Humanism*, 249, in *Torture and Eucharist*, 170.
[5] Cavanaugh, *Torture and Eucharist*, 187–189, 191–192, 198, 200–202.

officials and reticent church officials misread Maritain. In fact, the "failure of [Maritain's] project in [Chile's] context . . . may be instructive for Christian political practice in other contexts."[6] Whether looking to Europe or elsewhere, Cavanaugh's argument on Maritain's applicability needs revisiting in light of larger historical trends beyond Chile. As such, I turn toward the original text in question as well as Maritain's own activities in the region at a time of great political controversy.

To take up Cavanaugh's implicit challenge to evaluate the Chilean example, this article draws on evidence from Maritain's writings distinguishing the spiritual from the temporal. Maritain's distinction did not preclude the church from acting in the political sphere. Rather, reminding the church of its spiritual mandate even in political affairs buttressed it against political misuse. Second, it tests Cavanaugh's reading of Argentine and Brazilian debates occurring after Maritain visited during the 1930s upon publishing *Integral Humanism* (1935). Maritain traveled to Argentina (with a brief stop in Brazil), laying out his political vision for all to hear. This was before his thought gained serious traction in Chile and the series of lectures at The University of Chicago in which he clarified his distinction between the temporal and spiritual planes.[7] While Chile had a long electoral tradition which separated the church from the state, Argentina and Brazil had histories of subordinating church governance to political considerations and advocating Catholic public morality (i.e., *patronato*).[8]

Looking closely at debates around Maritain in these countries provides an alternative vision to Cavanaugh's. Because of the *patronato* tradition, intellectuals in these two countries did not see Maritain as advocating an apolitical stance. In their eyes, de-sacralizing politics itself was a political act. Argentine Catholic democrats and nationalists alike recognized in Maritain's writings a direct repudiation of Franco's vision for Spain. Meanwhile, Maritain's influence catalyzed a decisive political shift in Brazilian integralist Alceu Amoroso Lima, "one of the founders of Christian Democracy in Latin America." Cavanaugh rightly mentions Lima to highlight Maritain's reach in the region.[9] Lima wielded rare and outsized influence in Brazil's church hierarchy and among its electorally involved laity. His embrace of Maritain led moderate church officials

---

[6] Cavanaugh, *Torture and Eucharist*, 177.
[7] March Bloch, "Pour une histoire comparée des sociétés européennes," in *Mélanges Historiques* (Paris: SEVPEN, 1963), 17–19. Gabriella Pellegrino Soares, "A semear horizontes: leituras literárias na formação da infância, Argentina e Brasil (1915–1954)," PhD diss. (São Paulo: University of São Paulo, 2002), 19–20.
[8] Taylor C. Boas, *Evangelicals and Electoral Politics in Latin America: A Kingdom of This World* (Cambridge: Cambridge University Press, 2023), 114–115, 151–152.
[9] Cavanaugh, *Torture and Eucharist*, 152n.

and laity to eventually oppose Brazil's twenty-one-year dictatorship's repression in order to protect the church's right to social action.

This article answers a limited question with nevertheless broad implications. Some might argue that intellectual ideas are received in specific historic contexts and so coming to a definitive conclusion about Maritain's political efficacy is impossible. This article cannot offer *the* definitive reading of Maritain. It can reasonably answer whether it is more likely Maritain's thought naturally led to being silent on authoritarian atrocities or that authoritarians and their accomplices willfully misread Maritain and human rights activists adopted that reading to try to make sense of the Chilean Church's reticence.

This is a question worth answering. First, Cavanaugh's reading of Maritain is widely accepted, even in qualified form, among the latter's theological and political admirers, such as Luke Bretherton, who focuses on Maritain's relationship with community organizer Saul Alinsky.[10] This portrait coincides with the image of Maritain as a washed-up reactionary, the province of Catholic conservative elites (especially in the United States) looking to depoliticize the faith, sideline the laity, or turn it to conservative causes such as Cold War anti-Communism.[11] Indeed, historian Olivier Compagnon has noted Maritain's fall into political irrelevance as being tied to this latter rift with a younger generation of liberation theologians who saw him as outdated at best.[12]

Gustavo Gutierrez, one of Latin America's founding liberationists, derided Maritain's philosophy as "ecclesial narcissism" affirming that the church is "at the center of salvation work . . . a timid, and deeply ambiguous articulation" leading to "a nostalgia of the past."[13]

---

[10] Luke Bretherton, *Resurrecting Democracy: Faith, Citizenship, and the Politics of a Common Life* (Cambridge: Cambridge University Press, 2015), 36–37, 39–40; Luke Bretherton, *Christianity and Contemporary Politics* (London: Wiley-Blackwell), 94–95. See also Sarah Shortall, *Soldiers of God in a Secular World: Catholic Theology and Twentieth-Century French Politics* (Cambridge, MA: Harvard University Press 2021), 82; Leonard Taylor, "Catholic Cosmopolitanism and the Future of Human Rights," *Religions* 11, no. 566 (October 2020): 12, www.mdpi.com/2077-1444/11/11/566/html.

[11] Carlo Invernizzi Accetti, *What is Christian Democracy? Politics, Religion, and Ideology* (Cambridge: Cambridge University Press, 2019), 77–79; Paul Hanebrink, *A Specter Haunting Europe: The Myth of Judeo-Bolshevism* (Cambridge, MA: Harvard University Press, 2018), 210–211, 218–225.

[12] Olivier Compagnon, "Un philosophe hors de son temps?," in *Jacques Maritain et l'Amérique du Sud: Le modèle malgré lui* (Villeneuve d'Ascq: Presses universitaires du Septentrion, 2003). Even Maritain's supporters admit his influence waned after 1968. See Mario Ramos-Reyes, "Latin American Democracies at the Crossroads," in *The Common Things: Essays on Thomism and Education*, ed. Daniel McInerny (Washington, DC: The Catholic University of America Press, 1999), 248.

[13] Gustavo Gutierrez, *Teología de la Liberación* (Salamanca: Sígueme, 1973), 64, 75–76, 87–88. "Lima las aristas, suaviza los ángulos, evita los aspectos más conflictuales,

Gutierrez saw Maritain's distinction of the temporal and spiritual planes as sidelining the church when right wing authoritarian states could not co-opt it with corporativist reasoning. Cavanaugh endorses this reading, although he does think the church's spiritual salvation work should play a more central role in liberatory projects.[14] This view still holds currency in theological circles. Raúl Zegarra considers Maritain's theology "a powerful . . . but problematic articulation of faith and politics," limiting the "church proper" to "its hierarchy, ordained ministers, and members of religious orders," which would merely "inspire the temporal order, not intervene directly in political action."[15]

Second, far from a simple intergenerational dispute, disagreements over Maritain touch on core questions of movement development and the relationship of Catholicism to human rights and social justice. Did Maritain or his adherents really disavow a specifically Christian politics? Did Maritain's philosophy, which Cavanaugh acknowledges was at the vanguard of Catholic activism in the 1950s and 1960s, succumb to an inherent theological flaw, thereby absolving the church of responsibility to act? Does this give credence to those, like Samuel Moyn, who have categorized Maritain's vision as merely a layman's recapitulation of Pius XII, which sought to save Catholic teaching by inventing a new basis for the rights of the person?[16]

These questions have significant implications for assessing Maritain's global impact. To see Maritain's philosophy as apolitical or undergirding Chilean neoliberal right-wing governance flies in the face of a Chilean Church which prided itself on social action even during the conservative governments of the early twentieth century.[17] It also belies the fact, recognized by Cavanaugh himself, that controversies over Maritain in 1940s Chile centered on his followers' *political* break from the Conservative Party and opposition to outlawing the Communist Party.[18] Finally, the description runs against

---

rehúye las formas más agudas de los enfrentamientos entre clases sociales y entre países" (64).

[14] Gutierrez, *Teología de la Liberación*, 96; Cavanaugh, *Torture and Eucharist*, 179.

[15] Raúl E. Zegarra, *A Revolutionary Faith: Liberation Theology between Public Religion and Public Reason* (Stanford: Stanford University Press, 2023), 7–8, 21–22.

[16] Samuel Moyn, *Christian Human Rights* (Philadelphia: University of Pennsylvania Press, 2015), 16.

[17] Susana Monreal, "Catolicismo social en el Cono Sur: Genealogía de un ideario," in *Catolicismo social chileno: Desarrollo, crisis y actualidad*, ed. Fernando Berríos, Jorge Costadoat, and Diego García (Santiago de Chile: Centro Teológico Manuel Larraín, 2009), 29–31; Ana Maria Stuven, "'Cuestión social' y Catolicismo social: De la nación oligárquica a la nación democrática," in *Catolicismo social chileno*, 62–63.

[18] Stephan Ruderer, "The Controversies over Maritain in Chile and Argentina: Precursors of Different Progressive and Conservative Catholicisms," *International*

much recent scholarship tying Maritain's personalism to Polish freedom fighters, France's anti-torture movement, the Italian Christian Democrats favored by future Pope Paul VI (who would go on to appoint Latin American authoritarians' most vociferous critics), Léopold Sédar Senghor's Senegal, and Julius Nyerere's Tanzania.[19]

In a time of persistent authoritarian ideologies, engaging in this questioning can help us evaluate if one of the twentieth century's most important thinkers helps or hurts the cause of democracy and human rights today.[20] Maritain's vision of a church standing firmly independent of state political projects spawned movements opposing authoritarian regimes on spiritual and political grounds. While liberationists may have legitimate critiques about the usefulness of Maritain's political vision today, the contention that a serious reading of his works would encourage silence in the face of authoritarian atrocities, or even buttress them, is at best a selective reading.

MARITAIN: FROM REACTIONARY TO PLURAL DEMOCRAT

Jacques Maritain was born in 1882 to Paul Maritain and Geneviève Favre. He was an unlikely figure to become the Catholic standard-bearer for contemporary Thomistic thought. He was born into a Protestant household, attended the elite high school Lycée Henri-IV, which while having a Catholic heritage was immersed in the secular milieu of its time, and later attended the Sorbonne (to which the high school was related as a preparatory school). As Bernard Doering points out, his mother was a very good friend of the liberal Catholic essayist Charles Péguy and his grandfather was Jules Favre, a founder of the Third French Republic, fruit of a revolutionary secular political system that hardly exuded Catholic values. He also married Raïssa,

---

Journal of Latin American Religions 6 (2022): 12, doi.org/10.1007/s41603-022-00162-w; Cavanaugh, *Torture and Eucharist*, 155.

[19] See Rachel M. Johnston-White, "The Christian Anti-Torture Movement and the Politics of Conscience in France," *Past & Present* 257, no. 1 (Dec. 2021): 14, doi.org/10.1093/pastj/gtab025; Piotr H. Kosicki, *Catholics on the Barricades: Poland, France, and "Revolution," 1891–1956* (New Haven: Yale University Press, 2018), 53; Peter Hebblethwaite, *Paul VI: The First Modern Pope* (London: Harper Collins, 1993), 208; Gary Wilder, *Freedom Time: Negritude, Decolonization, and the Future of the World* (Durham, NC: Duke University Press, 2015), 210. Nyerere took an egalitarian view of social rights, claiming each person must "realiz[e] that his rights in society ... must come second to the overriding need of *human dignity* [italics mine] for all" (*Nyerere on Socialism* [Dar es Salaam, 1969], 19; in Samuel Moyn, *Not Enough: Human Rights in an Unequal World* [Cambridge, MA: Harvard University Press, 2018], 103).

[20] Leonard Francis Taylor, *Catholic Cosmopolitanism and Human Rights* (Cambridge: Cambridge University Press, 2020), 4.

from a Jewish family, and befriended a defender of the Jewish role in the plan of salvation, Léon Bloy.[21]

Maritain's background gives his critics ample evidence to accuse him of being a closeted reactionary. First and foremost, he began as one, falling under the influence of Father Humbert Clérissac, a reactionary who later became his confessor. In the early years after his conversion in 1906, Maritain uncritically took the advice of these confessors, and even in later years, stretched to defend their thinking. Doering highlights a particular letter in which Maritain wrestled with his mentor's attempts to justify an authoritarian political solution, efforts that would bring the Vatican to censure the French Catholic fringe:

> But what could Father Clérissac have been thinking . . . ? Here is how I explain it to myself: the restoration of the monarchy seemed to Father Clérissac indispensable to the restoration of the Church in our society; in his eyes, the monarchy alone was able to reestablish the Church in the fullness of its rights. He noted with horror all that the Church had been forced to abandon in fact or to leave . . . since the Revolution . . . He recognized the source of the blows struck against the notions of hierarchy, and order, which are essential to the life of the Church, and he placed the Church above all else; hence he detested democracy as an evil . . . he knew the dangers which at that particular time "Modernism" posed to the dogmatic teaching of the Faith.[22]

Second, Maritain had an anti-Semitism problem. Despite marrying a Jewish convert, Maritain wrote in 1921 that a Jewish race that rejected Christ as their savior necessarily played "a fatal role of subversion" because their spiritual inclinations towards justice turned toward a warped "messianic" political vision.[23] His critics are also right that he continued his scathing anti-Modernism and Catholic triumphalism well after his rejection of reactionary politics and anti-Semitism. In his 1938 lecture, "Integral Humanism and the Crisis of Modern Times," delivered at The University of Chicago, Maritain elaborated on Enlightenment philosophies which separated the material and supernatural worlds. He decried an attempt at "development from pure reason apart from the Gospel," because it sidelined "prayer, divine love, supra-rational truths, the idea of sin and

---

[21] Bernard E. Doering, *Jacques Maritain and the French Catholic Intellectuals* (South Bend, IN: University of Notre Dame Press, 1983), 7.

[22] Doering quoting Maritain on Father Clérissac, *Jacques Maritain and the French Catholic Intellectuals*, 11.

[23] Bernard Doering, "The Origin and Development of Maritain's Idea of the Chosen People," in *Jacques Maritain and the Jews*, ed. Robert Royal (South Bend, IN: Notre Dame University Press, 1994), 27, quoting Jacques Maritain, "À propos de la question juive," in *Le Mystère d'Israël* (Paris: Desclée De Brouwer, 1965), 305f.

grace, the evangelical beatitudes, the necessity of asceticism, of contemplation, of the way of the cross."[24]

He was also dismissive of the day's Protestant theologies. He scorned Kierkegaard and an "archaic and reactive" Barth. He saw two of the leading neo-orthodox theologians of the early twentieth century as studying the themes of the "intelligence which comes from the serpent," as well as trying to resurrect a "primitive reformation" to achieve "purification by a reversion to the past."[25] In a passage which may have pleased both fascists and communists alike, he dismissed these "noble" forms of thought which belied the emptiness of liberal promise, "of lying optimism and illusory moralities," in response to which the working class demands radical solutions to rid society of "the liberty which starves workmen and burns the stacks of grain."[26] Over against this liberally-imbued Protestant philosophy, Maritain proposed his vision of a plural society based on anti-liberal, but pluralistic, Christian values that held on to universal truths while progressing into an uncharted future. If Maritain's anti-modernism backed the church as a "perfect society, the protection of whose institution and organization was the principal duty of the hierarchy," such a view would present moral problems, especially since it would imply separation from politics at best and an emphasis on culture wars and clericalism at worst.[27]

But it was Maritain's very orthodoxy, not a radical shift toward theological progressivism, which compelled him to oppose the political solutions Charles Maurras's *Action Française* offered. As articles published in the 1920s for *La revue universelle* show, Maritain saw that Maurras and extreme liberalism drew from the same well: positivism.[28] In Maritain's view, politicized Catholics and anti-clerical zealots relied on the same sort of individualistic Darwinism and positivism that rejected the very dignity of the human person in exchange for setting up idols to concrete political philosophies. The same philosophy which drove him to disdain distant liberal Protestants and neo-orthodox thinkers instilled in him a begrudging admiration for communists. Yes, Maritain's ideal Christian humanism rejected both extremes. It emphasized a spiritual "person" instead of a utilitarian "individual" as the proper base for reason, as the way to "remake anthropology" and rediscover the "dignification" of the individual through openness to the world of the divine and superrational."[29]

---

[24] Jacques Maritain, "Integral Humanism and the Crisis of Modern Times," *Review of Politics* 1, no.1 (1939): 2–3, doi:10.1017/S0034670500000188.
[25] Maritain, "Integral Humanism," 4.
[26] Maritain, "Integral Humanism," 4–6.
[27] Bernard Doering, "Ambiguity (Letter to the Editor)," *America*, September 15, 2003.
[28] Doering, *Jacques Maritain and the French Catholic Intellectuals*, 21.
[29] Maritain, *Scholasticism and Politics*, 9.

Crucially, Maritain did not take the easy route of simply blaming both sides. In the same breath that he credited wayward communists, he fully denounced racist right-wing ideologies. At least communism wished to replace the Christian message with another universalizing message, no matter how unsustainable. Maritain saved his harshest criticism for a generalized racist ideology "which sets itself against Christianity by rejecting all universalism, and by breaking even the natural unity of the human family, so as to impose the hegemony of a so-called higher racial essence."[30] Maritain affirmed that while communism triumphed via the legitimate demands of an ill-informed working class, racism, which also "detested" capitalism, conquered through pure war helped along by the "strong privileged interests blindly anxious to safeguard their own position."[31] In contrast to both of these systems, Maritain proposed an "integral" system that would attend to workers' rights and dignity, as well as "substitute for bourgeois civilization, and for an economic system based on the fecundity of money."[32] His new temporal order entailed "not a collectivistic economy, but a 'personalistic' civilization and a 'personalistic' economy, through which would stream a temporal refraction of the truths of the Gospel." In a more secular sense, Maritain hoped for a spiritual transformation, a "profound renewal of the interior energies of conscience."[33] In contrast to the popes with whom he is often yoked, his vision pushed him to support an alliance with the Soviets and France's Popular Front.[34]

Much of Maritain's democratic political philosophy emerged in opposition to the Spanish Civil War, in which Francisco Franco claimed to defend monarchy and traditional Catholicism against a degenerate Spanish republic. Maritain began to wonder whether the heavily Catholic Basque region's support for the Spanish Republicans might not prove an important point about mainstream Catholics' distance from on-the-ground realities of the peasants and workers.[35] As the leader of the French dissent to the *franquistas*, he wrote a series of essays in which he put economic justice first and foremost among Catholic priorities. He argued that if the church did not deal with the

---

[30] Maritain, "Integral Humanism," 15.
[31] Maritain, "Integral Humanism," 15.
[32] Maritain, "Integral Humanism," 15.
[33] Maritain, "Integral Humanism," 16.
[34] James Chappel, *Catholic Modern: The Challenge of Totalitarianism and the Remaking of the Church* (Cambridge: Harvard University Press, 2018), 111–113.
[35] Bernard Doering, "Jacques Maritain and the Spanish Civil War," *Review of Politics* 44, no. 4 (Oct. 1982): 490, doi.org/10.1017/S0034670500041462.

full range of human problems and remained distant, workers would quickly confuse Catholicism with a reactionary philosophy.[36]

Expanding on Pius XI's concern with the working class, Maritain was extremely attentive to the need to join Catholic faith and political practice.[37] He even invoked the broken body of Christ to drive home the cost of war. In a March 1937 article in the French journal *Esprit*, which he helped found but would later part ways with, Maritain directed the blame for the rise of socialism at those who had abandoned the working class, calling on Catholics to "live with the people" in order to emulate what had made socialism so effective while correcting its errors.[38] In an April 1937 article in the Spanish journal *Sur* he highlighted working class problems in Spain as some of the most severe in Europe.[39]

Even if Franco claimed to defend the church, that claim alone did not sanctify conflict, and stopping one evil could simply bring about another. In a passage which directly challenges Cavanaugh's claim that Maritain did not connect political atrocities to a theology of the Body of Christ, Maritain wrote, "A man who does not believe in God might think: after all . . . this is the price of a return to order and *one crime deserves another*. A man who believes in God knows that there is *no worse disorder*. It is as if the bones of Christ, which the executioners could not touch, were *broken on the Cross* by Christians."[40] Maritain made clear that a web of political and economic interests drove the conflict, with religion merely the pretext.

Maritain's political philosophy must be understood in light of the Spanish Civil War, the cloud of the impending Nazi military buildup, and the exile which led to his embrace of US democracy.[41] But a close reading of the passages Cavanaugh cites makes clear that there are certainly times when the church itself can and should intervene in politics. While Maritain distinguished between religious and temporal (political action), he also permitted a third plane in which the two met. To clarify further, Maritain asserts that "these two orders [the temporal

---

[36] Doering, "Jacques Maritain and the Spanish Civil War," 493. See also J. Lassaigne, "L'Espagne sera-t-elle fasciste!," September 21, 1934, in Doering, "Jacques Maritain and the Spanish Civil War," 493–494.

[37] Pius XI, *Quadragesimo Anno* (1931), nos. 3, 44, 57, 59, 64, 101, www.vatican.va/content/pius-xi/en/encyclicals/documents/hf_p-xi_enc_19310515_quadragesimo-anno.html.

[38] Jacques Maritain in *Esprit* 5, no. 1 (March 1937), cited in Doering, "Jacques Maritain and the Spanish Civil War," 50.

[39] Jacques Maritain, "De la guerre sainte," *La nouvelle revue française* 49 (1 July 1937): 34, n. 2, cited in Doering, "Jacques Maritain and the Spanish Civil War," 502.

[40] Jacques Maritain, "De la guerre sainte," 22, 30, 32, cited in Doering, "Jacques Maritain and the Spanish Civil War," 508–509, emphasis added.

[41] Juan Manuel Burgos, "French Personalism," in *An Introduction to Personalism*, trans. R. T. Allen (Washington, DC: The Catholic University of America Press, 2018), 52.

and spiritual] are distinct, but they are not separate."[42] The Chilean hierarchy's later response to Pinochet's persecution of Christians would also be permitted in Maritain's formula, which allows for a specific "apostolate" to "interven[e] in politics *in the very name of Christianity* when politics touches the altar."[43] On the other hand, Maritain cautioned that "it is not by trying to find *in one* particular *camp* an instrument for religion . . . but rather by laying *every political camp whatsoever* under the necessity of respecting these rights and values."[44] Maritain called on the church to "distinguish" the political and religious spheres, not to give them an excuse for inaction, but to "unite" diverse Catholics into the Body of Christ.[45]

While Cavanaugh suggests even Maritain's language about "touching the altar" leaves *Christian* politics fully by the wayside, Maritain later called for the moral formation of Christian conscience on matters related to "civil peace and international peace, the sanctity of treaties, social justice, the rights of the human person, [and] the rejection of means of violence."[46] He admitted the importance of all spheres and called for the "cooperation of Catholics and non-Catholics." In a direct rebuke of the paranoia of Catholic nationalists, he decried "those looks of scorn and detestation which people have for traitors, for hopeless madmen and outcast dogs."[47] In short, it is a stretch to imagine that a good-faith reading of his distinction of the temporal and spiritual planes could support inaction against Catholic nationalist ideologies such as those of the Argentine and Chilean dictatorships. To be sure, Maritain rejected the domination of the spiritual over the temporal order, which had been a mainstay of medieval thought lionized by these philosophies.[48] But by the same token, he rejected the religious utilitarians of his day: Maurras (an avowed atheist), Franco, and their Latin American allies foremost.

While this first section has acknowledged viable reasons for Maritain's reputation as a conservative at best and reactionary at worst, it has also suggested alternative readings and usages of the distinction of planes that so troubles Maritain's radical critics. Since Latin American theologians and their allies debate Maritain's overall regional influence, I will next move to revisit in detail his interactions

---

[42] Maritain, *Scholasticism and Politics*, 212, emphasis added.
[43] Maritain, *Scholasticism and Politics*, 195–196.
[44] Maritain, *Scholasticism and Politics*, 212, emphasis added.
[45] Maritain, *Scholasticism and Politics*, 212.
[46] Maritain, *Scholasticism and Politics*, 214n.
[47] Maritain, *Scholasticism and Politics*, 215–216, 218.
[48] Patrick McKinley Brennan, "Jacques Maritain: Philosopher of Law, Politics, and All That Is," in John Witte, Jr., and Frank S. Alexander, eds., *The Teachings of Modern Christianity on Law, Politics, and Human Nature*, vol. 2 (New York: Columbia University Press, 2006), 125.

with and influence over Argentine and Brazilian intellectuals. This comparative frame will hopefully make clear how Maritain's vision played out in pre-Allende contexts, where resisting authoritarianism and embracing plural politics put him on one side of active fault lines of theological debate. We shall see that Latin American democrats did not just praise Maritain but took his thought as a mandate to resist rising authoritarianism in their own countries. Sympathizers to dictatorship saw him as a theological and political threat.

MARITAIN DIVIDES ARGENTINA'S CATHOLICS: THE CÓRDOBA VISIT AND THE TRAJECTORY OF JULIO MEINVIELLE AND LEONARDO CASTELLANI

One of Maritain's most prominent visits to South America brought him to potentially hostile territory. The Argentina of the 1930s boasted a significant Catholic Nationalist wing stemming from a tradition of fierce anti-Liberalism which in the Catholic stance meant joining church and state and rejecting any role of inculcating civic virtue.[49] Mainly a group of middle-class students, the Catholic Nationalists rejected Radical Party populist rhetoric and sought to distance themselves from the working-class issues to which the early twentieth century Catholic Church had been confined.[50]

While they contemplated the possibility of a democracy which worked toward the common good, they assumed that most democracies would fall into moral relativism; the Catholic faith seemed to them more secure under a unified government supporting the customs and traditions of the people and rejecting abstract, foreign, universal ideas.[51] For them, those traditions derived from classical "Latin"-based Western civilization. Since the 1920s, they had seen themselves defending the latter from intellectuals fascinated with

---

[49] Federico Finchelstein, *The Ideological Origins of the Dirty War: Fascism, Populism, and Dictatorship in Twentieth Century Argentina* (Oxford: Oxford University Press, 2014), 19–21, 24; Alberto Spektorowski, *The Origins of Argentina's Revolution of the Right* (Notre Dame, IN: Notre Dame Press, 2003), 138; Roberto Di Stefano and Loris Zanatta, *Historia de la iglesia argentina: Desde la conquista hasta fines del siglo XX* (Buenos Aires: Grijalbo S. A., 2000), 247–248.

[50] Fernando J. Devoto, "Los proyectos de un grupo de intelectuales católicos argentinos entre las dos guerras," in Carlos Altamirano, ed., *Historia de los intelectuales en América Latina: Los avatares de la "ciudad letrada" en el siglo XX*, vol. II (Buenos Aires: Katz, 2010), 351, 357; John J. Kennedy, *Catholicism, Nationalism, and Democracy in Argentina* (South Bend, IN: University of Notre Dame Press, 1958), 12, 19.

[51] Juan Fernando Segovia, "La legitimidad entre la teología y la política. Reflexiones sobre el orden político católico en Meinvielle y Castellani (1930–1950)," *Anales de la Fundación Francisco Elías de Tejada* 10 (2004): 85–88, 90–92.

foreign civilizations like a nebulous East, or from those like Maritain, who would relativize its virtues.[52]

The French philosopher's visit to Córdoba, Argentina, was a highlight of his thought's reception in Latin America. His visit was controversial precisely because he took a political stand against Franco.[53] Before he had even stepped off the boat in Buenos Aires, he had already made a name for himself in the liberal journal *Sur* which had translated his arguments for embracing social Catholicism while rejecting fascism, communism, and the baptizing of political projects.[54] That said, Argentines now saw more clearly how Maritain, basing himself in Thomas Aquinas, rejected modernism as a whole, but argued that Aquinas was "the saint of the *intelligentsia*" still relevant to modern society. They listened to his warnings that Catholic militants could not revive the Middle Ages *per se* and should instead consider how to preach classical Catholic values in a modernist setting.[55]

Liberal Catholics responded positively. Agosto J. Durelli cited Maritain in his article for *Sur*, praising his supposed lack of partisanship in spiritual affairs. Quoting Maritain directly, Durelli highlighted his shift from the merely political to the spiritual, arguing that the Gospel does not compel one to follow a party but "to learn with intimacy the word of God." This intimacy, argued Maritain and Durelli, would stop "the good from calling down the fire of God upon the bad." They hoped, foreshadowing Christian pacifists, that such intimacy should cause devout Catholics to think of Christ's death for his enemies instead of a God that would command them to kill for him.[56]

As the introduction of Maritain at the University of Córdoba on October 6, 1936, by philosopher Alfredo Fragueiro (following a visit to the September P.E.N. Conference in Buenos Aires) showed, many Argentine scholars warmly welcomed Maritain. They lauded his philosophical rigor and also his social conviction. They found his

---

[52] Martín Bergel, "'Los bárbaros están otra vez sobre Roma': Acerca de la reacción antioriental del pensamiento nacionalista católico argentino de los años 1920," *Iberoamericana* 10, no. 40 (2010): 7–26.

[53] José Zanca, "La teología política de la secularización: Pedro de Basaldúa y el exilio vasco en Argentina," *Historia Contemporánea* 63 (2020): 555–556.

[54] "Conferencia de Jacques Maritain a propósito de la 'Carta Sobre la Independencia,'" *Sur* 6, no. 7 (1936): 7. www.borges.pitt.edu/sites/default/files/files/Sur/Sur%20no.27%20%281936%29.pdf.

[55] José Zanca, *Cristianos antifascistas: Conflictos en la cultura católica argentina* (Buenos Aires: Siglo Veintiuno, 2013), 38–48, 50–51.

[56] Citing Maritain's *Questions de Conscience* (Paris: Desclée De Brouwer, 1939), in Agosto J. Durelli, "El Cristianismo y El Reposo," *Sur* 11 (Septiembre de 1939): 74–76. Durelli also chronicles a debate between Maritain and Claudel involving Maritain's emphasis on social justice and possible social revolution. Claudel believed such issues could be handled within the confines of the state (76–80).

encompassing views refreshing, especially his rejection of the use of the scientific method as an *ethical* tool, and his updating of a living versus an "archeological" Thomism.[57] Not all intellectuals agreed, however. Leopoldo Lugones called democracy a "cadaver" and wrote against the failure of the "bourgeois democracy."[58] According to Córdoba philosopher Fernando Martínez Paz, Charles Maurras's dialectic "seduced" many of Argentina's Catholic intellectuals into taking authoritarian positions due to their healthy skepticism of participatory processes. The problem, according to Martinez's reading of Maritain, lays in the fact that governments involved in pure action are not worried about human dignity. Despite these challenges, Paz believed Maritain opened up a way to a "Catholic political integralism," a "second liberation" that constituted a "true metaphysics."[59]

Even in Argentina, Maritain broke with nationalists to condemn Franco's authoritarianism by *distinguishing* the sacred from the temporal. He did not rule on the Spanish Civil War as just or unjust defense on the part of the Franco regime (he eschewed such categories as unfair mixing of the temporal and spiritual). Instead, Maritain criticized the Spanish Civil War for creating a savior-like mentality that denied the balance between "force, justice, and civil friendship."[60] For Maritain there was a contradiction in attempting to construct the kingdom of God on "political realism and hate" and thus allowing liberty to "open the way to dictatorships."[61] He also took issue with the classification of the Spanish Civil War as a "holy war," saying that the term was anachronistic in a time where the "sacred" was clearly separated from the "profane."[62] His vision, later interpreted by his Argentine supporters in *Revista Sur*, rejected "a Church with excessive submission to the temporal powers."[63] Such a vision clearly condemned "all *dictatorships* . . . all forms of *oppression* . . . all forms

---

[57] "Buenos Aires host to P.E.N. Congress," *New York Times*, September 6, 1936, 7, timesmachine.nytimes.com/timesmachine/1936/09/06/issue.html; Alfredo Fragueiro, *Jacques Maritain en la Universidad de Córdoba: Octubre 1º. De 1936* (Córdoba: Imprensa de la Universidad, 1937), 7–8, 14.
[58] Fernando Martínez Paz, *Maritain, Política, e Ideologia: Revolución cristiana en la Argentina* (Buenos Aires: Editorial Nahuel, 1966), 75.
[59] Martinez Paz, *Maritain, Política, e Ideología*, 74–77. See also Carlos Alberto Torres, *The Church, Society, and Hegemony: A Critical Sociology of Religion in Latin America*, trans. Richard A. Young (Westport, CT: Praeger, 1992), 133, 183–184.
[60] Martínez Paz, *Maritain, Política e Ideologia*, 118–119.
[61] Martínez Paz, *Maritain, Política e Ideologia*, 118–119.
[62] Martinez Paz, *Maritain, Política e Ideologia*, 118–119.
[63] "Posición de Sur," *Sur*, no. 35 (1937): 7–8. Quoted in Nora Pasternac, "Corrientes Cristianas durante los años 30 en la Revista *Sur*," in *Varia lingüística y literaria: 50 años del CELL: III. Literatura: siglos XIX y XX*, ed. Yvette Jiménez de Báez, Martha Linia Tenorio (D.F.: Colégio de México, 1997), 283.

of ignorance exercised over the gray mass of people which has been called the holy *plebs* of God."[64]

Such statements must have perturbed nationalists such as Father Julio Meinvielle who mixed religion and anti-Semitism in support of authoritarianism. Meinvielle wrote in 1937 regarding the Spanish Civil War that Franco, "a most illustrious *caudillo*," had put an end to the Popular Front, led by the "masonic" government of Portela Valladares, and stopped the Jewish-led "third blow" against an already defunct Christendom—communism—from spreading.[65] Argentina's Catholic *Criterio* magazine echoed Meinvielle's sentiments, putting the Spanish Civil War in the context of a spiritual struggle against modernity itself: "Our state is no longer a skeptical state, nor is it a people that rests," it asserted. "Our state rejects Rousseauian skepticism. It knows that truth and justice are permanent categories of reason, and not arbitrary decisions of the will. Our state knows, as does the people, the truth of God and the Truth of Spain."[66] This same magazine published the words of the Toledo Archbishop, Cardinal Dr. D. Isidro Gomá y Tomás: "Man through the demand of his very nature, is tied threefold: to God, to his parents, and to the Fatherland."[67]

Maritain received initial support from one Catholic nationalist during the visit, Leonardo Castellani. Born in Santa Fe, Argentina, Castellani received a degree in psychology from the Sorbonne, where Maritain taught in 1935.[68] Along with Meinvielle, he is considered "one of the best Argentine writers, essayists, novelists, journalists, literary critics, poets, philosophers, and theologians."[69] Castellani wrote approvingly of the philosopher in the liberal Argentine journal

---

[64] "Posición de *Sur*," "Corrientes Cristianas durante los años 30 en la Revista *Sur*," 283, emphasis added.
[65] Julio Meinvielle, *¿Qué saldrá de la España que sangra?* (Buenos Aires: Asociación de los jóvenes de la Acción Católica, 1937), 6–8.
[66] "El ser o no ser de España," *Criterio* 11, no. 532 (May 12, 1938): 39. "Nuestro Estado no es ya un Estado escéptico, como no lo es tampoco el pueblo que descansa. Nuestro Estado rechaza el sofisma roussoniano y sabe que la verdad y la justicia son categorías permanentes de la razón y no son decisiones arbitrarias de la voluntad. Nuestro Estado conoce, como conoce el pueblo, la verdad de Dios y la verdad de España."
[67] Isidro Gomá y Tomás, "Catolicismo y Patria (Carta del Cardenal Arzobispo de Toledo, Msgr. Dr. D. Isidro Gomá y Tomás)," *Criterio* 12, no. 581 (April 20, 1939): 376. "Y la Patria es España.... Y somos hijos de la Patria, que no es más que una prolongación y una ampliación del hogar paterno donde recibimos la plenitud de nuestra vida natural... Así el hombre por exigencia de su misma naturaleza está atado con triple vínculo: a Dios, a sus padres y a la Patria."
[68] Alfredo Sáenz, *El apocalipsis según Leonardo Castellani* (Pamplona: Fundación Gratis Date, 2005), 2.
[69] Juan Fernando Segovia, "La legitimidad entre la teología y la política. Reflexiones sobre el orden político católico en Meinvielle y Castellani (1930–1950)," *Anales de la Fundación Francisco Elías de Tejada*, Madrid, 2005, 98–99.

Sur. Castellani called Maritain's melding of current history with his theory of a "New Christianity" to replace the old, "full of clarity" and saying "the latest works of Maritain are a must read."[70]

Gustavo Franceschi, another conservative editor, was also influenced by Maritain; near the end of World War II, he endorsed the practical alliance between the Allies and the Soviet Union against Nazi Germany using the same rationale Maritain had laid out in his University of Chicago lectures. Nazism was a graver threat than Communism, he argued, even though Catholics should reject the latter, too. He also enthusiastically supported Maritain's nomination as French ambassador to the Vatican.[71]

Julio Meinvielle, however, was not impressed by Maritain's postwar political philosophy. He rejected what he saw as the dialectical and revolutionary view of history in Maritain's *The Rights of Man and the Natural Law* (1945), where Maritain endorsed Roosevelt's Four Freedoms, just wages, and even the right to strike.[72] By 1951, Castellani had also turned against Maritain, hurling an anti-Semitic slur after Maritain invoked Bartolome de Las Casas's report on indigenous mistreatment to condemn the racism frequent among theologians. In 1951, in his work *So is Christ Returning or Not? [Cristo vuelve o no vuelve]*, Castellani condemned the vague attacks of the French Catholic philosopher directed at "certain Spanish theologians [*ciertos teólogos españoles*]."[73] Castellani responded by questioning the integrity of Maritain's anonymous attack, saying it "should make one cry." Castellani mocked Maritain's international reputation saying "What disgusts us quite a bit is the Jew in service to propaganda, even if he is Christian and a philosopher. . . . The French philosopher has left aside philosophy and is left only with the French, and not even that. . . . What a disaster!"[74]

This break widened at the Second Vatican Council, as Argentina polarized even further over issues such as church-state relations and the liturgy. With the onset of a series of dictatorships, those who supported Maritain's vision had been isolated, and those with Catholic

---

[70] Leonardo Castellani, "Jacques Maritain," *Sur* 6 (August 1936): 65–67.

[71] Gustavo Franceschi, "Jacques Maritain, embajador ante la Santa Sede," *Criterio* 17, no. 885 (March 1, 1945): 161–169; Gustavo Franceschi, "Democracia y Comunismo," *Criterio* 18, no. 892 (April 19, 1945): 329–332.

[72] Jacques Maritain, *The Rights of Man and Natural Law*, trans. Doris C. Anson (London: Centenary, 1945), 42, 54; Julio Meinvielle, *De Lamennais a Maritain*, 2nd ed. (Buenos Aires: Theoría, 1967), 15–18.

[73] "El racism," in Leonardo Castellani, *¿Cristo vuelve o no vuelve?*, 2nd ed. (Buenos Aires: Biblioteca Dictio, 1976), 196–197.

[74] "El racismo," 196–197. "El que nos disgusta bastante es el judío puesto al servicio de la propaganda, aunque sea cristiano y filósofo. La *Información Católica Internacional* anda repartiendo un folleto de Jacques Maritain, titulado *Por qué no somos racistas ni antisemitas*. Es cosa de ponerse a llorar cuando uno lo lee…! que desastre!"

nationalist leanings had entered the hierarchy. Argentina's 1976 dictatorship was one result of this split and the democrats' unsuccessful struggle.[75]

MARITAIN CHANGES BRAZILIAN CATHOLICS' TRAJECTORY: THE CASE OF ALCEU AMOROSO LIMA

Comparative historians such as Ana Maria Koch, William de Souza Martins, and José Luis Bendicho Beired agree that both structural and theological issues, such as a less developed grassroots Brazilian Church and a more accommodationist approach to liberalism, made Brazil's episcopate more open to criticizing the military dictatorship than their Argentine counterparts. Despite that, the bishops had also passed through a similar process of emergence from political marginalization in the 1930s. Getúlio Vargas, a politician-turned-military dictator who ruled between 1930 and 1945 (from 1937 as a dictator), made a political alliance with revived Catholic movements. The latter tied culture to economic development to support his authoritarian *Estado Novo*. But as Brazil fought with the Allies in World War II, dictatorship at home became untenable, even for the pro-Vargas Catholic intelligentsia.[76]

Their gradual turn toward resisting the 1964 military dictatorship, especially in the Northeast, made Brazil's Catholic Church "one of the few institutions capable of confronting the state [and] . . . appear[ing] like the defender of human rights *par excellence*."[77] This "defender

---

[75] Fernando Carlos Urquiza, "Las transformaciones a la iglesia argentina: Del concilio Vaticano II a la recuperación democrática" (Universidad Nacional del Centro, 2006), 3–4, dialnet.unirioja.es/servlet/articulo?codigo=5028502.

[76] Cândido Moreira Rodrigues, *A Ordem: uma revista de intelectuais católicos (1934–1945)* (Belo Horizonte: Autentica; Fapesp, 2005), 220; Dain Borges, "Catholic Vanguards in Brazil," in *Local Church, Global Church: Catholic Activism in Latin America from Rerum Novarum to Vatican II*, ed. Stephen J. C. Andes and Julia G. Young (Washington, DC: The Catholic University of America Press, 2015), 21–50; Ana Maria Koch, "Cruzada pela democracia: militantes católicos no Brasil republicano," *Revista Brasileira de História* 33, no. 66 (2013): 288; William de Souza Martins, "Igreja e Estado no Brasil oitocentista: um diálogo com La Iglesia católica y la formación del Estado-nación en América Latina en el siglo XIX. El caso colombiano, de Luis Javier Ortiz Mesa," *Almanack. Guarulhos*, no. 6 (2nd semester, 2013): 27, 29; Getúlio Lira Neto, *Do governo provisório á ditadura do Estado Novo (1930–1945)*, 1st ed. (São Paulo: Companhia de Letras, 2013), 143–144; Luiz Carlos Bresser-Pereira, "Getúlio Vargas: O estadista, a nação e a democracia," in *A Era Vargas: Desenvolvimentismo, economia, e sociedade*, ed. Pedro Paulo Zahluth Bastos and Pedro Cezar Dutra Fonseca (São Paulo: Unesp, 2012), 101–105; José Luis Bendicho Beired, *Sob o signo da nova ordem: Intelectuais autoritários no Brasil e na Argentina* (São Paulo: Loyola, 1999), 67–68; Roberto Romano, *Brasil: Igreja Contra Estado: Crítica ao populismo católico* (São Paulo: Kairos, 1979), 11–15.

[77] Romano, *Igreja Contra Estado*, 28, 45–46.

par excellence" largely owed such a stance to the influence of Jacques Maritain. Christian Democratic resistance to Brazil's twenty-one-year dictatorship suggests that Maritain's philosophy does not necessarily create a false dilemma between spiritual faith and praxis.

Alceu Lima, potentially "modern Brazil's greatest Catholic intellectual," embodied the political transformation that could occur when previously integralist theologians embraced Maritain.[78] He was the principal Catholic intellectual guiding the hierarchy after the death of Jackson de Figueiredo and during the height of Getúlio Vargas's first government (1930–1945), which embraced ideals of social harmony with a mandate for redistribution at the service of material sufficiency for all.[79] Lima's dominance in Brazilian Catholic circles shows through his command of electoral machines which delivered votes. His relationship with the church hierarchy shows through in the praise he received from intellectuals as divergent as Gustavo Corção and Leonardo Boff. A "disciple" of Maritain, he is also considered one of the founders of Christian Democracy in Latin America, the principal conduit for French Catholicism in Brazil, and a "prophetic" voice against the military regime.[80] Given his position in that social hierarchy, Lima, covered extensively in Brazil's Catholic press, remains a singular figure to analyze Maritain's reception in the region.

Lima traces a trajectory similar to Maritain's. Born in 1893, Lima became an esteemed literary critic in the 1920s, finally converting to Catholicism in 1928 under the influence of Figueiredo, then editor of Brazil's largest Catholic journal *A Ordem*. Figueiredo was known for radical religious zeal. He would take up the call to bring about a "restoration" of order in Brazil. His attitudes reflected broader European disillusionment with the failures of liberalism and the rise of communism in the interwar period. Figueiredo saw liberalism as antithetical to the common good, and willing to aid the middle class, but unwilling to regulate it when necessary. From his religious point

---

[78] Kenneth Serbin, *Secret Dialogues: Church-State Relations and Social Justice in Authoritarian Brazil* (Pittsburgh, PA: University of Pittsburgh Press, 2000), 45.

[79] Robert Levine, *Father of the Poor?: Vargas and His Era* (Cambridge: Cambridge University Press, 1998), 37. John D. French, *Drowning in Laws: Labor Law and Brazilian Political Culture* (Chapel Hill: University of North Carolina Press, 2004), 64–67, 179, n. 11, n. 12.

[80] Michaël Löwy and Jésus Garcia-Ruiz, "Les Sources françaises du christianisme de la libération au Brésil," *Archives de sciences sociales des religions* 97 (1997): 11, 14; Josué Montello, *Diário da noite iluminada, 1977–1985* (Rio de Janeiro: Nova Fronteira, 1994), 71; Leonardo Boff, "A Presença de Alceu Amoroso Lima," *Revista Eclesiástica Brasileira* 43, no. 171 (1983): 440; Sister M. Ancilla O'Neill, *Tristão de Athayde and the Catholic Social Movement in Brazil* (Washington, DC: The Catholic University of America Press, 1939), v.

of view, the Middle Ages served as a Golden Age to be recovered, much like thinkers of the Renaissance valued Antiquity.[81]

Unlike his mentor, and much like Maritain, Lima had an eclectic group of acquaintances, including Alfonso Reyes, Mexico's ambassador to Brazil during the Cristero Rebellion. This openness led him to assess the truth of an argument fairly, irrespective of whether the latter came from friendly Catholics or Mexican and Soviet adversaries.[82] He believed in the importance of interpersonal communication, not of mere political action. He emphasized a "dialogue culture" between educated adversaries who, while on opposite sides of a fundamental divide, shared the virtues of charity and love for the common good.[83]

Still, the Alceu Lima of the 1930s did share many common traits with Figueiredo. Like Maritain, he garnered a reputation as anti-Modernist. Looking back, he admitted his embrace of integralism's role in reviving Brazilian Catholicism: "a crusade never done before in Brazil! A Crusade of servants for the Return of Christ that was like that . . . of the 13th Century" guided not by swords but adolescents' "clarity of conscience."[84] As director of the Catholic Electoral League during the 1930s, Lima had also pushed for politicians at the local, state, and national level that would emphasize religious education and resist the legalization of divorce.[85] Though reserved toward Franco, under his leadership the journal *A Ordem* supported Portugal's dictatorship because it sought to "organize the nation on the foundations of Corporatism" while also "reserv[ing] for individual liberty and initiative a sliver of autonomy in the constructing of its economy," such as press debates on "a work contract between factory workers and industry leaders."[86]

At heart, however, Lima was not a reactionary. In his 1932 work *Política* he had already discussed the idea of "necessity" and "liberty"

---

[81] Francisco Iglesias, *Historia e Ideologia* (São Paulo: Perspectiva, 1969), 109–114, 115.

[82] Marcelo Timotheo da Costa, "La espada y el arado: El conflicto religioso en México y la intelectualidad católica brasileña, los casos de Jackson de Figueiredo y Alceu Amoroso Lima," cited in Jean Meyer, *Las Naciones Frente Al Conflicto Religioso en México* (D.F: CIDE, 2010), 84, 88; Robert Patrick Newcomb, *Nossa and Nuestra América: Inter-American Dialogues*, vol. 52 (Lafayette, IN: Purdue University Press, 2012), 165; João Etienne Filho, *Alceu Amoroso Lima, Jackson de Figueiredo: Correspondência, harmonia dos contrastes (1919–1929)* (Rio de Janeiro: Academia Brasileira de Letras, 1992), 89.

[83] Renato Augusto Carneiro Junior, "Amor em tempos de ressentimento: Alceu Amoroso Lima, política e resistência à ditadura militar de 1964," PhD Dissertation (Curitiba: UFPR, 2011), 5, 12.

[84] Tristão de Athyde, *Adeus Á Disponibilidade* (Rio de Janeiro: Agir, 1969), 22.

[85] Lira Neto, *Getúlio*, 143.

[86] "Os acontecimentos na Espanha," *A Ordem*, October 1937, 88.

as two essential features in individual searches for the common good. He shared with Maritain a healthy critique of a mechanistic modernity pitted against the soul of the human person. In his view, socialism presented a synthetic, not organic, unity, based on a dualistic vision of class struggle. The common good, on the other hand, welded various societies together into a corporate structure, a cohesive social unit.[87] Lima followed the Argentine debates over Maritain's visits through contacts in Buenos Aires, and personally took Maritain to visit Lima's Centro Dom Vital during a short 1936 stop in Brazil on the way back to France.[88] By 1945, he had fully embraced Maritain and democracy, writing the preface to *Christianity and Democracy's* Portuguese edition. For Lima, democracy in the twentieth century would "represent for Christianity a *political instrument* in defense of Liberty against the advance of Totalitarianism."[89]

Maritain's influence spread rapidly in Brazil, in part through Lima's efforts and undergirded the church's engagement with the world. Lending a copy of *Integral Humanism* (1936) to Dom Hélder Câmara, who would later go on to be a towering figure of liberation theology, proved crucial to Câmara's embrace of pluralism as a political ideal. Like Maritain, he saw a disordered list of priorities on the part of traditional clergy. For Câmara, this position constituted a political transformation that began upon reading Lima's recommended book. Echoing Maritain's skepticism of the middle class, he questioned "the Pharisaic [attitude] of determining that we the bourgeois represent social order and virtue and that Communists embody disorder, disequilibrium and disenchantment, and the forces of evil. . . . We have our own faults and sins . . . because we cover up social injustices with generous and spectacular offerings."[90] Though some factions, especially Jesuits in Rio Grande do Sul, emphasized his previous anti-modernism and downplayed his democratic shift, Maritain influenced a generation of Catholic activists in the 1950s. While many of these groups moved beyond Maritain, his influence continued to be felt in the work of priests such as Louis-Joseph Lebret.[91]

---

[87] Tristão de Athayde, *Política* (Rio de Janeiro: Livraria Catholica, 1932), 18, citing Jacques Maritain, *Trois Réformateurs* (Paris: Plon, 1925), 22, 28–29.
[88] "Manhã com Maritain," *Revista Portuguesa de Filosofia* 29, no. 4 (1973): 432–433.
[89] Alceu Amoroso Lima, "Introduction," in Jacques Maritain, *Cristianismo e Democracia*, 2nd ed. (Rio de Janeiro: Agir, 1945), 10–11, emphasis added.
[90] Quoting Helder Câmara in Nelson Piletti and Walter Praxedes, *Dom Hélder Câmara: Entre o Poder e a Profecia* (São Paulo: Ática, 1997), 158, in Martinho Condini, "Dom Hélder Câmara: Modelo de esperança na caminhada para a paz e justiça social" (Diss. de Mestrado, PUC-SP, 2004), 81, 80–82.
[91] Lorena Madruga Monteiro and André Drumond, "A democracia na obra de Jacques Maritain e sua recepção pelos círculos católicos brasileiros," *Revista do Núcleo de Pós-Graduação Pesquisa em Ciências Sociais* 18 (2011): 67–68; Marcelo Ridenti,

Lima would build on the importance of spiritual-temporal distinction to Christian Democracy in 1948, following an important meeting in Montevideo the previous year. Maritain had "distinguish[ed] [the spiritual and worldly] to unite."[92] Per Lima, when Maritain's thought had merely influenced "in the spiritual and metaphysical" plane, everyone had accepted him "without reservation." When his thought had touched on politics, "especially the happenings in Spain, everything changed all of a sudden." While the post-World War II period may have brought a risk of reducing everything to politics and economics, "in those moments . . . one needed to push back *against the separation* of the temporal and spiritual, between the political or economic, and the ethical."[93]

Lima himself soon pushed back in Brazil against separating social and political concerns from spiritual ones. He "opposed the coup and fearlessly criticized the censorship and torture perpetrated by the military regime."[94] Writing in one of Brazil's leading Catholic dailies during the first months of the regime, he put the blame for the coup indirectly at the feet of racist Brazilian elites who refused even moderate reforms. In this critique he echoed Maritain's dismissal of middle-class German ideology as self-interested and thus worse than communism. Reflecting upon the death of US President John F. Kennedy half a year before, he criticized middle-class regime opponents of land reform as "small samples of social inertia" who called themselves "disinterested" while they merely looked after their own interests. He believed this type of cynical citizen, be it the racist in Texas or the small landowner that went against their own interests in opposing land reform, constituted the true murderers of the idealist president.[95]

Lima passionately argued there could be no order without liberty. Order meant both "unity and variety," not "social immobility . . . hierarchical rigidity or . . . the exclusion of contradictory elements."[96] He was blunt on the state of Brazil's military regime: "To confuse order with an authoritarian regime, with the maintaining of the social status quo, with political traditionalism or with a government of brute force is to misrepresent [Order's] very nature."[97] His position gained

---

"Ação Popular: cristianismo e marxismo," in *História do marxismo no Brasil*, ed. Marcelo Ridenti and Daniel Aarão Reis (Campinas: UNICAMP, 2002), 216, 219–222.

[92] Alceu Lima, "Maritain y la América Latina," in *Jacques Maritain: Su obra filosófica* (Buenos Aires: Desclée de Brouwer, 1959), 35.

[93] Lima, "Maritain y la América Latina," 35, emphasis added.

[94] Kenneth Serbin, *Secret dialogues*, 73.

[95] Tristão de Athayde, "Os anti-Kennedy," *O Diário*, May 1, 1964.

[96] Tristão de Athayde, "Ordem e Progresso," *Diário de Belo Horizonte*, June 21, 1964.

[97] Athayde, "Ordem e Progresso."

wider acceptance among the bishops and even some center-right papers as the military regime cracked down on what the bishops perceived as legitimate Catholic social militancy.[98] He instead promoted a culture of dialogue, as an anti-conservative concept that allows variety in society and opposes "isolationism and the justification of wars and Revolutions [the self-given name of the regime]."[99] Two years later, he reminded readers that the coup, led by "false saviors," had been "completely useless and counterproductive, capable of creating evils even worse than those against which we all complained."[100]

Like Maritain, Lima condemned general violence on both sides, but that did not stop him from continuing to speak out on human rights abuses and advocate for social transformation. In a challenging speech before the State Assembly of Minas Gerais, Lima condemned an "armed" mentality that amounted to "collective robbery from a hungry world."[101] Calling for a redistribution of wealth and the beginning of a "social revolution," he called on the church to leave its "attack or defense" mentality to live "in the midst, at the service, and at the side of all men of goodwill against alienation. [Especially] the alienation of underdevelopment." His most controversial line reflected Maritain, when Lima warned against creeds and instead promised to work with "all men of good will, be they Protestants, Spiritists, Communists, or Atheists."[102]

Another speech likely made him unpopular with some religious figures who advocated armed revolution. Warning of a "Third World War," Lima criticized the violence advocated by Communist manifestos. Armed force to end colonialism in the Western Hemisphere would only reinforce the most reactionary governments of the region through "maximum consolidation of the military mentality and . . . fanaticism of the 'rights,' like we have seen here since 1964."[103]

This is not to say that some Catholics did not attempt to co-opt Maritain's earlier writings for authoritarian ends, such as the

---

[98] "Dom Helder Camara defende as reformas como anseio da justiça social," *O Diário de Belo Horizonte,* April 14, 1964; "Arcebispo de Brasília louva Dom João: Manifesto de Ação Católica," *O Diário,* March 6, 1965; "Bispo desfaz calúnias contra Ação Católica," *O Diário,* April 18, 1964; Paulo Fernandes, "Dom Helder," *O Diário,* May 23, 1965.
[99] Tristão de Athayde, "Filosofia da dialogação," *O Diário,* May 9, 1965.
[100] Tristão de Athayde, "Falsos Salvadores," *O Diário,* April 20, 1966.
[101] Antônio Otaviano and Antônio Nilso, "Alceu Amoroso Lima na assembléia Legislativa de Minas," *O Lutador,* September 17, 1967.
[102] Otaviano Nilso, "Alceu Amoroso Lima na assembléia Legislativa de Minas."
[103] Tristão de Ataíde, "As guerrilhas representariam em nossos países sul-americanos o melhor pretexto para consolidar o militarismo," *O Lutador,* February 18, 1968.

aforementioned Jesuits in Rio Grande do Sul.[104] However, unlike their Christian Democratic counterparts in Argentina, Lima and his ecclesial associates exercised a singular influence to shape the debate. A key lay figure on Brazil's Catholic scene, he had always embraced dialogue in the abstract. But in his advocacy for Maritain's work with friends in the hierarchy, Lima managed to channel the legitimate critiques of middle-class Catholicism and liberalism away from integralist rhetoric in a more democratic direction from bishops down to the laity.

Brazilian newspapers even shed light on perceptions of Maritain's favorite Latin American political figure, Chile's Eduardo Frei. In 1967, when Maritain decried alleged excesses of post-Second Vatican Council modernist theology and overly broad ecumenical efforts, he still extolled the "authentic 'Christian Revolution'" of Eduardo Frei's Chile (as well as the efforts of Chicago's "staunch organizer . . . and . . . anti-racist leader" Saul Alinsky).[105] At this time, the international arena considered Frei a reformer, not a centrist reactionary.[106] In fact, possible military intervention was not lost on Frei's Christian Democratic supporters in Brazil who, themselves under a military regime, still reported on Frei's denunciation of a June 1966 coup in Argentina.[107] If one reads the 1960s Frei as a zealous reformer, it should come as no surprise that some Brazilian liberation theologians

---

[104] Monteiro and Drumond, "A democracia na obra de Jacques Maritain e sua recepção pelos círculos católicos brasileiros," 67–68.

[105] Jacques Maritain, *The Peasant of the Garonne: An Old Layman Questions Himself about the Present Time*, Michael Cuddihy and Elizabeth Hughes (New York: Holt, Rinehart, and Winston, 1968), 23, 23n. Alinsky is most visibly identified with the left.

[106] Many look back on Frei as a reformist with ambiguous-to-supportive positions toward the Pinochet regime, though he did oppose the 1954 US overthrow of Guatemala's Jacobo Arbenz. Mark T. Hove, "The Arbenz Factor: Salvador Allende, US-Chilean Relations, and the 1954 US Intervention in Guatemala," *Diplomatic History* 31, no. 4 (September 2007): 631, 635, 644. doi.org/10.1111/j.1467-7709.2007.00656; Joaquín Fermandois, "Multiple Christian Democratic Exiles: Debating the Road Back to Democracy," in *Political Exile in the Global Twentieth Century: Catholic Christian Democrats in Europe and the Americas*, ed. Wolfram Kaiser and Piotr H. Kosicki (Leuven: Leuven University Press, 2022), 260–261; Élodie Giraudier, "Chilean Christian Democrats in Exile in the Americas and in Europe: Impact on Networks and Ideas," in *Political Exile in the Global Twentieth Century*, 275, 278. Andrew J. Kirkendall points out that "in almost any other South American country during the Cold War era," Frei's proposed and implemented reforms "would have resulted in a military coup." They did not in Frei's case presumably because Lyndon Johnson still held out the possibility of combating communism through development. See Andrew J. Kirkendall, *Paulo Freire and the Cold War Politics of Literacy* (Chapel Hill: University of North Carolina Press, 2010), 88.

[107] Carlos Newton, "Denúncia do Golpe no Chile," *Diário de Belo Horizonte*, July 30, 1966.

such as Frei Betto recognized a theological debt to Maritain for the emergence of liberation theologies themselves.[108]

In summary, tracing Lima's life as well as the newspaper coverage of him and the early dictatorship more generally, we see that church participants did not absolve the church from engaging in political denunciations of authoritarianism. In Brazil, church publications and organizations criticized dictatorship, embraced dialogue, and called for political diversity.

CONCLUSION

This article has traced reactions to Maritain's work in two countries with similar ecclesial trajectories, but radically different trajectories in responding to dictatorship to offer a comparison to the appropriation of Maritain in the Chilean context. In both Argentina and Brazil, we find examples of Maritain's influence on opponents of authoritarianism. Maritain divided Argentina's Catholics in 1936 specifically because he opposed the Spanish Civil War. Intellectuals and the press across the region acknowledged Maritain's political engagement. With the Conciliar reforms, even some right-wing supporters quickly turned against Maritain for his anti-nationalist views. I have also shown how Alceu Lima, a highly influential Brazilian layperson, continued to advocate for Maritain's vision of forging a path away from ideological extremes while embracing social transformation.

Though they differ on how to frame the role of the church in society, both Gutierrez and Cavanaugh see Maritain's centering of spirituality as the relic of a bygone era, superseded by more robust personalist and liberationist philosophies. Even Lima himself covered Maritain's trajectory from obvious champion of a church engaged more with the people than the bourgeois elite and state to alleged reactionary.[109] But simple binaries lack nuance. A spiritual vision could be said to have propelled the vision that won out at Vatican II and during the following years. Even those French theologians who broke with Maritain's formulations framed the church as a primarily spiritual institution which could and should leaven society (ironically through Catholic Action). The distinction between the church's spiritual and earthly role did not prevent Marie-Dominique Chenu, with whom Gutierrez studied, from embracing Maritain's "profane

---

[108] María Soledad Del Villar Tagle, "The European Roots of *A Theology of Liberation*: Gustavo Gutiérrez and the *Nouvelle Théologie*," *International Journal of Latin American Religions* 6 (2022): 32, dx.doi.org/10.1007/s41603-022-00163-9.

[109] Alceu Amoroso Lima, "The Influence of Maritain in Latin America," *New Scholasticism* 46 (1972): 70–85.

Christendom." He used it to develop his theology on labor, later echoed in Karl Rahner and liberation theologians themselves.[110]

While critics of Maritain deplore the use of his thought by Latin American authoritarians, its more coherent usage by one outspoken archbishop, Óscar Romero, suggests it did not inevitably serve as an opiate for inaction. Facing censorship, bombing threats, and the burial of his Jesuit friend and colleague Rutilio Grande, Romero stressed the importance of using radio communications to go beyond the walls of the Cathedral. He stressed the same spiritual dimension which undergirded Maritain's New Christendom: "The *mystical body* of Christ is one in which every last Christian, every persecuted, silenced, *tortured* Christian participates."[111] Attributing a quote to Pius XI that could have easily come from Maritain, Romero exclaimed, "The church does not do politics, but when politics touches its altar, the church defends her altar."[112] Like Maritain, Romero elaborated, "The rights of man concern the church, life in danger concerns the mother church. The mothers who suffer are very much in the heart of the church at this moment. Those who cannot speak, those who suffer, those who are tortured, silenced, matter to the church."[113]

That is not to say Maritain would have agreed with some liberation theologies' focus on political praxis *over* Catholic spirituality. Maritain reasonably concluded that the church's service of a political theology (in his day Christ the Restorer but today perhaps even a secularized Christ the Liberator) ultimately hurts its prophetic witness, a witness nurtured by the "growth and maturing within the conscience which is produced with the spontaneity of life."[114] As he continues, fleeting "chimeras" limit charity, preclude tolerance, and "wound the Christ within [politically co-opted Christians]."

This conflict over how far specific political projects should intrude on spiritual considerations drives readings of Maritain's legacy as conservative. This defense put him at odds with a new generation which sought to put "faith-praxis" above rational theology based on natural law. "Faith-praxis" advocates such as Leonardo Boff argued that traditional spiritual and rational approaches were merely "adhesions to truth" which "supposes an economically carefree theologian, who has

---

[110] Shortall, *Soldiers of God in a Secular World*, 52, 59, 173; Tagle, "The European Roots of *A Theology of Liberation*," 34.
[111] Oscar Romero, "La misión de la Iglesia," in *Homilías monseñor Óscar Romero* (Managua: UCA, 2005), 58–59, emphasis added.
[112] Romero, "La misión de la Iglesia," 58–59.
[113] Romero, "La misión de la Iglesia," 58–59.
[114] Maritain, *Scholasticism and Politics*, 218–219, 222.

a lot of time, a lot of books, a lot of money to buy them, and a lot of peace."[115]

This division between faith and praxis did not play out as clearly as Maritain's critics suggest. Yes, distinguishing the spiritual from the worldly put Maritain on the side of certain "reformer" German theologians, such as Karl Rahner and Joseph Ratzinger, who expressed skepticism toward full engagement with the world over against French prelates who argued for a fuller embrace. These theologians argued for a distinction between world and church.[116] Additionally, a rejection of Maritain's distinction between the spiritual and temporal provided aid to theologians like Boff, radical pastoral agents in struggle. But this approach often baptized the extremes, as exemplified in Emmanuel Mounier's alleged support, through his emphasis on the immanent over the spiritual, for the Vichy French and Soviet states respectively.[117] In short, even if one gauges Maritain's theology by its relation to later politically engaged currents, the record does not favor a primarily apolitical reading of Maritain but a desacralizing one.

Scholars and activists should view Maritain's ideas and the political reactions within the context of their initial articulation. Doing so, they might see why Maritain's democratic pluralist ideas appear to the present day in expected places, such as inspirations for the United States' second Catholic president.[118] They also appear in unexpected places in Latin America such as in union halls, among left-wing politicians, and in preparations for an international conference on racism.[119] Ecclesial feuds aside, activism from some of Latin America's leading Christian Democrats also suggests that his philosophy did not lose its power to inspire. While the Chilean Church may have been slow to act against the Pinochet regime, we can safely rule out Maritain's advocacy of a spiritually-based plural democracy as a culprit. Legitimate debate over Maritain's usefulness does not need to imply that his philosophy aided authoritarians. Perhaps now,

---

[115] Leonardo Boff, *Teologia do Cativeiro e da Libertação* (São Paulo: Vozes, 2014), 29, 46–47.

[116] John O'Malley, *What Happened at Vatican II* (Cambridge, MA: Harvard University Press, 2008), 256–257.

[117] Piotr H. Kosicki, *Catholics on the Barricades: Poland, France, and "Revolution," 1891–1956* (New Haven, CT: Yale University Press, 2018), 54–55, 57–58, 67.

[118] David Brooks, "Has Biden Changed? He Tells Us," *New York Times*, May 20, 2021, www.nytimes.com/2021/05/20/opinion/joe-biden-david-brooks-interview.html.

[119] Jonathan Power, "Rethinking Militancy in Brazil," *International Herald Tribune*, February 1, 1985, 4; Hamar de Oliveira, "Patrus Ananias: Testemunho Cristão na Política," *O Lutador*, February 9–15, 1997, 3; Carlos Alves Moura, "O papel do governo na promoção da igualdade," in Ministério de Justiça, *Seminários Regionais Preparatórios para Conferência Mundial Contra o Racismo, Descirminação Racial, Xenofobia, e Intolerância Correlata* (Brasília: SEDH, 2001), 325, citing Maritain's *Man and the State*, 34.

politically center-left Catholics can once again see promise in Maritain's emphasis on plurality in pursuit of the common good. **M**

Travis Knoll received his PhD in History from Duke University in 2022. He is a History Instructor at Wingate University.

Rescuing Maritain from His Reception History: A Reappraisal of William T. Cavanaugh's Critique in *Torture and Eucharist*

Brian J. A. Boyd

Abstract: The influential writings on church and state of philosopher Jacques Maritain, who died in 1973, possessed a mid-twentieth century hopefulness about a new birth of freedom and lay-led Christian humanism. In light of the next twenty-five years—particularly the experience of the regime of Augusto Pinochet in Chile—William T. Cavanaugh, in his 1998 book *Torture and Eucharist: Theology, Politics, and the Body of Christ,* argued that Maritain's work facilitated the marginalization of faith in the modern nation-state. Another quarter-century later, this essay reappraises Cavanaugh's criticisms of Maritain's views on the nature of the church, the role of the laity, and the power of the state. It argues that while Cavanaugh's concerns about sovereignty, subsidiarity, and formation have been vindicated, a careful reading of Maritain's lesser-known and later works suffices to justify Maritain's views on the laity and the church. Maritain remains a vital resource for theologians who seek to avoid both, on the right hand, resurgent integralism and Christian nationalism and, on the left hand, a relativizing of the Gospel in what Maritain called "kneeling before the world."

INTRODUCTION: TORTURED BODIES AND TWISTED READINGS

Jacques Maritain counts among the greatest Catholic intellectuals of the twentieth century, having written over fifty books on topics from aesthetics to metaphysics to politics, with a legacy that continues to be promoted through twenty-odd national associations devoted to his work.[1] Yet it has been largely philosophers and political theorists who have continued this discussion into the twenty-first century, as none of the major recent work directly on Maritain and Christian political practice has been written by theologians.[2] This relative neglect of the philosopher Maritain by

---

[1] William Sweet, "Jacques Maritain," *Stanford Encyclopedia of Philosophy* (Summer 2022 edition), plato.stanford.edu/archives/sum2022/entries/maritain.
[2] William McCormick, "Jacques Maritain on Political Theology," *European Journal of Political Theory* 12, no. 2 (2013): 175–94, doi.org/10.1177/1474885112471263; Miguel Vatter, "Politico-Theological Foundations of Universal Human Rights: The Case of Maritain," *Social Research: An International Quarterly* 80, no. 1 (Spring 2013): 233–260, doi.org/10.1353/sor.2013.0039; Thomas Pink, "Jacques Maritain and the Problem of Church and State," *The Thomist* 79, no. 1 (January 2015): 1–42, doi.org/10.1353/tho.2015.0020; Jerónimo Molina-Cano, "Jacques Maritain y la teología

contemporary theologians is partly due to disciplinary boundaries. Another contributing factor is theologian William T. Cavanaugh's criticism of Maritain in his 1998 book *Torture and Eucharist: Theology, Politics, and the Body of Christ*, which criticized Maritain to clear the ground for Cavanaugh's constructive project. Cavanaugh makes a strong case that Maritain's work proved deeply harmful to Christian political practice, directly in Chile and indirectly for the church at large. In the quarter-century since *Torture and Eucharist* was written, no sustained reply on behalf of Maritain has been made.[3]

Cavanaugh lived and worked in a co-op in Chile during the closing years of the Pinochet dictatorship, and this experience animates his criticism of Maritain.[4] In 1966, Maritain had cautiously endorsed Pinochet's ideological predecessor, writing "I know only one example of an authentic 'Christian revolution,' and that is what President Eduardo Frei is attempting at this very moment in Chile, and it is not sure that he will succeed."[5] Frei's "revolution" did not succeed: in 1970, Frei was succeeded in office by Salvador Allende, who professed Marxism rather than Christian democracy. The threat of communism was then used as justification for the military junta's *coup* in 1973, initiating General Pinochet's seventeen-year reign of terror. Yet the junta's "Declaration of Principles" positioned itself as precisely the New Christendom which Maritain had sought— espousing the "dignity of the human person," affirming "natural rights anterior and superior to the state" in "protecting the weak from all abuses by the strong," seeking "the common good" by allowing each and every citizen "to reach their full personal fulfillment," and pursuing this good through subsidiarity in an "organic, social, and

---

política de la democracia contemporánea," *Scripta Theologica* 52, no. 1 (2020): 39–72, doi.org/10.15581/006.52.1.39-71; V. Bradley Lewis, "Thomism, Personalism, and Politics: The Case of Jacques Maritain," *Quaestiones Disputatae* 9, no. 2 (Spring 2019): 151–173, doi.org/10.5840/qd2019929; D. Q. McInerny, "The Social Thought of Jacques Maritain," *The Catholic Social Science Review* 12 (2007): 155–172, www.pdcnet.org/collection/fshow?id=cssr_2007_0012_0155_0172&pdfname=cssr_2007_0012_0155_0172.pdf&file_type=pdf; Timothy Fuller and John P. Hittinger, eds., *Reassessing the Liberal State: Reading Maritain's* Man and the State (Washington, DC: American Maritain Association, 2001).

[3] The closest that can be found are some clarifications in Maritain's favor, in Matthew A. Shadle, "Cavanaugh on the Church and the Modern State: An Appraisal," *Horizons* 37, no. 2 (2010): 246–270, doi.org/10.1017/s0360966900007271. At the time of writing, *Torture and Eucharist* had 750 citations listed on Google Scholar, a very large number for a contemporary work of theology. The lack of rebuttal combined with its widespread popularity implies that Cavanaugh's criticism of Maritain has been conceded, if not embraced, by his fellow theologians.

[4] William T. Cavanaugh, *Torture and Eucharist* (Malden, MA: Blackwell, 1998), 17.

[5] Jacques Maritain, *The Peasant of the Garonne: An Old Layman Questions Himself about the Present Time*, trans. Michael Cuddihy and Elizabeth Hughes (New York: Holt, Rinehart, and Winston, 1968 [1966]), 23.

participatory" democracy.⁶ This self-professedly Christian civilization was maintained, we now know, in part by torturing at least 27,255 of its citizens.⁷

Cavanaugh emphasizes that the "great" and "holy" Maritain would have been the first to denounce the regime's injustice, had he not died a few months before the coup;⁸ yet Cavanaugh also makes a strong case that Maritain's understanding of church and state nonetheless "has sapped the church's ability to resist regimes such as that of General Pinochet."⁹ As democracy currently seems shakier in the Global North than at any point since the 1930s, and as Maritain's ideas—developed but not replaced—remain foundational for non-integralist Thomistic Catholics, Cavanaugh's claim is of urgent interest.

This paper will not dispute Cavanaugh's telling of the reception history of Maritain's work. Cavanaugh appears to be entirely correct in his assessment of the Chilean injustice as having been rationalized through readings of Maritain. However, these rationalizations were possible only by misreading or selectively reading Maritain: his influence in Chile was largely due to his main political writings in the early and mid-twentieth century; attention to his later ecclesial and theological work supplements and contextualizes his earlier political philosophy.¹⁰ It is no small tragedy that these clarifications failed to influence the tyrannical Pinochet regime.

Cavanaugh's critique of Maritain in *Torture and Eucharist* was offered in order to clear the ground for his constructive project, which over the past twenty-five years has flourished in Augustinian soil.¹¹

---

⁶ Quoted in Cavanaugh, *Torture and the Eucharist*, 198–199. These themes are at the heart of Maritain's political thought; for brevity, in this essay I am presuming the reader's general familiarity with the main lines of Maritain's views on church and state, which sought a *concordat* with the democratic nation-state and were deeply influential in the *aggiornamento* of the Second Vatican Council. For a refresher, see John P. Hittinger, "The Political Philosophy of Jacques Maritain," *Liberty, Wisdom, and Grace: Thomism and Democratic Political Theory* (New York: Lexington, 2002), 3–20.

⁷ "Report of the Chilean National Commission on Truth and Reconciliation," *United States Institute for Peace*, www.usip.org/sites/default/files/resources/collections/truth_commissions/Chile90-Report/Chile90-Report.pdf.

⁸ In a 1971 letter to his dear friend Saul Alinsky, Maritain heaps praise on *Rules for Radicals* but expresses dismay that Alinsky claims that "in war the end justifies almost any means." Maritain rhetorically offers a list of self-evidently unjustifiable means: "Torture? Indiscriminate bombing? Annihilation of cities?" Quoted in Bernard E. Doering, "Jacques Maritain and His Two 'Authentic Revolutionaries,'" *Thomistic Papers III* (Houston, TX: Center for Thomistic Studies, 1987), 103.

⁹ Cavanaugh, *Torture and the Eucharist*, 177, 202.

¹⁰ Joseph M. de Torre, "Maritain's 'Integral Humanism' and Catholic Social Teaching," in *Reassessing the Liberal State: Reading Maritain's* Man and the State.

¹¹ Cavanaugh, *Torture and the Eucharist*, 197. Among his many subsequent works, of particular note is *Field Hospital: The Church's Engagement with a Wounded World*

While Thomistic theologians ought to engage with and learn from Cavanaugh's postliberal perspective, they need not follow him in leaving Maritain's seeds on the shelf and planting new ones elsewhere. Instead, they ought to return to "the peasant of the Garonne" and do some careful cultivation, weeding included. For this is how the peasant-professor hoped to be remembered: as "a kind of spring-finder who presses his ear to the ground in order to hear the sound of hidden springs, and of invisible germinations."[12]

CAVANAUGH'S THREE MAIN CRITICISMS OF MARITAIN

Which views of Maritain would, in Cavanaugh's view, prove so disastrous? This paper will focus on Cavanaugh's objections to Maritain's understanding of the church, laity, and state. First, that the church is to the state as the soul to the body, an immaterial animating principle: Cavanaugh charges that this leads to a view of the church as ghostly, insubstantial, with some power to spook but none to compel. Second, that the laity have a rightful autonomy in their realm of action, one which will require that they dirty their hands in a fallen world: Cavanaugh charges that this neglects the way in which charity transforms and infuses moral virtue. Third, that the state which wrongly claims sovereignty can nonetheless rightly take responsibility for subsidiarity among and formation of its citizens: Cavanaugh demonstrates that there is an irreconcilable tension between sovereignty, subsidiarity, and formation, and that the internal logic of the modern nation-state is to at once expand and harden. While Maritain can be defended on the first two charges, the third must be conceded to Cavanaugh.

The first critique is the most fundamental. St. Thomas Aquinas compares the subordination of things temporal to things spiritual with the subordination of the body to the soul, and Maritain largely "considers it unproblematic to identify Thomas's medieval 'temporal' with the modern 'state.'"[13] In analogizing the state as body and the church as soul, Cavanaugh charges that Maritain "seems unable to

---

(Grand Rapids, MI: Eerdmans, 2016). The present author would like to thank the two anonymous reviewers who pressed this point, and also through many other suggestions greatly improved this paper.

[12] Jacques Maritain, *Notebooks*, trans. Joseph W. Evans (Albany, NY: Magi, 1964), 3. Born and educated in Paris, Maritain was not literally a peasant; he calls himself one towards the end of his life to justify a willingness to risk putting "his foot in his mouth" while seeking to "call a spade a spade" (Maritain, *Peasant of the Garonne*, Preface).

[13] Cavanaugh, *Torture and the Eucharist*, 161. Cavanaugh recognizes Maritain's distinction between the "sacral" Middle Ages and the "secular" modern age, but is right to imply that it is not pertinent to this point.

contemplate the possibility that the modern distinction of temporal and spiritual, body and soul, has also served to subjugate the church by creating a sphere of purely temporal power." Further, Maritain is "maddeningly vague" on how the Christian is to fulfill her responsibility to animate, influence, inspire, vivify, and elevate the temporal order.[14] Maritain hoped for a soul as Aristotle defines it, a principle of organization which instantiates and unifies an organism; in the conditions of modernity, what results instead is a soul as understood by Descartes, an increasingly irrelevant ghost in an increasingly inexorable machine. And so the "very distinction of [spiritual and temporal] planes can function to augment the power of the state by eliminating the interference of the church. . . . Once the church has been individualized and eliminated as Christ's body in the world, only the state is left to impersonate God."[15]

Cavanaugh illustrates the life-and-death urgency of the problem by recounting a story Chilean Bishop Alejandro Jimenez told him. The bishop had an old friend who was an army lieutenant in the early days of the junta. Bishop Jimenez sought to convince his friend to stand against the regime's kidnapping, torture, and lawless executions, but his friend replied that while "the authority of a bishop . . . goes directly to the conscience," it can be disregarded, whereas the soldiers "form part of a body in which not they but their superiors have the final word."[16] The moral, as Cavanaugh interprets it, is that the status of the church as mystical body is inferior for being spiritual. The discipline that matters is material, embodied; the army's orders must be obeyed.

More precisely, Cavanaugh says that true discipline is that which, "by taking hold of our bodies," forms our souls into virtue or vice, as "body and spirit are but one."[17] A properly Thomistic psychosomatic unity wherein the soul is directly, without mediation, related to the body, entails that the soul-like church has the right to impose sacramental discipline on Catholics in the state without any intermediaries or interference. However, Cavanaugh claims that "for Maritain the power of the spiritual in the temporal must take the form of inspiration and mere counsels which do not require obedience. The result is a dysfunction between body and soul, a [Cartesian] false soul haunting a body which receives its orders from elsewhere."[18]

As his second point, Cavanaugh argues that this abstracted view of the church entails a false view of the laity. Cavanaugh is scandalized—in the traditional, proper sense of the term—by Maritain's position that the laity must accept "that there can be justice in employing horrible

---

[14] Cavanaugh, *Torture and the Eucharist*, 161, 186.
[15] Cavanaugh, *Torture and the Eucharist*, 193.
[16] Cavanaugh, *Torture and the Eucharist*, 95–96.
[17] Cavanaugh, *Torture and the Eucharist*, 196.
[18] Cavanaugh, *Torture and the Eucharist*, 196.

means," as worldly work entails that none will have "clean hands . . . [we] cannot touch the flesh of the human being without staining our fingers. To stain our fingers is not to stain our hearts."[19] These quotes seem to place Maritain in the company of Machiavelli[20] and suggest how a country claiming Maritain's mantle in its Declaration of Principles could embrace torture as policy. This relates to Cavanaugh's further objection that, by sharply distinguishing the material from the spiritual, Maritain divorces the moral from the theological virtues. Maritain, he charges, grants that charity "influence[s]" and "elevate[s]" the natural virtues, but neglects the virtues' full transformation and infusion and moreover fails to show how virtues, as habituated, must be learned within communities of practice.[21] While Cavanaugh concedes that Maritain follows St. Thomas in holding "that the politician who is caretaker of the common good must be *bonus vir*, a virtuous man in every respect, that is, natural and supernatural," he claims that Maritain's prudent ruler will merely "take into account" the supernatural end.[22] Accounting for our supernatural end and yet accepting "horrible means" to justified earthly ends, Cavanaugh charges, undermines the possibility of sanctity for the laity.

Cavanaugh's third criticism is the most complex and compelling. Maritain understood the liberal order in the later twentieth century to be in an unstable equilibrium, hoping that "our civilization has a chance to right itself," but fearing it would sink deeper into "capitalist materialism" or "communist totalitarianism," each of which are "rendered more formidable, and more similar, by technocracy."[23] The cause of this instability is the tension between sovereignty, subsidiarity, and formation in the modern nation-state, each of which requires some discussion.

MARITAIN'S SHORTCOMINGS ON SOVEREIGNTY, SUBSIDIARITY, AND FORMATION

---

[19] Maritain, *Integral Humanism,* quoted in Cavanaugh, *Torture and the Eucharist*, 170.
[20] Whose company he utterly disavows. See Jacques Maritain, "The End of Machiavellianism," *Review of Politics* 4, no. 1 (January, 1942): 1–33, doi.org/10.101 7/s0034670500003235.
[21] Cavanaugh, *Torture and the Eucharist*, 182–183.
[22] Cavanaugh, *Torture and the Eucharist*, 182.
[23] Jacques Maritain, *On the Church of Christ*, trans. Joseph W. Evans (Notre Dame, IN: University of Notre Dame Press, 1973), 92.

In *Man and the State*, Maritain asserts that only God is truly sovereign, "*transcendently* supreme."[24] God grants the social body limited autonomy, but for the state to claim sovereignty is for it to claim power without accountability. Maritain argues that the very use of the concept of sovereignty "must be scrapped" by political philosophy, since it only belongs in metaphysics as an attribute of God.[25] Despite "the sovereign state" being a key concept for centuries, Maritain holds that its association with democracy is only a bad accident of history, that can in principle be remedied with a "New Christendom" (run by the people, not the monarch) to replace the modern sovereign state. Cavanaugh agrees that state sovereignty is a category error but argues it was no accident. Rather, asserting sovereignty in principle from God and in practice over the church was essential to the creation of the modern state. From Rousseau onward, "the object of the state [has been] to make citizens as independent as possible from each other and as dependent as possible on the state."[26] Some individual leaders of modern states may work against this inherent logic; but what Maritain saw as the natural growth of the state to protect its citizens' expansive and expanding rights, Cavanaugh demonstrates, in fact requires that the state aggrandize itself indefinitely.[27]

The problems this causes for Maritain's willingness to work with the nation-state become clearer when considering the principle of subsidiarity. A society governed by subsidiarity is one, as Cavanaugh explains, where "the organic City would be ruled not by the wheels of a bureaucratic machine but by decisions taken by men chosen as leaders of their several organizations."[28] The many guilds, corporations, fraternal societies, churches, schools, and community organizations which make up the lifeblood of society are to be as independent and self-directing as possible, with the state only interfering to protect individuals when fundamental rights are infringed. Maritain famously upheld this view of subsidiarity in his close friendship with Saul Alinsky and support of community organizing as a counterweight to institutional power.[29] Yet in hoping that the state machinery could

---

[24] Jacques Maritain, *Man and the State* (Washington, DC: Catholic University of America Press, 1998 [1951]), 51.
[25] Maritain, *Man and the State*, 49–53, emphasis in original.
[26] Cavanaugh, *Torture and the Eucharist*, 165, 190–193.
[27] See William T. Cavanaugh, "Killing for the Telephone Company: Why the Nation-State is Not the Keeper of the Common Good," *Modern Theology* 20, no. 2 (2004): 243–274, doi.org/10.1111/j.1468-0025.2004.00252.x.
[28] Cavanaugh, *Torture and the Eucharist*, 194. See also William T. Cavanaugh, "The Road Not Taken: Figgis, Subsidiarity, and Catholic Social Teaching," in *Neville Figgis, CR: His Life, Thought and Significance*, ed. Paul Avis (Leiden: Brill, 2021).
[29] C. J. Wolfe, "Lessons from the Friendship of Jacques Maritain with Saul Alinsky," *Catholic Social Science Review* 16 (2011): 229–240, doi.org/10.5840/cssr20111620.

restrain and even efface itself, Maritain failed to contend with the Iron Law of Oligarchy, memorably paraphrased as "Bureaucracy happens. If bureaucracy happens, power rises. Power corrupts."[30] In order to adjudicate disputes—particularly if the state claims to serve the common good, which Maritain wants—over time, Cavanaugh notes, "the state will find it necessary to build such strong controls of the intermediate associations into the system that meaningful participation and autonomy for these groups will be squelched."[31] Examples in American democracy are plentiful: the trajectory from federalism towards statism, the constriction of religious freedom (whose concept itself was a grab for power by the state),[32] and the nationalization and bureaucratization of organizations such as political parties and unions.[33]

A sovereign state which undermines subsidiarity in order to have an increasingly direct relationship with citizens has final power over the formation of its citizens. This secular formation is the third, and worst, problem for Maritain's conception of the state. Cavanaugh points out that "Christians in modernity have often bought into a devil's bargain in which the state is given control of our bodies while the church supposedly retains our souls. . . . But the state cannot be expected to limit itself to the body; it will colonize the soul as well . . . . The secular god is a jealous god."[34] Maritain promoted the teaching of civics and even a *"civic or secular* faith, not a religious one" within democratic societies, but only as an interim measure.[35] In the long run, "States will be obliged to make a choice for or against the Gospel. They will be shaped either by the totalitarian spirit or by the Christian spirit."[36] In an age where American presidents worked closely with the Papacy against tyrants,[37] professed the country to be "a Christian

---

[30] Darcy K. Leach, "The Iron Law of *What* Again? Conceptualizing Oligarchy across Organizational Forms," *Sociological Theory* 23, no. 3 (September 2005): 312–337, doi.org/10.1111/j.0735-2751.2005.00256.x.

[31] Cavanaugh, *Torture and the Eucharist*, 195.

[32] William T. Cavanaugh, "Are We Free Not to Be a Religion? The Ambivalence of Religious Freedom," in *Field Hospital*, 234–248.

[33] Perhaps the most compelling account of the anti-democratic nature of bureaucracy is to be found in David Graeber, *The Utopia of Rules: On Technology, Stupidity, and the Secret Joys of Bureaucracy* (New York: Melville House, 2015).

[34] Cavanaugh, *Torture and the Eucharist*, 196.

[35] Maritain, *Man and the State*, 110, 119–126, emphasis in original. Maritain presumably had in mind the French tradition, going back to the Revolution, of required courses in *éducation civique*.

[36] Maritain, *Man and the State*, 159.

[37] W. David Curtiss and C. Evan Stewart, "Myron C. Taylor, Part Two: President Franklin D. Roosevelt's Ambassador Extraordinary," *Cornell Law Forum* 33 (2007), heinonline.org/HOL/P?h=hein.journals/corlawfofe33&i=76.

nation" in great need of "a renewal of faith,"[38] and claimed in the State of the Union that "religion [is] the source of . . . democracy and international good faith,"[39] Maritain may be forgiven for a hope that looks in hindsight to have been ill-founded. The use of American civil religion to turn the nation itself into an idol had not yet been made clear.[40] Citizens of the United States are not formed into a civic faith that tends towards Christian civilization; rather, as Cavanaugh demonstrates, they have been formed as citizens in a patriotic liturgical cycle that grounds the present reality on past sacrifice which created order from chaos, leading to indebtedness requiring fresh sacrifice and "new good wars."[41] Moreover, the nation-state in "ordinary time" forms citizen-consumers, as the market is the closest thing there is to a common good.[42] Here again, Maritain foresaw possible dangers, and he strongly condemned the bourgeois state which sees economic growth as its highest end.[43] Yet his belief that America could be much more than the colossus of the market has turned out to be in vain, and not just accidentally. For if the state has ultimate and increasing responsibility for the protection of the rights of its citizens, and the Lockean rights of "life, liberty, and property" are foremost in American jurisprudence, then an ever-increasing

---

[38] Harry S. Truman, "Exchange of Messages with Pope Pius XII," *American Presidency Project*, www.presidency.ucsb.edu/documents/exchange-messages-with-pope-pius-xii.

[39] Franklin D. Roosevelt, "Annual Message to Congress," *American Presidency Project*, www.presidency.ucsb.edu/documents/annual-message-congress.

[40] The classic article is Robert N. Bellah, "Civil Religion in America," *Daedalus* 96, no. 1 (Winter 1967): 40–55. Bellah prefaces his article by writing, "I conceive of the central tradition of the American civil religion not as a form of national self-worship but as the subordination of the nation to ethical principles that transcend it [and] in terms of which it should be judged." Frederick Douglass's 1852 speech "What to the Slave is the Fourth of July?" exemplifies the kind of self-scrutiny offering a path towards national self-improvement, the positive sense of American civil religion. Yet Bellah wrote during the Vietnam War and saw that this tradition of self-scrutiny was losing ground to self-worship alternating with self-hatred; since then, the language of civil religion has arguably become a comforting myth, a now-fraying mask to hide from Americans the reality of the United States' impact in the world. See William T. Cavanaugh, "Telling the Truth about Ourselves: Torture and Eucharist in the US Popular Imagination," *The Other Journal*, no. 15 (Fall 2009), theotherjournal.com/2009/05/telling-the-truth-about-ourselves-torture-and-eucharist-in-the-u-s-popular-imaginat/.

[41] William T. Cavanaugh, "The Liturgies of Church and State," *Liturgy* 20, no. 1 (2005): 29, doi.org/10.1080/04580630590522876. Eighteen years later, one wonders to what extent Cavanaugh would extend this analysis of "new good wars" to present calls for increased intervention in Ukraine.

[42] Lizabeth Cohen, *A Consumer's Republic: The Politics of Mass Consumption in Postwar America* (New York: Vintage, 2003).

[43] Maritain, *Man and the State*, 110. See also his posthumous exploratory essay on political economy, "A Society Without Money," *Review of Social Economy* 43, no. 1 (April 1985): 73–83, doi.org/10.1080/00346768500000022.

idolatry of money will necessarily mirror and complement the growth of the state.[44]

That the state falsely considers itself sovereign, an authority higher than God; that the principle of subsidiarity might fall prey to the bureaucratic machinery upholding individual rights; and that citizens would be formed by means intrinsically opposed to faith—these all occurred to Maritain as risks for democratic nation-states. However, Cavanaugh is right to argue from a more contemporary standpoint that these defects are more akin to fatal flaws. It is understandable that, in 1951, Maritain hoped that "the totalitarian State," acting as "the old spurious God of the lawless Empire bending everything to his adoration," would be defeated by the joint cause of freedom and the church, "one in the defense of man."[45] In hindsight, it becomes clear that any such victories were temporary, indeed partly illusory.

DEFENDING LATER MARITAIN ON THE CHURCH AND THE LAITY

Cavanaugh is right that the nation-state has used its false sovereignty to undermine subsidiarity and distort the formation of Christian citizens, and thus the *concordat* which Maritain sought with the modern state is a lost cause. Yet that does not mean that there is nothing of worth to be found in Maritain for the contemporary theologian. Rather, Maritain's thought, particularly his later work, can fully respond to Cavanaugh's other criticisms concerning the relationship of church and body politic and the dirty hands of the laity. Offering a clarification and defense of Maritain on these two points gives grounds to seek a renewal of Maritain's influence in theology.

Return first to the criticism that Maritain held the church to be in psychosomatic unity with the body politic, yet it became a mere Cartesian haunting ghost. Cavanaugh is right to decry this disembodiment of the church as a pernicious development in modernity, one particularly ubiquitous after the Second Vatican Council. To remedy it, he calls for a deepened appreciation of the way in which "to participate in the Eucharist" is "to be caught up into what is really real, the body of Christ," to be given a more fundamental identity than any of "the state's [attempts] to define what is real."[46]

---

[44] These claims are contentious and deserve further support than space allows. Proper elaboration would draw on Cavanaugh, "Telephone"; "Are Corporations People?"; *Field Hospital*; *Being Consumed: Economics and Christian Desire* (Grand Rapids, MI: Eerdmans, 2008). See also Michael Sandel, "The Skyboxification of Everyday Life," in *What Money Can't Buy: The Moral Limits of Markets* (New York: Farrar, Straus, and Giroux, 2012), and Alasdair MacIntyre, "Introduction," in *Marxism and Christianity*, 2nd ed. (New York: Bloomsbury, 1995).

[45] Maritain, *Man and the State*, 187.

[46] Cavanaugh, *Torture and the Eucharist*, 279. As noted above, developing this positive vision is the main purpose of the book.

Yet in this there is no disagreement with Maritain—either Jacques or Raïssa, his wife and intellectual partner. They jointly wrote that in order to understand terms such as "fraternal love" and "social justice," Christians must pursue a "liturgical renewal" which helps "the faithful to realize better, through their union with the public prayer of the Church, their belonging to the Mystical Body" as their primary identity.[47] While the view of the ghostly, Cartesian church-soul described above is deeply harmful, it is not Maritain's position.

The first point to press on is Cavanaugh's attribution to Maritain of the view that "the power of the spiritual in the temporal must take the form of inspiration and mere counsels."[48] This claim seems plausible in light of Maritain's more general comments.[49] Moreover, Cavanaugh is right about the harms that come from too complete a separation of spiritual and temporal.[50] However, in this distinction which Maritain makes, he is careful to emphasize that the church is restricted in its counsels concerning material things *per se,* but her binding teachings on faith and morals do concern material things *per accidens.*[51] That this distinction makes a real difference can be seen by referring back to Cavanaugh's example of the lieutenant and the bishop. In interpreting the text wherein Aquinas compares the church to the soul of the body politic, Maritain approvingly quotes Cajetan's commentary:

> The spiritual power by its very nature has authority over the temporal power *in view of the spiritual* end. . . . That means that the secular power is not subject absolutely and in every respect to the spiritual power: for instance . . . in the military order the Commander of an army [must be obeyed], rather than the Bishop, who has no business to meddle in such matters unless in relation to spiritual things. But *should anything whatsoever in temporal things in any way jeopardize eternal salvation,* the prelate then intervening in that demand by a command or a prohibition is not thrusting his scythe into another man's harvest but legitimately exercising his own authority: because *all secular powers are subject on that score to the spiritual power.*[52]

---

[47] Jacques and Raïssa Maritain, *Liturgy and Contemplation,* trans. Joseph W. Evans (New York: P. J. Kenedy & Sons, 1960), 78.

[48] Cavanaugh, *Torture and the Eucharist,* 196.

[49] For instance: "'Authentically and vitally Christian' [political activity,] while drawing its inspiration from the Christian spirit and Christian principles, would involve only the initiative and responsibility of the citizens who conduct it, without being in the slightest degree a politics dictated by the Church" (Maritain, *Peasant of the Garonne,* 22).

[50] William T. Cavanaugh, "'A Fire Strong Enough to Consume the House:' The Wars of Religion and the Rise of the State," *Modern Theology* 11, no. 4 (October 1995): 397–420, doi.org/10.1111/j.1468-0025.1995.tb00073.x.

[51] Jacques Maritain, *The Things That Are Not Caesar's,* trans. J. F. Scanlan (New York: Charles Scribner's Sons, 1931), xiii.

[52] Maritain, *Things That Are Not Caesar's,* 129–130, emphasis in original.

Things jeopardizing eternal salvation are things concerning grave matter, wherein sins committed with full knowledge and intent become mortal (*Reconciliatio et Paenitentia,* no. 17). In order to know his authority to intervene, the Chilean bishop need not have read Maritain or Cajetan (although he could have); he need only have read *Gaudium et Spes,* no. 27, promulgated not even a decade before the coup. The Council expressly condemned "torments inflicted on body or mind" as "violat[ing] the integrity of the human person" and thus one among many grave "infamies." It is only through culpable ignorance and dereliction of duty that a bishop could fail to see widespread torture and unjust executions as falling under his authority to forbid on pain of excommunication. By 1980, the bishops of Chile finally did come to see their duty, excommunicating "not only those participating in the actual torture but also those who order[ed] it or [were] in a position to stop it but [did] not."[53] This is the kind of intervention which Maritain had endorsed in a case where the evil was far less obvious, namely the Pope's forbidding Catholics to participate in the political movement *Action Française.*[54] For the church to have right of intervention in mundane matters which touch on salvation is for the church to have right of intervention on the gravest issues in social, economic, and political life, as *Gaudium et Spes* implies.[55]

Through excommunication, a Catholic is shown to have expelled him- or herself from the Body of Christ, and thus is forbidden from approaching the altar and receiving Christ in the Eucharist. Cavanaugh faults Maritain for insufficiently appreciating "the church's own character as a *contrast society,* a counter-performance of the body to that of the state," a "social body," and indeed "a body *sui generis.*"[56] It is true that the embodied church receives little emphasis in Maritain's chief political writings, such as *The Person and the Common Good* (1947) and *Man and the State* (1951), but they are not altogether missing.[57] Moreover, Maritain details this truth in his later

---

[53] Cavanaugh, *Torture and the Eucharist,* 116.
[54] See Maritain, *Things That Are Not Caesar's,* 44–77.
[55] It is important to keep in mind Maritain's close connection with Vatican II. Hittinger compellingly argues that Maritain inspired the Council's declaration that the "split between the faith which many profess and their daily lives deserves to be counted among the more serious errors of our age" (*Liberty,* 286).
[56] Cavanaugh, *Torture and the Eucharist,* 180, emphasis in original.
[57] "For the believer the Church is a supernatural society, both divine and human—the very type of perfect or achieved-in-itself, self-sufficient, and independent society— which unites in itself men as co-citizens of the Kingdom of God and leads them to eternal life, already begun here below; which teaches them the revealed truth received in trust from the Incarnate Word Himself; and which is the very body of which the head is Christ, a body *visible,* by reason of its essence, in its professed creed, its worship, its discipline and its sacraments, and in the refraction of its supernatural

works, particularly *The Peasant of the Garonne* (1967) and *On the Church of Christ* (1973). In the former, Maritain warns against two opposed errors: one which through a deficit of charity and a surplus of moralism, fear, and self-denial would condemn the world as evil, irredeemably corrupt for practical purposes; and the other, a *"kneeling before the world"* which seeks nothing more than to be accepted by and become part of it.[58] Instead, he would have the church live the Gospel truth that contrasts "the world *in its concrete and existential connections"* with the church which is *"the kingdom of God,* already present in our midst . . . at once visible in those who bear the mark of Christ and invisible in those who, without bearing the mark of Christ, share in his grace." Maritain emphasizes that because "Jesus came not to condemn the world but to save it, the kingdom of God, which is not of the world, is itself growing in the world."[59] Cavanaugh considers it of utmost importance that the church not be held on a separate plane from the world, but rather that the two offer competing performances on the same stage, one a Divine Comedy and the other a mundane tragedy.[60] In this Cavanaugh is echoing Augustine on the two cities—precisely as Maritain had done decades before.[61] In offering the world a new performance of human life, Maritain's ideal is to become a contemplative "on the roads of the world," a lofty state only reached through bodily practices such as "asceticism, mortification, or

---

personality through its human structure and activity" (Maritain, *Man and the State*, 151), emphasis in original.

[58] Maritain, *Peasant of the Garonne*, 48, 54, emphasis in original. Maritain extended this line of thought in *On the Church of Christ:* "Those Churchmen who bend the knee before the world, fabricate for it a religion made to measure, and believe themselves dedicated to the social progress and to the happiness of man here on earth, know moreover very badly the world; and the command optimism displayed by them with regard to the future of a civilization which in fact, and for the moment, finds itself in full decadence is nourished by as many illusions as by holy desires" (*On the Church of Christ: The Person of the Church and her Personnel*, Joseph W. Evans [Notre Dame, IN: University of Notre Dame Press, 1973], 92).

[59] Maritain, *Peasant of the Garonne*, 37, emphasis in original.

[60] William T. Cavanaugh, "From One City to Two: Christian Reimagining of Political Space," *Political Theology* 7, no. 3 (2015): 299–321, doi.org/10.1558/poth.2006.7.3.299.

[61] "The world is the domain *at once* of man, of God, and of the devil. Thus appears the essential ambiguity of the world and of its history; it is a field common to the three. The world is a closed field which belongs to God by right of creation; to the devil by right of conquest, because of sin; to Christ by right of victory over the conqueror, because of the Passion. The task of the Christian in the world is to contest with the devil his domain, to wrest it from him; he must strive to this end, he will succeed in it only in part as long as time will endure. . . . Divided between two opposing ultimate ends, the history of the temporal city leads at one and the same time toward the kingdom of perdition and toward the kingdom of God" (Maritain, *Peasant of the Garonne*, 35–36), which in turn echoes a theme of his much earlier work, *True Humanism*.

penance."[62] For Maritain equally as for Cavanaugh, ascetical and liturgical practices confirm us in and conform us to the church as our primary membership. For while the state is a body analogously, lacking the kind of full integration which an animate body possesses, the church is not only a true body—the Body of Christ—but even a true person—the Bride of Christ. Maritain would have us take these traditional concepts not as analogies but as archetypes, great mysteries of divine splendor and fundamental truth. Our mundane citizenship, which can be revoked or renounced, is but a faint echo of our membership in the church, which literally makes the Christian a "new creation," one now bearing "the likeness of the man from heaven."[63] That few of the lay baptized believe this or have even seriously considered it is a great tragedy, "the true and authentic need of our age" to remedy, so that contemplative love may "go out of doors and spread its wings" to reach the four corners of the earth.[64]

The church can only serve as a living, forming soul for the body politic, then, if the laity have already been formed and found their true identity as the Body of Christ. Maritain holds that the Christian's relation to the world is best understood through spelling out what it means for her to have been born and then born again. She was first "*born of the world*, and in original sin," and then "by baptism" was born again, "*born of God*."[65] This latter birth is second in time but first in importance. From the day of baptism, the Christian is not a member of the world, but of the church. To be in the world but not of it means that the laity do not have two separate vocations, one temporal and the other spiritual, but rather one vocation with a mundane object and a spiritual mode. That is, the object of lay discipleship, "absolutely basic and *necessary for all*," is simply to enact the daily labors of the life of the world, but to do each thing in the mode of "*the spirit . . . as a Christian.*"[66] To claim that the spirit of Christ will radiate from the Christian, giving "witness to the Gospel, not by preaching it, but by living it, and by the *manner* in which [s/]he carries out the most banal

---

[62] Maritain and Maritain, *Liturgy and Contemplation*, 74; Maritain, *Peasant of the Garonne*, 54.
[63] Maritain, *On the Church of Christ*, chap. 3.
[64] Maritain and Maritain, *Liturgy and Contemplation*, 73.
[65] Maritain, *Peasant of the Garonne*, 207, emphasis in original. Maritain emphasizes that one is a true member of the church, indeed ontologically one has full personhood precisely because one is a branch from the vine that is the Body of Christ; one is analogously a member of one's society because man is by nature a political animal; but one is not a member of the world *per se* because the world lacks organic unity (208).
[66] Maritain, *Peasant of the Garonne*, 208–210, emphasis in original.

tasks" is precisely to claim that charity, an unearned gift from God, infuses all the virtues and hence all their acts.[67]

For Maritain, one can and must not only rule or philosophize as a Christian; all of life, in his example extending even to having a drink at the pub with one's friends, is lived as a Christian. This requires not constant preaching but rather constant integrity, which means allowing the Gospel's radiance to shine through mundane mediums such as a friendly word or even a spontaneous reaction or gesture. This is the straightforward but difficult means to healing the centuries-long cleavage between "the temporal work of the lay Christian and [her] spiritual vocation," which "for many centuries our Western civilization has suffered from" as among its gravest evils.[68] Cavanaugh calls for the Christian to offer a counter-performance to the ways of the world; yet this is precisely the result of the transformation in charity of one's every action, as insisted upon by Maritain. Maritain paraphrases the famous quote from his "old godfather," Léon Bloy, that "there is only one sadness; it is not to *be a saint.*"[69] Thus the church offers a soul to the social body: by offering saints who uplift its life.

In response to Cavanaugh's charge that Maritain undervalues the role of charity in forming the cardinal virtues, consider the conclusion to *The Peasant of the Garonne*. Maritain quotes an entry from his wife Raïssa's journal, published posthumously, which insists that "what one must first and foremost tell men, and go on telling them, is to love God—to know that he is Love and to trust to the end in his Love."[70] The foremost and final word is the love of God, and this applies also, Jacques makes clear earlier in the work, to "those who take charge of guiding [political] parties of Christian inspiration."[71] Such leaders require a solid formation in doctrine and character in order to fulfill their "mission to transform the world," a literal transformation so that the world might be informed by "the spirit of Christ and of his

---

[67] Maritain, *Peasant of the Garonne*, 208–210, emphasis in original.

[68] Maritain, *Peasant of the Garonne*, 210.

[69] Maritain, *Peasant of the Garonne*, 212, emphasis in original. In *Man and the State*, 139–141, Maritain more explicitly relates sanctity to social life in speaking of the "prophetic shock-minorities" who are the people's "inspired servants." Although he warns against false prophets and speaks of the need for discernment of spirits, one may wish he wrote in a more expressly theological mode. His full treatment of the question of how much one saint may inspire and elevate the life of a people is offered in considering St. Joan of Arc in *On the Church of Christ*. A fuller exposition of Maritain's view on the lay life would take into account the way in which the true common good is found in the Kingdom of God, and the autonomy of the political sphere is not full sovereignty but freedom with respect to a subordinate order of creation hierarchically ordered towards life in God.

[70] Maritain, *Peasant of the Garonne*, 260.

[71] Maritain, *Peasant of the Garonne*, 201.

kingdom."[72] For "justice without love is inhuman, and love for men and for peoples . . . is itself fragile without theological charity. Without the love of charity, work as we might, we will work *nothing*."[73]

This call for charity to inform justice and prudence at first glance sits uneasily with Maritain's assertion that none of the laity can have "clean hands." While this claim might seem to imply a compromise with Machiavelli, Maritain's writings on the laity in context and development in fact are profoundly opposed to any "end justifies the means" view. His suggestion that the laity ought to have dirty hands does not undermine his insistence that intrinsic evils must be avoided. Rather, it comes in the context of explaining his understanding of the relationship of means to ends, which he considers "*the* basic problem in political philosophy."[74]

Maritain describes a hierarchy of means. The highest actions are "pure spiritual means directed towards eternity" (e.g., prayer and fasting for the conversion of sinners); next are "spiritual means directed towards the material world" (e.g., prayer and fasting for an increase of integral human development); then come temporal means, richer or poorer to the extent that they serve the spiritual order (e.g., spiritual works of mercy taking priority over corporal works).[75] The point of this gradation of means is to help us identify which means are proportionate to their end, in traditional Thomistic fashion. For example, the right to self-defense includes, in the most dire circumstances, the right to kill one's aggressor; but a higher material means to be sought when possible would be incapacitating the aggressor, a higher still material means would be nonviolent resistance, and a spiritual means would be the use of one's dignity to forestall aggression altogether.[76] The virtuous Christian officer of order will be prepared to kill, but will regard this as a failing in almost every circumstance, and will seek in prudence to elevate his means and reduce his violence wherever possible.[77]

---

[72] Maritain, *Peasant of the Garonne*, 204.

[73] Maritain, *Peasant of the Garonne*, 204.

[74] Maritain, *Man and the State*, 54, quoted in Nicholas C. Lund-Molfese, "Maritain's Contribution to the Development of the Magisterium on Means," in *Reassessing the Liberal State*.

[75] Lund-Molfese, "Maritain's Contribution," 229.

[76] Lund-Molfese, "Maritain's Contribution," 234–237. For a compelling illustration of this kind of spiritual means defusing aggression before it strikes a blow, see Gichin Funakoshi, "No Weapons: An Important Lesson," *Karate-Do: My Way of Life* (New York: Kodansha America, 1981), 21–29. Magisterial practitioners of the martial arts often find pacifism to be an aspirational ideal.

[77] Lund-Molfese, "Maritain's Contribution," 237–240. See also Maritain's appreciation of Mahatma Gandhi in *Man and the State*, 68–71. For an overview, see Gregory M. Reichberg, "Jacques Maritain: Christian Theorist of Non-Violence and Just War,"

Maritain's hierarchy of means can give the impression that in contrasting material means with "pure" spiritual ones, he condemns the material as impure and thereby sinful. To avoid this misunderstanding, Maritain emphasizes the inevitability and necessity of dirty hands, leading to the passages in *True Humanism* to which Cavanaugh objects. What Maritain means by insisting that Christians will not have "clean hands" is absolutely not that they are to commit evil acts expecting good to come. Instead, his point is that they cannot expect to detach themselves from the material world, that they cannot serve as the Body of Christ and leaven of the world if they are not engaged in tilling the soil. Maritain's emphasis on dirty hands is not much different from Pope Francis's insistence that priests be close to the poor, like shepherds living with the smell of the sheep.[78]

CONCLUSION: RETRIEVING MARITAIN WHILE RETAINING CAVANAUGH

Jacques Maritain was no optimist or naïve idealist. He worked on behalf of the Free French during World War II, and believed that the Allies' victory at best bought some time for deep reforms, both of nation-states and the church. He poured substantial efforts into the Universal Declaration of Human Rights and the founding of UNESCO.[79] He also served as an inspiration in the lead-up to the Second Vatican Council, with Pope St. Paul VI naming himself "a disciple of Maritain."[80] While Cavanaugh in *Torture and Eucharist* focused on Maritain's reception in Chile, Maritain also had an extensive impact in Europe.[81] Yet towards the end of his life, in the works which have been the focus of this article, Maritain seemed to

---

Journal of Military Ethics 16, nos. 3-4 (2017): 220–238, doi.org/10.1080/15027570.2017.1413216.

[78] Pope Francis, "Chrism Mass Homily," March 28, 2013, www.vatican.va/content/francesco/en/homilies/2013/documents/papa-francesco_20130328_messa-crismale.html. There are interesting parallels in Jacques Maritain, "To Exist with the People," in *The Range of Reason* (New York: Scribner, 1952). The comparison falters when it comes to war, but even here, Maritain cautions that "those who claim to be the champions of Order and of the Spirit must serve Order and the Spirit even in the means they employ to defend them" ("'Right' and 'Left,'" *Blackfriars* 18, no. 212 [November 1937]: 809, www.jstor.org/stable/43811003).

[79] Jacques Maritain, "The Goal of UNESCO," *Modern Schoolman* 25, no. 4 (May 1948): 211–223, doi.org/10.5840/schoolman194825436.

[80] Quoted in Brooke W. Smith, "The Jacques Maritain Controversy in Perspective," *Thought* 50, no. 199 (December 1975): 394, doi.org/10.5840/thought197550434.

[81] See James Chappel, *Catholic Modern: The Challenge of Totalitarianism and the Remaking of the Church* (Cambridge, MA: Harvard University Press, 2018). I thank an anonymous reviewer for the reference. For Maritain's impact on Italy in particular, see Mehmet Ciftci, "A Case Study of Catholic Social Thought in Action: Giorgio La Pira, Politician, Jurist, and the Saintly Mayor of Florence," *Journal of the Oxford Graduate Theological Society* 2, no. 2 (2021): 78–87, www.coursesidekick.com/arts-humanities/3181764.

intuit that his legacy would be ambiguous. One reviewer called *The Peasant of the Garonne* "quite literally a bomb" thrown into the discourse; others felt that the book was "a betrayal of the Council and his own life's work."[82]

It is understandable that in the quarter-century since publishing *Torture and Eucharist*, Cavanaugh has not drawn on Maritain as a resource. Cavanaugh's work on politics and economics is instead perhaps best summed up by Pope Francis's metaphor of the church as "field hospital": a site on the battlefield yet ordered towards healing, not fighting; a physical presence that makes an immediate difference for those who encounter it; a shelter open to any in need, but a waystation more than an entrenchment. While calling for a profound change in the political work of Christians, Cavanaugh does not offer a systematic plan of action, endorsing instead the personalist revolution of Dorothy Day and the call for improvisation made by Samuel Wells.[83] He would have Christians regain an Augustinian politics, which rather than empires prefers small political units in peaceable concord with their neighbors, and above all emphasizes the Christian's primary status as pilgrim towards the City of God who has renounced her birthright citizenship in the City of Man.[84] He thus makes the case for pacifism and "fugitive democracy," as well as "working alongside other people of good will from other faiths and none" while still "knit[ting] together our spiritual lives with our material lives."[85]

Cavanaugh's perspective offers essential insights which must be taken up by theologians who consider themselves Thomists. He offers a third way, an escape from the false dilemma which characterizes too much Christian political discourse, especially popular discussion of political theology—a dilemma which suggests that the only alternative to (mal)formation by the sovereign state and subsequent 'kneeling before the world' is the imperative to conquer the world through a renewed integralism or 'political Catholicism.'[86] These are not mere

---

[82] Quoted in Smith, "The Maritain Controversy," 381.

[83] Respectively, in Cavanaugh, "'We Are to Blame for the War': Dorothy Day on Violence and Guilt," in *Field Hospital*, 249–263; and Cavanaugh, "From One City," 317. Pointing this out is not meant as a criticism. It is a sign of prudence and humility, not an intellectual failing, when Cavanaugh elsewhere writes "I am not in the business of setting forth models for a new global order. I tend to think such global models are inherently problematic" ("If You Render Unto God What Is God's, What Is Left for Caesar?," in Daniel Philpott and Ryan T. Anderson, eds., *A Liberalism Safe for Catholicism?: Perspectives from* The Review of Politics [Notre Dame, IN: University of Notre Dame Press, 2017], 572).

[84] Cavanaugh, *Field Hospital*, 153.

[85] Cavanaugh, *Field Hospital*, 54, 155.

[86] Pink, "Jacques Maritain," argues that since history has proven Maritain a failure, the only faithful position is integralism. By contrast, a Thomistic perspective harmonious with Cavanaugh's is offered in Andrew Willard Jones, "The End of

ivory-tower disputes. Misreading Maritain had a lethal impact in Chile, and Cavanaugh is right to generalize the point by claiming that Christian nationalism inevitably involves a "collective narcissism" which requires "the identification of God with the 'we' [in] a blatant form of idolatry."[87] Moreover, when integralism leaves blue-sky theorizing and moves towards concrete plans for a common-good constitutionalism—with the common good defined by a small minority and asserted through force if necessary—the only paths forward seem to lead in the same direction as Chile's junta.[88]

Yet, having now gained sufficient distance from Maritain to understand the deep harm caused by his understatement of the problem of sovereignty, we can also retrieve insight from the old peasant, who both foresaw and lived through the horrors of last century's polarization. In a 1937 essay, Maritain decried political extremism, writing that "to array hate against hate is to head for catastrophe and the utter destruction of all political life. Neither impatience nor violence—no matter under what provocation—can ever work the good of society or nation."[89] What was necessary then and is necessary now is to transcend the dichotomy of Right and Left altogether. One must be a "true conservative" with reverence for the life handed on by tradition, and yet also look to the "needs of the future" through a commitment to innovation and "the most radical of revolutions" which can only come about through "the spirit of Faith in God."[90] In his emphasis that the laity must be formed liturgically and spiritually into the Body of Christ, so that they might be salt, light, and leaven to the world; in his careful distinctions among spiritual and material means, so that prudence might find the most apt means to attain a just and good end; and more generally, in his emphasis upon the both/and nature of the person in relationship to the common good as the church's alternative to the zero-sum mindset of both totalitarian collectivism and technocratic individualism,[91] Jacques Maritain continues to offer vital insights to contemporary theologians. Those

---

Sovereignty: An Essay in Christian Postliberalism," *Communio* 45 (Fall-Winter 2018): 408–456, www.communio-icr.com/files/45.3-4_Jones_WEB.pdf.

[87] William T. Cavanaugh, "The Splendid Idolatry of Nationalism," *Pro Publico Bono – Public Administration* 9, no. 2 (2021): 4–25, doi.org/10.1093/oso/9780197679043.003.0007.

[88] To which the integralist might offer a *tu quoque:* in the words of President Obama, "we tortured some folks," but "it's important for us not to feel too sanctimonious in retrospect about the tough job that those folks [i.e., the torturers] had" (Roberta Rampton and Steve Holland, "Obama Says that After 9/11, 'We Tortured Some Folks,'" *Reuters* [August 1, 2014]).

[89] Maritain, "'Right' and 'Left,'" 808.

[90] Maritain, "'Right' and 'Left,'" 809.

[91] Although not central to this essay, Maritain's most enduring work is almost surely to be *The Person and the Common Good*, trans. John J. Fitzgerald (Notre Dame, IN: University of Notre Dame Press, 2006 [1946]).

who read him will find that the last lines of his last book, published in 1973, speak with a prophetic humility: "What I have tried to furnish here is the last testimony of an old solitary. . . . I have an idea that today it will displease many. But who knows? In fifty years, one will find perhaps that all of this has been very poorly said, but that after all, it was not so stupid."[92] M

Brian J. A. Boyd, PhD, is a moral theologian serving as Research Assistant Director of the Center for Ethics and Economic Justice at Loyola University New Orleans. His research in Thomistic ethics ranges from political economy and peacemaking to prudence and discernment around novel technologies. He is a strategic consultant to *The New Atlantis* and a member of the Initiative for the Study of a Stable Peace and the International Society for MacIntyrean Enquiry.

---

[92] Maritain, *On the Church of Christ*, 241.

Revisiting Maritain in the Present Context—
A Response to Gilbrian Stoy, Travis Knoll, and Brian Boyd

William T. Cavanaugh

Abstract: In this article, William Cavanaugh responds to Brian Boyd's critique of Cavanaugh's use of Jacques Maritain's work in Cavanaugh's book *Torture and Eucharist*. The article reassesses Maritain's views on the state, the church, and the laity in light of Boyd's analysis, which accepts Cavanaugh's critique of Maritain on the state but rebuts aspects of Cavanaugh's critique of Maritain's views on the church and the laity. Cavanaugh accepts some of Boyd's rebuttals, such as his defense of Maritain's views on the formation of laity and the temporal authority of bishops, but Cavanaugh pushes back on others, such as Maritain's views of the relationship of ends to means and eternity to time. After discussing the differences among Maritain's context, the context of Pinochet's Chile, and the present context of the church in Latin America and Europe, Cavanaugh argues for a different form of Christian politics that rises from the grassroots rather than tries to sway elites.

One of my prized possessions is a framed photo of Jacques Maritain given me by Wallace Fowlie, the late and great professor of French literature at Duke University. Maritain had been Fowlie's sponsor when he entered the Catholic Church. The photo is a copy of an official portrait taken, I think, by John Howard Griffin in Maritain's later years. Maritain is seated, his hand emerging from the shadows like a ghostly apparition, gripping a cane he uses to steady himself. His facial expression is dour and brooding, a shock of white hair dipping down toward his eyes. When Fowlie heard I was working on Maritain as part of my doctoral dissertation at Duke, he summoned me for lunch, regaled me with stories of his correspondence with Jim Morrison of the Doors, and gave me the portrait of Maritain to watch over me as I wrote. I often felt the old master looking down on me disapprovingly as I critiqued his work. While critical, I tried to be fair, recognizing Maritain's holiness and acknowledging that the misuse of Maritain in Chile was a matter of unintended consequences in a context different from the one in which Maritain wrote. Nevertheless, I wish I had succeeded in being as charitable to Maritain as Brian Boyd has been to me in his response to the book my dissertation became.

I was asked to respond to Boyd's article, and my response follows. Just before this issue of the journal went to press, I was made aware that Travis Knoll and Gil Stoy had also contributed articles that address my critique of Maritain. Without the time to gracefully shoehorn responses to Knoll and Stoy into my response to Boyd, I have nevertheless briefly addressed both Knoll[1] and Stoy[2] in footnotes.

---

[1] I learned a lot from Travis Knoll's analysis of Maritain's influence in Argentina and Brazil. I have no doubt that most of Maritain's followers in those two countries were opposed to right-wing Catholic politics and military dictatorships. I am not sure, however, that Knoll has accurately rendered my criticisms of Maritain. Knoll believes I "see Maritain's philosophy as apolitical or undergirding Chilean neoliberal right-wing governance," and pushes back against my supposed "contention that a serious reading of [Maritain's] works would encourage silence in the face of authoritarian atrocities, or even buttress them." Furthermore, "Cavanaugh does not claim Pinochet's right-hand officials and reticent church officials misread Maritain." In my book, however, I write of the junta's ideologues: "Certainly they are a corruption of Maritain's intentions. I do not wish to argue that New Christendom thought is responsible for the rise of the Pinochet regime. What I want to argue is rather that this type of ecclesiology has sapped the Church's ability to resist regimes such as that of General Pinochet" (*Torture and Eucharist: Theology, Politics, and the Body of Christ* [Oxford: Blackwell, 1998], 202). The problem with Maritain's ecclesiology is not that his church is apolitical or stays silent on state-sponsored atrocities; but that it is disembodied, serving only to try to influence the temporal via "counsels" or "inspiration" or "animation." Maritain's admonition to act as Christians, but not as Christians as such, in the temporal realm, mutes Christian social action and filters it through individuals, not the church as a body. When combined with a failure to fully appreciate the power and ambition of modern states, I think Maritain's ecclesiology falls short, despite his intentions, of an embodied practice of resistance to the powers and principalities. I have no doubt that Christian Democrats in many countries have been a force for good and opposed tyranny. As I explain in my response to Boyd, however, the Christian faith of the first generation of Christian Democrats has not been replicated in succeeding ones. What is needed is a more direct embodiment of the Gospel in facing the issues of the day.

[2] I think that Gil Stoy's critique of Maritain on temporal ends is very interesting. Stoy shows that Maritain deviates from Thomas Aquinas in describing the end of the temporal plane as "ultimate," though it is still subordinate to the spiritual end. Making the temporal common good ultimate causes the state to reach for transcendence to anchor it. For Stoy, the ambition of the state for hegemony over both body and soul I criticize is thus embedded in Maritain's philosophy. But Stoy thinks my attempt to overcome this problem in Maritain is also problematic. "By claiming that the supernatural virtues not only elevate human nature, but 'transform' the acquired virtues and direct them towards their 'proper' ends, Cavanaugh erases any possibility of natural human goods *qua* nature. Human nature is not merely elevated, but destroyed and replaced by something new when grace introduces a new end." I don't see how my language of grace transforming nature necessarily entails grace destroying nature. In my brief treatment of Maritain's use of Aquinas, I attempt nothing more than to side with Henri de Lubac's critique of neo-scholastic distortions of Thomas and his view of the permeation of nature by grace without thereby

I am hoping that my response to Boyd is also in some ways a response to Knoll and Stoy, if only insofar as it indicates how my thinking on Maritain and the church has evolved. I will hope to continue the conversation with Knoll and Stoy at another time or in another venue.

I am genuinely grateful to Boyd for his careful and sympathetic reading of my critique and Maritain's writings twenty-five years after *Torture and Eucharist* was published. It has given me an opportunity to think about how I and Chile have changed in the years since I lived there. The story I told in the book was overall a positive one for the Catholic Church in Chile, which had summoned its resources to become a center of resistance to the military dictatorship. Since the end of the Pinochet regime, however, the Catholic Church in Chile has seemingly lost its way, pulling back from social involvement and suffering the necessary consequences of its failure to curb sexual abuse by priests. In the *estallido social* (social outburst) that rocked Chile in 2019–2020, the Catholic Church was a target, not a catalyst, of the protests; several churches were looted and burned. Membership in the Catholic Church has fallen precipitously in Chile in the last three decades, and the same can be said of other countries across Europe and Latin America. In light of this unfolding situation, the task of reassessing Maritain's work is about more than the reputation of a scholar who died fifty years ago. It is rather about constructing practical ecclesiologies and political theologies that can help the church live faithfully in contexts increasingly unmoored from their Christian past.

In responding to Boyd's article, therefore, I will address both text and context. I will respond to Boyd's analysis of Maritain's writings in each of the three areas of critique he identifies in my book. I will also make comments about the French context in which Maritain wrote and the Chilean context into which his writings were received, and relate both to the broader needs of the church today for a truly Gospel-based theory and practice of the political.

STATE

---

destroying nature. De Lubac sees the interpenetration of the natural and supernatural in Thomas, which early modern Dominican commentators like Cajetan had separated. Stoy appears to think he is disagreeing with me and de Lubac in positing "pure nature" as a hypothetical state, but this was in fact de Lubac's own position. He thought Aquinas entertained "pure nature" as a hypothetical, but Cajetan and others turned it into an actuality. See Henri de Lubac, *The Mystery of the Supernatural*, trans. Rosemary Sheed (London: Herder & Herder, 1967), 80–81, 94. When I write, "De Lubac showed that the Dominicans' understanding of a hypothetical state of 'pure nature' and the resultant dual finality of human nature was nowhere to be found in Thomas" (*Torture and Eucharist*, 184), I mean that Aquinas thought *natura pura* was only hypothetical, and the way the early modern Dominicans understood it was not how Aquinas did.

Of the three main criticisms Boyd identifies in the fourth chapter of my book—of Maritain's views of the Church, the laity, and the state—Boyd concedes the last one and contests the other two. Maritain's view of the state, Boyd agrees, was insufficiently critical. Assigning to the state the sovereignty that belongs to God alone was not an historical accident but a consequence of the centralization of power that is part of the basic logic of modern states. Maritain tried to balance the necessary power of the state with an emphasis on subsidiarity, a central theme of Catholic social thought. The passage Boyd quotes about the "organic City" ruled not by a bureaucratic machine but by "men" is in fact a quote not from me but from Maritain's *Freedom in the Modern World*, which I quote in *Torture and Eucharist*.[3] The principle of subsidiarity is meant to delegate a task to the lowest level of authority capable of handling it, thus preferring local control and decentralization whenever possible. The key problem with subsidiarity is the question of who does the delegating; who decides at which level tasks will be handled? The principle of state sovereignty ensures that the state itself decides and, as Boyd notes, bureaucracies are not usually very good at relinquishing their own prerogatives to those outside their control.[4] Maritain was unable fully to appreciate this essential conflict between the state and subsidiarity.

As Boyd points out, Maritain knew that the civil religion or secular faith a modern state requires was unstable, and it would either evolve toward a Christian-inspired civilization or devolve toward idolatry. He expressed his hope for the former path in his *Man and the State*, published in 1951. Maritain can be forgiven, says Boyd, for allowing his postwar optimism and confidence in the *Pax Americana* to cloud his judgment: "The use of American civil religion to turn the nation itself into an idol had not yet been made clear." I am not sure, however, what could be clearer evidence of idolatry than the detonation of a nuclear weapon under the code name "Trinity" in July of 1945 and the subsequent use of the same type of weapon to obliterate tens of thousands of civilians a few weeks later. Nagasaki was the center of Catholicism in Japan; the American crew that dropped the bomb used the spires of Immaculate Conception cathedral as a landmark.[5] Boyd

---

[3] In Boyd's article, the quote comes after "as Cavanaugh explains" and the footnote simply cites *Torture and Eucharist*, without making clear that the quote is Maritain's, not mine.

[4] I deal with these matters in much greater detail in my chapter "The Road Not Taken: Figgis, Subsidiarity, and Catholic Social Teaching," in *Neville Figgis, CR: His Life, Thought and Significance*, ed. Paul Avis (Leiden: Brill, 2021), 220–245.

[5] The death rate from leukemia in Hiroshima and Nagasaki peaked between four and six years after the bombings, when *Man and the State* was published. Leukemia was

is right not to cast stones at Maritain for his hopefulness. The important and broader question is why Christians on the whole have been reluctant to name the idolatry of various kinds of state violence. Boyd acknowledges in his footnote to the above comment that the idolatry of American civil religion is still not clear to the majority of Americans, which includes Christians. Maritain's confidence in the evolution of American civil religion was based on the conviction that places like America and Chile are already Christian, a conviction increasingly difficult to maintain today. But even among practicing Christians, the church has not been clear on the ambivalence of loyalty to nation-states that claim an ever-more-perfect monopoly on power and violence.[6] This failure is why I find Maritain's comments not only on the state, but on the church, inadequate.

CHURCH AND LAITY

This brings us to Boyd's defense of Maritain's thought on the church and the laity. Boyd is right, of course, that Maritain's shortcomings do not mean there is nothing of worth in his thought for the contemporary theologian. Boyd cites a passage in *Liturgy and Contemplation* (1960) in which Maritain seeks to root "social justice" and authentic social life, as I do, in participation in the liturgy. For Maritain, thus belonging to the "Mystical Body" should be the Christian's primary identity. Mystical Body is Maritain's favored image for the church, including in his later works.[7] In the fifth chapter of my book, I do a genealogy of the term "Mystical Body," following Henri de Lubac, and show how the shift in terminology from the church as *corpus verum* to the church as *corpus mysticum* often accompanied a certain disincarnation of the church. According to de Lubac, the shift occurred around the twelfth century as the gap widened between the visible and invisible church, the church as institution and as spiritual reality. De Lubac went on to criticize the twentieth-century rage for Mystical Body theology, worrying that the church as Mystical Body was not a real social body, but hovered above

---

the most deadly long-term effect of radiation from the bombs, and children were the population most severely affected. See Dan Listwa, "Hiroshima and Nagasaki: The Long-Term Health Effects," Columbia University Center for Nuclear Studies, August 9, 2012, k1project.columbia.edu/news/hiroshima-and-nagasaki.

[6] In a footnote, Boyd wonders how I would apply my critique of sacrifice in "new good wars" to the situation in Ukraine. I have in fact published an article recently on that very topic. See "No War is Good," *Commonweal* 150, no. 5 (May 2023): 28–30.

[7] See for example, Jacques Maritain, *The Peasant of the Garonne: An Old Layman Questions Himself about the Present Time*, trans. Michael Cuddihy (New York: Holt, Rinehart, and Winston, 1968), 176–83.

such bodies.[8] The popularity of Mystical Body theology culminated in Pope Pius XII's encyclical *Mystici Corporis Christi*, published in 1943 in the middle of World War II. Pius XII wanted to provide hope for Christian unity above the fray, but the earthly reality was that belonging to the Mystical Body of Christ did not prevent Christians from slaughtering one another. The Body of Christ had been overly spiritualized; one could recognize the spiritual unity of Christians in the church precisely when they were trying to blow each others' limbs off.

Merely using the term "Mystical Body" for the church does not suffice to show that Maritain's church is disincarnated. Dorothy Day used the term, but rather than seeing the church as hovering over the war, she thought belonging to the same Body of Christ demanded that Christians refuse to kill one another. The key question is how body language for the church shakes out in social and political practice. Boyd acknowledges that "the embodied church receives little emphasis in Maritain's chief political writings," but points to language in Maritain's later works *The Peasant of the Garonne* (1966) and *On the Church of Christ* (1973) that emphasize the concrete temporal effects of the church on earth. Though these works were too late to have much effect in pre-Pinochet Chile, I appreciate Boyd's recovery of Maritain's mature ecclesiology. I recognize that Maritain was deeply concerned with the formation of the Christian in the church, especially by its liturgy; that Maritain had a profound sense of the action of the living Christ in the lives of Christians; that he wanted Christians' membership in the church to be their primary loyalty; that he wanted Christians to help witness to the Kingdom of God on earth, already present though always incomplete; that the temporal vocation of the Christian, though not the same as her spiritual one, was always and in everything animated by it; and that the church should neither shun the world nor kneel before it. Maritain certainly cannot be accused of being apolitical or attempting to derive politics from secular sources. At the same time, he was rightly trying to free the church from the entanglement of clerics with political power. I can see why Christians engaged in politics and business were excited by his call to overcome the separation between their temporal and spiritual vocations without asking the church to rule the world. None of this is discontinuous with the earlier Maritain—in discussing the church's role in politics in *Peasant of the Garonne,* he quotes extensively from his *Letter on Independence* from thirty years prior.

---

[8] I lay out this argument in detail in chapter five of *Torture and Eucharist*. Those interested in de Lubac's thought can follow the footnotes there, most especially to his works *Corpus Mysticum* and *The Splendor of the Church.*

And yet there remains ambiguity in Maritain's thought represented by his declaration in that same section of *Peasant of the Garonne* that "I see in the Western world no more than three revolutionaries worthy of the name—Eduardo Frei in Chile, Saul Alinsky in America, . . . and myself in France."[9] But Frei and Alinsky are very different figures. Frei was a devout Catholic and president of Chile, representing the Christian Democratic party, from 1964 to 1970. Alinsky was a pioneering community organizer, an agnostic who wrote *Reveille for Radicals* (1946) and *Rules for Radicals* (1971). Frei was a reformist, not a radical. Gustavo Gutiérrez wrote in 1971 that the followers of Maritain in Latin America had gone since the 1930s from the vanguard to being defenders of the status quo.[10] To them, the structures of the world—the state and market—seemed given; Christians were to animate, shine the radiance of the Gospel within them, but were not called to change them fundamentally. Alinsky, on the other hand, wanted to change the world from the bottom up. He eschewed party politics, and instead focused on organizing local communities to change economic and political structures that kept them mired in poverty and exclusion. Alinsky began his career by working with local Catholic churches and the Archdiocese to create the Back of the Yards Neighborhood Council, which would challenge the meatpacking industry in Chicago. He would go on to found the Industrial Areas Foundation with Bishop Bernard Sheil, and worked with other grassroots organizations to reclaim the social capital of poor people against the power of corporations and the exclusionary—often racist—politics of the Democratic Party machine in Chicago.[11]

There remains, it seems to me, an unresolved tension between Maritain's two favorite "revolutionaries" (besides himself). Maritain's ecclesiology most often favors Frei. As Boyd writes, even for the late Maritain "the church offers a soul to the social body: by offering saints who uplift its life." The church is still the soul of another body, and the spiritual enters the social body by way of influential individual Christians. The social body is something the church forms individuals to join, and once there, they allow "the Gospel's radiance to shine through mundane mediums such as 'a simple brotherly word' or 'the spontaneous manner of reacting to an event.'" Well-formed Christians work for corporations and join political parties in order to transform the world.

---

[9] Maritain, *Peasant of the Garonne*, 23; the ellipsis is in the original.
[10] Gustavo Gutiérrez, *A Theology of Liberation*, revised ed., trans. Sister Caridad Inda and John Eagleson (Maryknoll, NY: Orbis Books, 1988), 36–41.
[11] Maritain maintained a lively correspondence with Alinsky. See Bernard E. Doering, ed., *The Philosopher and the Provocateur: The Correspondence of Jacques Maritain and Saul Alinsky* (Notre Dame, IN: University of Notre Dame Press, 1994).

They are *helped* in this battle by the counsels they receive from the Church, and without which they could do no good; and they can even be *helped* in that respect by the Church in another fashion, in particular cases, when her ministers, facing an especially serious situation, judge it their duty to raise their voices and to intervene in the temporal order by a word of truth, giving witness to divine precepts. In any case, for the Church it is always only a question of helping the world to resolve its problems, not resolving them for it.[12]

Alinsky's radical democracy, on the other hand, sees the church not as well-formed individuals working in the system to achieve top-down change, but as communal bodies organizing at the grassroots to transform society from the bottom up by creating spaces of genuine economic justice and participation. This kind of church as body was able to resist the Pinochet regime in Chile; this is the story I tell in chapters five and six of *Torture and Eucharist*.

If Maritain is to be useful for the church going forward in a world where states and corporations together continue to centralize power, I would hope for a little more of the critical edge Alinsky brings. In *Peasant of the Garonne*, Maritain rightly warns against the Promethean tendencies of Marx and Teilhard, which would make humans gods in trying to divinize the world. But Maritain does not critique the idolatry of the state and market to which people are also sacrificed. In short, if Maritain's view of the state is insufficiently critical, as Boyd concedes, then his view of the church as individuals working within the state to animate it also is insufficiently critical. Others may disagree, but I would have liked his friendship with Alinsky to have penetrated his political thought and ecclesiology more deeply.

A more critical attitude to state violence would have helped in the case of Chile once the military took control. Boyd is right that Maritain recognizes the right of bishops to use their authority in the temporal realm when eternal salvation is at stake. Maritain's quote from Cajetan that Boyd cites is sufficient to refute my overstated critique of Maritain, for whom the power of the spiritual in the temporal is not always that of mere counsels. The Chilean Bishops' Conference did eventually issue a blanket order of excommunication for anyone participating in torture. The problem was not with the bishops but with the soldiers and secret police, most of them Catholics, who planned and facilitated and carried out the torture. The efficacy of a "word of truth" in the temporal sphere, as the block quote above puts it, depends in this case on well-formed soldiers who would recognize the bishops' moral authority. The problem is that the soldiers were trained to regard torture as a matter of state security and not of eternal salvation; the

---

[12] Maritain, *Peasant of the Garonne*, 205, emphasis in original.

soldiers were quite capable of a complete separation of the temporal from the spiritual when the security of the state was at stake. This complete separation is the fault of those elements of the church that regard the state's monopoly on violence as fully compatible with Christianity and loyalty to the nation-state simply as part of a Christian's duty. This wider problem with Christian formation is not Maritain's fault, but it does point to the need for a more critical attitude toward the state and its equation of security with violence.

With regard to the role of charity in the lives of individual laypeople, I accept Boyd's defense of the later Maritain against my charge that he denies direct access of the theological virtues to the temporal. Boyd points to passages in *Peasant of the Garonne* in which Maritain clearly states that love transforms justice, and does not merely provide an inchoate motivation for the Christian in the world. Maritain here does indeed want the love of God to have a transformative effect on every action the Christian takes. I would add that, in the same book, Maritain goes some way toward specifying the actual contours of love through the contemplative encounter with Jesus, whom we meet in the poor, sick, imprisoned, and so on.[13] My complaint that Maritain writes mostly about "the spiritual" and not about the concrete shape of Jesus's life, death, and resurrection is answered here.

I am less ready to concede Boyd's rebuttal to my critique of Maritain on the relationship of ends to means and eternity to time. Boyd assimilates Maritain's passages on the necessity of dirty hands to Pope Francis's "insistence that priests should be close to the poor, like shepherds living with the smell of the sheep." Indeed, Pope Francis has recently used the metaphor of dirty hands himself, telling a group gathered at a center for the poor, elderly, and disabled in Lisbon that "there is no such thing as an abstract love, it doesn't exist," and that real love "gets its hands dirty" in the concrete circumstances of people's lives.[14] But when Maritain uses the metaphor, he is talking explicitly about the Christian use of violence. He writes

> It is clear that force and, generally speaking, what I have called the carnal means of war are not intrinsically bad, because they can be just. Theologians and moralists explain to us on what conditions these are just, and thereby they perform a work of mercy, enabling us to live on this earth. They do not take the lead, it is not their business to open new doors to violence; but once these doors are open, they justify what can be done, and give us light in order to advance into the dark defiles

---

[13] Maritain, *Peasant of the Garonne*, 234–239.
[14] Pope Francis, quoted in "Impromptu Pope Says Real Love 'Gets its Hands Dirty,'" *Crux*, August 4, 2023, cruxnow.com/world-youth-day-lisbon/2023/08/impromptu-pope-says-real-love-gets-its-hands-dirty.

of history.... The worst anguish for the Christian is precisely to know that there can be justice in employing horrible means.[15]

The passage about staining our fingers without staining our hearts follows. For Francis, the metaphor calls us to the corporal works of mercy, summoning the relatively privileged to enter into the messiness and chaos of the lives of the marginalized. Dirty hands means a descent from power to love. For Maritain, by contrast, the metaphor is used to justify the necessary violence of those who exercise power for the common good. What Maritain calls "a work of mercy" is performed by moral theologians who "justify what can be done" once "new doors to violence" are opened. This must be one of the spiritual works of mercy which, as Boyd writes, outrank the corporal works of mercy in Maritain's thought.

I fully recognize that Maritain forbids doing intrinsically evil acts and does not think the end justifies any and all means. The corporal works of mercy are lower on Maritain's hierarchy of means than they are on Francis's, but I have no doubt that Maritain prefers nonviolent to violent means and less to more violence. For Maritain, however, the hierarchy of means for the state is different than it is for the individual. Maritain differentiates "individual ethics" from "political ethics" in the following passage from *Man and the State* I quote in my book:

> For human life has two ultimate ends, the one subordinate to the other: an ultimate end *in a given order*, which is the terrestrial common good, or the *bonum vitae civilis;* and an *absolute* ultimate end, which is the transcendent, eternal common good. And individual ethics takes into account the subordinate ultimate end, but *directly aims* at the absolute ultimate one; whereas political ethics takes into account the absolute ultimate end, but its *direct aim* is the subordinate ultimate end, the good of the rational nature in its temporal achievement. Hence a specific difference of perspective between those two branches of Ethics.
>
> Thus it is that many patterns of conduct of the body politic, which the pessimists of Machiavellianism turn to the advantage of political amorality—such as the use by the State of coercive force (even of means of war in case of absolute necessity against an unjust aggressor), the use of intelligence services and methods which should never corrupt people but cannot help utilizing corrupt people, the use of police methods which should never violate the human rights of people but cannot help being rough with them, a lot of selfishness and self-assertion which would be blamed in individuals, a permanent distrust and suspicion, a cleverness not necessarily mischievous but yet not candid with regard to the other States, or the toleration of certain evil deeds by the law, the recognition of the principle of the lesser evil and the recognition of the *fait accompli* (the so-called "statute of limitations") which permits the retention of gains ill-gotten long ago, because new human ties and vital relationships

---

[15] Jacques Maritain, *Integral Humanism*, trans. Joseph W. Evans (New York: Charles Scribner's Sons, 1968), 246–248.

have infused them with new-born rights—all of these things are in reality ethically grounded.

The fear of soiling ourselves by entering the context of history is not virtue, but a way of escaping virtue.[16]

The hierarchy of means in political ethics demands that we prefer "the lesser evil." In history, we nevertheless cannot avoid "soiling ourselves"; the intelligence services "cannot help utilizing corrupt people," and the police "cannot help being rough." This is a far cry from what Pope Francis means by "dirty hands," which is the unavoidable consequence of incarnated love that pours itself out for and with the powerless.

For Maritain, the drama of dirty hands takes place because there is a tragic element to time. In *Integral Humanism*, he emphasizes that the fullness of the Kingdom of God is "outside time,"[17] and writes that those engaged in the building of culture "are engaged in time and in the vicissitudes of time. Moreover, it can be said that none of them has clean hands."[18] In *Peasant of the Garonne*, as Boyd points out, he puts more emphasis on the Kingdom of God as already present in the world, but still the Gospel "forbids us to mix up the orders of finality by imagining that the goal of the temporal mission of the Christian is the coming of the kingdom of God on earth."[19] Maritain is rightly trying to emphasize that God, not we, brings the Kingdom, but the Kingdom will come in fullness only when God brings an end to time.[20] By way of contrast, Pope Francis has a more positive view of time; he juxtaposes it not with eternity but space, as in his oft-repeated phrase "Time is always much greater than space."[21] In *Evangelii Gaudium* he writes "One of the faults which we occasionally observe in sociopolitical activity is that spaces and power are preferred to time and processes. Giving priority to space means madly attempting to keep everything together in the present, trying to possess all the spaces of power and of self-assertion; it is to crystallize processes and presume to hold them back. Giving priority to time means being concerned about initiating processes rather than possessing spaces."[22]

---

[16] Jacques Maritain, *Man and the State* (Chicago: The University of Chicago Press, 1951), 62–63.
[17] Maritain, *Integral Humanism*, 101.
[18] Maritain, *Integral Humanism*, 98.
[19] Maritain, *Peasant of the Garonne*, 203.
[20] "The coming of the kingdom would not, in that case, be a simple interruption of a becoming with no final term, it would be rather an *eruption* by which the divine glory would interrupt the earthly becoming, but in order to lead it, through a miraculous begetting, to that final term toward which it is tending with no power to reach it: no longer natural happiness, but supernatural beatitude" (Maritain, *Peasant of the Garonne*, 203).
[21] Pope Francis, *Lumen Fidei*, no. 57. See also Pope Francis, *Laudato Si'*, no. 178.
[22] Pope Francis, *Evangelii Gaudium*, no. 223.

Francis agrees that we cannot achieve perfection in time through human effort. But his emphasis is on time not as a fallen condition but an opportunity to let grace unfold. Rather than dominating spaces, for which coercive power is required, we are called to initiate processes of accompaniment lower on the social scale. Appreciating time also means giving up obsession with short-term results, but Francis is interested not only with the quantity but also the quality of time. He wants Christians to look in hope to the Kingdom of God as a model for the present, unconstrained by what the world says is possible. I don't think Maritain would disagree, but a lot depends on the differing contexts for which Maritain and Francis are writing; Maritain seems to be writing for Christians in positions of power, whereas Francis is writing for a church he would like to seek the margins.

PAST AND PRESENT

Jacques Maritain was a significant figure in Catholic Europe and Latin America in the twentieth century because he helped the church navigate the end of Christendom. He tried to envision a Catholic political practice that would neither be nostalgic for its former direct access to state power nor simply succumb to the privatization of the faith and leave the secular world unchallenged by the Gospel. In France, the former tendency was represented by *Action Française*, the latter by those Catholics who so separated the natural from the supernatural—as was typical of neoscholastic thought—that they could not see the contradiction between their faith and support for the Vichy regime. Maritain envisioned cadres of well-formed lay Christians acting in public as Christians—but not "as Christians as such"[23]—to make a better world in concert with non-Christians.

The results were mixed. In Europe, Christian Democrats inspired by Maritain led the rebuilding of Europe after World War II, helping to establish welfare states, the European Union, and NATO. Over time, Christian Democratic parties in Europe have drifted rightward; they are now the main conservative party in countries such as Germany, Belgium, and Switzerland. In Latin America, Gutiérrez had noted the same rightward drift by the 1970s. Maritain's distinction of planes "amounted to a timid and basically ambiguous attempt."[24] It bred moderates, children of the elites with an increasing tendency toward bourgeois developmentalism. In Chile, Christian Democrats have tended to be center-left; Frei and friends founded the Christian

---

[23] "On the plane of the temporal, I do not act *as a Christian as such*, but I should act *as Christian*, engaging only myself, not the Church, but engaging my whole self" (Maritain, *Integral Humanism*, 294).
[24] Gutiérrez, *Theology of Liberation*, 36.

Democratic party and, once elected president, Frei's administration launched an ambitious series of social programs aimed at alleviating poverty. In other Latin American countries, like El Salvador and Mexico, Christian Democrats have been right wing parties. In other countries, Maritain had other followers who were not Christian Democrats and took hard-right stances. In Chile, Jaime Guzmán, chief ideologue of the Pinochet regime, was a disciple of Maritain, and El Maestro's vocabulary leaps off every page of the Declaration of Principles Guzmán wrote for the military junta shortly after it assumed power: the individual's eternal end and transcendence over the social body, the differentiation of the political from the social, the responsibility of the state for the common good, the principle of subsidiarity, and more.[25] Frei himself supported the coup,[26] though he would later become a critic of the Pinochet regime.

Maritain, of course, would have hated the military regime in Chile. He anticipated that Christians in politics would take a range of different positions, but the Pinochet regime was clearly beyond the pale. There is no direct line from Maritain to Pinochet; that was never my point, as Boyd acknowledges. I am, however, interested in what lessons we can learn for the continued political relevance of the Gospel from the uses and misuses of Maritain's thought in Chile and elsewhere. The variety of positions associated with Maritain's followers indicates to me that the political relevance of the Gospel remains underspecified in Maritain's thought. The personal piety of the original cadres of Christian Democrats was not enough to ensure that the Gospel mandates to love enemies and embrace the poor were actually put into practice.

Gutiérrez was not the only one who thought so. Giuseppe Dossetti in Italy left the Christian Democratic party in the 1950s over its embrace of NATO and resistance to land reform, and instead became an advocate for what he called the "Gospel *sine glossa*": as Joseph Komonchak puts it, "He began to work for a renewal of the Church that might be able to promote a badly needed different form of politics."[27] In his interventions at Vatican II, Dossetti advocated for a

---

[25] Junta Militar de Gobierno, *Declaración de Principios del Gobierno de Chile*, www.archivochile.com/Dictadura_militar/doc_jm_gob_pino8/DMdocjm0005.pdf.
[26] He expressed his support in November 1973 in a letter to Mariano Rumor, the head of the worldwide Christian Democratic Union. See "Carta a Mariano Rumor, Presidente de la Union Mundial de la Democracia Cristiana," www.memoriachilena.cl/archivos2/pdfs/MC0023241.pdf.
[27] Joseph Komonchak, "Augustine, Aquinas, or the Gospel *sine glossa*?: Divisions over *Gaudium et Spes*," in Austen Ivereigh, ed., *Unfinished Journey: The Church 40 Years after Vatican II: Essays for John Wilkins* (New York: Continuum, 2003), 106. For a fuller account, see my article "Ecclesial Ethics and the Gospel *Sine Glossa*: Sacramental Politics and the Love of the World," *Modern Theology* 36, no. 3 (July 2020): 501–523.

church that would embrace the active nonviolence of Jesus rather than issue bland calls for peace while accepting the compromises necessary for statecraft. He wanted a word from the council that would be "evangelical, which is the only discourse that can respond today to the anxiety of the peoples and that, for all its apparent unlikelihood, is the only true one, the only one that can banish war and make peace, not by human calculation but by the creative force of the Word of God."[28] Dossetti was disappointed with *Gaudium et Spes* for its acceptance of Just War and the possession of nuclear weapons for deterrence. The problem, according to Dossetti, is that the church did not know how to speak the Gospel into the world of politics. Instead, *Gaudium et Spes* offered a "rational sociology that allows the presentation of an objective discourse to all men, that all men should accept," leaving only "islands of a supernatural anthropology."[29] And so "Catholics acted like accomplices"[30] to the state and its machines of war.

Maritain thought he could rely on lay Christians, well-formed in the Gospel, to take the spirit of the Gospel into the political realm without having to actually speak the Gospel directly in a post-Christendom world. They would act as Christians, but not as Christians as such. The problem, I continue to think, is that—like an immigrant language that eventually dies in the second or third generation if not spoken outside the home—the Gospel will fade if not spoken in public. The years since Maritain's death seem to have borne this out; Christians went out to change the world and the world changed them instead. The piety of the first generation of Christian Democrats has not been replicated by succeeding generations. The Church in Europe and Latin America is shrinking for many reasons, but one is, I think, that it has been reluctant to enact the Gospel directly in addressing the problems of the day. Politics is understood solely as statecraft, and the compromises necessary to gain and keep power have either rendered the Gospel irrelevant or, worse, identified the Gospel with a narrow range of conservative positions on sexual and gender issues right-wing Catholics hope the state will coercively enforce.

In the current situation, I think the "badly needed different form of politics" of which Komonchak has written will not consist of getting more Christians into office and on the judiciary so that the Christian

---

[28] Giuseppe Dossetti, quoted in Joseph Komonchak, "The Redaction and Reception of *Gaudium et Spes*: Tensions within the Majority at Vatican II," 16, jakomonchak.files.wordpress.com/2013/04/jak-views-of-gaudium-et-spes.pdf.

[29] Giuseppe Dossetti, "Per una valutazzione globale del magistero del Vaticano II," in *Vaticano II: Frammenti di una reflessione* (Bologna: Il Mulino, 1996), 87, my translation.

[30] Dossetti, quoted in Komonchak, "Redaction and Reception," 18.

heritage of the West will be respected and promoted. It is likely, rather, to take the form of Christians acting as creative minorities, forming grassroots organizations—as in Pinochet's Chile—to enact the Gospel *sine glossa* while openly collaborating with those of other faiths or none. This is the kind of "politics" to which Pope Francis was calling the church when he asked every Catholic parish and religious community in Europe to take in one refugee family.[31] Had this call been heeded, not only would tens of thousands of refugees have found shelter, but the church itself would be energized. The Old and New Christendoms are both dead; Christianity will survive and thrive in the West only by groups of Christians embracing the fullness of the Gospel, changing the world by changing themselves. Were Maritain writing today amidst a greatly diminished church in Europe, perhaps the critical edge and prophetic freedom he admired in Alinsky would have brought him to a similar conclusion.

William Cavanaugh, PhD, is Professor of Catholic Studies and Director of the Center for World Catholicism and Intercultural Theology at DePaul University. He is the author of nine books, including most recently *The Uses of Idolatry* with Oxford University Press (2024), as well as *Torture and Eucharist* (1998), *The Myth of Religious Violence* (2009), *Migrations of the Holy: Theologies of State and Church* (2011), and *Field Hospital: The Church's Engagement with a Wounded World* (2016). He is the co-editor of seven volumes, including *The Blackwell Companion to Political Theology* (2003), and co-editor of the journal *Modern Theology*. He has published over a hundred journal articles and book chapters, has lectured on six continents, and his books and articles have been published in seventeen languages.

---

[31] Anthony Faiola and Michael Birnbaum, "Pope Calls on Europe's Catholics to Take in Refugees," *Washington Post*, September 6, 2015, www.washingtonpost.com/world/refugees-keep-streaming-into-europe-as-crisis-continues-unabated/2015/09/06/8a330572-5345-11e5-b225-90edbd49f362_story.html.

Partners in Forming the People: Jacques Maritain, Saul Alinsky, and the Project of Personalist Democracy

Nicholas Hayes-Mota

Abstract: At first glance, Jacques Maritain, the influential Catholic philosopher, and Saul Alinsky, the infamous "dean" of community organizing, could scarcely be more different, in temperament or reputation. Nevertheless, for nearly three decades, these two men were close friends and dedicated collaborators, drawn together by a passionate commitment to democracy. By reading them alongside each other, this article offers a new interpretation of both. After historically contextualizing the relationship between Maritain and Alinsky, it advances two major claims about their democratic thought. First, it shows that Maritain and Alinsky shared a commitment to a political project best described as "personalist democracy," insofar as it founded democratic politics upon a specific ethical (and, for Maritain, theological) conception of the human person. Second, the article argues that both thinkers understood personalist democracy to be realizable, in practice, only through a particular kind of democratic organization. They saw the process of organizing as the indispensable means for forming the diffuse persons who comprise society into a coherent "people," capable of acting for the common good and, in so doing, discovering their own dignity. The article concludes by offering reasons why the project of personalist democracy, as Maritain and Alinsky conceived it, may still have much to offer today.

INTRODUCTION: "THE PHILOSOPHER AND THE PROVOCATEUR"

At first glance, Jacques Maritain (1882–1973) and Saul Alinsky (1909–1972) present a striking study in contrasts. Maritain, the neo-Thomist philosopher, was a French Catholic intellectual of international renown, whose influence extended across Europe and the Americas. Known to friends as "gentle Jacques," he was deeply pious, principled and, by his own admission, much more a man of contemplation than an "agitator."¹ Alinsky, on the other hand, was an agitator par excellence. A self-professed agnostic of Russian Jewish descent, the "dean" of community organizing in the US was pugnacious, irreverent, and impatient with philosophical niceties that got in the way of decisive action. Alinsky also took delight in infuriating moralists of all stripes. He accordingly began his most notorious book, *Rules for Radicals* (1971) with an acknowledgment of "the very first radical known to man who rebelled against the establishment . . . Lucifer."²

Nevertheless, for all their differences, Maritain and Alinsky maintained a decades-long and surprisingly intimate friendship. As the title of their collected correspondence reveals, "the philosopher and the provocateur" felt a profound personal, intellectual, political, and even spiritual affinity for each other.³ Late in life, Maritain would refer to Alinsky not only as a "great friend" but as one of only two "authentic revolutionaries" he knew.⁴ For many years, he used his considerable influence to promote Alinsky's work, even arranging a meeting in Milan, in 1958, between the organizer and Archbishop Giovanni Montini, the future Pope Paul VI.⁵ For his part, Alinsky called Maritain "a man who has had more influence on me than anyone else I know and who is infinitely precious to me."⁶ He credited Maritain as the catalyst for his first book, *Reveille for Radicals* (1946); he also regarded him as a "spiritual father," to whom he confided in his darkest hours.⁷

---

¹ Jacques Maritain, *The Peasant of the Garonne: An Old Layman Questions Himself about the Present Time*, trans. Michael Cuddihy and Elizabeth Hughes (Eugene, OR: Wipf & Stock, 2011 [1968]), 23.
² Saul Alinsky, *Rules for Radicals* (New York: Vintage, [1971]xs 1989), ix. Contrary to legend, Alinsky did not actually dedicate the book to Lucifer, but rather "to Irene," his wife. His reference to the fallen angel appears later, on a separate page after the dedication proper. There, following epigraphs from Rabbi Hillel and Thomas Paine, Alinsky adds a third of his own, in which he makes an "over-the-shoulder acknowledgement to the very first radical . . . Lucifer." The epigraph exemplifies Alinsky's tongue-in-cheek humor, as well as his penchant for provocation. He would be highly amused to know that some of his more humorless critics have since mistaken this passage for a literal profession of fidelity to Satan.
³ Doering published their collected letters under this title in 1994. See Bernard Doering, ed., *The Philosopher and the Provocateur: The Correspondence of Jacques Maritain and Saul Alinsky* (Notre Dame, IN: University of Notre Dame Press, 1994).
⁴ The other "authentic revolutionary" was Eduardo Frei, the leader of the Chilean Christian Democrats (Maritain, *The Peasant of the Garonne*, 23). For background, see Bernard Doering, "Jacques Maritain and His Two Authentic Revolutionaries," in *Thomistic Papers*, ed. Leonard A. Kennedy, vol. 3 (Houston, TX: Center for Thomistic Studies, 1987), 91–116.
⁵ P. David Finks, *The Radical Vision of Saul Alinsky* (New York: Paulist, 1984), 114.
⁶ Letter XLIII (May 15, 1962), in Doering, *The Philosopher and the Provocateur*, 92.
⁷ For Maritain's role in moving Alinsky to write *Reveille,* see Sanford D. Horwitt, *Let Them Call Me Rebel: Saul Alinsky—His Life and Legacy* (New York: Vintage, 1989),

Though the biographical dimensions of their relationship are highly interesting, in this article I wish to explore the specifically *political* affinity between Alinsky and Maritain. What was the political vision Alinsky and Maritain shared, allowing them to regard each other not only as kindred spirits but as fellow "revolutionaries"? More specifically, what was it about Alinsky's approach to community organizing that led Maritain to proclaim it "a new way for *real* democracy, the only way in which man's thirst for social communion can develop and be satisfied, through freedom and not through totalitarianism in our disintegrated times"?[8] In response to these questions, I will advance two major claims. First, Maritain and Alinsky shared a commitment to a political project best described as "personalist democracy," insofar as it founded democratic politics upon a specific ethical (and, for Maritain, theological) conception of the human person. Second, both thinkers understood personalist democracy to be realizable, in practice, only through a particular kind of democratic *organization*. They saw the process of organizing as the indispensable means for forming the diffuse persons who comprised society into a coherent "people" capable of acting for the common good and, in so doing, discovering their own dignity.

In advancing this argument, I build on the work of several scholars who have previously treated the Maritain-Alinsky relationship.[9] This article contributes to existing literature by specifically foregrounding the personalist character of Alinsky and Maritain's shared democratic vision and analyzing the way in which that vision, in turn, underwrote their shared commitment to organizing. An additional aim of this article is to suggest that these democratic thinkers are best interpreted in dialogue with each other. Reading Maritain in dialogue with Alinsky draws out the practical implications of his democratic

---

164–165. On Maritain as Alinsky's "spiritual father," see Doering, *The Philosopher and the Provocateur*, xxxii–xxxv; see 112 for Alinsky's own reference to Maritain as such.

[8] Letter VI (August 20, 1945), in Doering, *The Philosopher and the Provocateur*, 11, emphasis in original.

[9] Beyond the works by Doering already cited, key contributions include Charles E. Curran, *Directions in Catholic Social Ethics* (Notre Dame, IN: University of Notre Dame Press, 1985), 147–175; Luke Bretherton, *Resurrecting Democracy: Faith, Citizenship, and the Politics of a Common Life* (Cambridge: Cambridge University Press, 2015), 35–40; Bradford E. Hinze, "Vatican II and US Catholic Communities: Promoting Grassroots Democracy," in *The Legacy of Vatican II*, ed. Massimo Faggioli and Andrea Vicini (Mahwah, NJ: Paulist, 2015), 152–181. All of this literature contradicts the tendentious analysis of C. J. Wolfe, which reads *Rules for Radicals* completely out of context and, as a result, fundamentally distorts Alinsky's views, as well as Maritain's. See C. J. Wolfe, "Lessons from the Friendship of Jacques Maritain with Saul Alinsky," *Catholic Social Science Review* 16 (2011): 229–240, doi.org/10.5840/cssr20111620.

philosophy, as well as its inherent radicalism, both of which might otherwise be missed. Reciprocally, reading Alinsky in dialogue with Maritain illuminates the ethical ideals deeply embedded, but not always explicit, within his organizing practice, countering the mistaken (though still quite prevalent) tendency to regard him as an amoral "Machiavellian."[10] On both counts, the article seeks to enrich the interpretation of each figure. Its overarching objective is to recover Alinsky and Maritain's democratic vision for constructive redevelopment in our own time.

The argument unfolds in four parts. In the first section, I historically contextualize Maritain and Alinsky's relationship. Situating the latter in the biography of each man, I describe how the two came to know, and admire, each other as friends and collaborators. Secondly, I show how Maritain and Alinsky converged on a common vision of personalist democracy, and analyze the core ethical ideas which defined that vision. Thirdly, I argue that both thinkers regarded "organization" as the critical, mediating process for translating the ideals of personalist democracy into institutional reality, focusing in particular on how Maritain and Alinsky understood organizing as a way of "forming the people." Finally, in my conclusion, I offer some reasons why the project of personalist democracy, as they conceived it, may still have much to offer today. Indeed, in a moment where democracy around the world seems to be degenerating, it could scarcely be more relevant.[11]

DRAWN TOGETHER BY DEMOCRACY: THE MEETING OF JACQUES MARITAIN AND SAUL ALINSKY

Jacques Maritain and Saul Alinsky were first introduced to each other in Chicago sometime between 1941 and 1944, most likely by a

---

[10] Brian Stiltner's article, elsewhere in this issue, offers an illuminating discussion and rebuttal of the "Machiavellian" reading of Alinsky, as does Bretherton, *Resurrecting Democracy,* 196–200. For broader background on the demonization of Alinsky by the US Right, see Dylan Matthews, "Who Is Saul Alinsky, and Why Does the Right Hate Him So Much?," *Vox,* www.vox.com/2014/10/6/6829675/saul-alinsky-explain-obama-hillary-clinton-rodham-organizing. Negative misconceptions about Alinsky are notably widespread in conservative Catholic circles, where one also sometimes hears the organizer denounced as a "communist"—an irony, given that Alinsky, like Maritain, advocated personalist democracy precisely as an alternative to communism. *A Wolf in Sheep's Clothing*, a video distributed by the Eternal Word Television Network (EWTN), is in part to blame for the spread of these misconceptions within the US church. Though the video purports to be "a documentary," it is in fact little more than a propaganda piece offering a highly selective, misleading, and distorted account of Alinsky's life and legacy.

[11] A comprehensive analysis of this troubling trend is offered in Craig Calhoun, Dilip Parameshwar Gaonkar, and Charles Taylor, *Degenerations of Democracy* (Cambridge, MA: Harvard University Press, 2022).

mutual acquaintance.[12] Though the precise circumstances of their meeting remain unclear, it seems each man quickly identified a kindred spirit in the other: "In spite of the radical differences in their personalities and educational backgrounds," Bernard Doering recounts, "Maritain was immediately attracted to this truculent genius of social reform, and the two men recognized their profound intellectual affinities."[13] They would remain close friends, confidants, and practical collaborators until Alinsky's death in 1972, which preceded Maritain's by only a year.

Historically speaking, as Doering notes, it is difficult to assess the degree to which Maritain and Alinsky actually influenced each other intellectually.[14] By the time they met, both had already arrived at many of the fundamental ideas informing their respective conceptions of democracy. Maritain had begun to develop his democratic theory in the late 1920s when, having abandoned Action Française, the French Thomistic philosopher underwent a dramatic political conversion. Alarmed by the rise of European fascism, he shifted his attention from speculative to political philosophy, devoting much of the next decade to working out an alternative vision to guide Catholic and secular politics.[15] In *Integral Humanism* (1936), his major political work of the 1930s, Maritain accordingly offered an account of "New Christendom," a "concrete historical ideal" premised on principles such as "personalism," "communalism," "pluralism," and the "autonomy of the temporal."[16] Though in that work he had relatively little to say about democracy, in the following years, informed by his first experience of democratic life within the United States, Maritain

---

[12] It remains unknown exactly when they were introduced, and by whom. Doering speculates that George Schuster, the former editor of *Commonweal*, made the connection; Sanford Horwitt, Alinsky's biographer, regards it as equally possible that John Nef (a University of Chicago historian) or Chicago auxiliary bishop Bernard Sheil, did. See Doering, *The Philosopher and the Provocateur*, xviii, 4; Horwitt, *Let Them Call Me Rebel*, 166.

[13] Doering, *The Philosopher and the Provocateur*, xviii.

[14] Doering, *The Philosopher and the Provocateur*, xx; Horwitt, *Let Them Call Me Rebel*, 197.

[15] On Maritain's political conversion, and his passionate embrace of anti-fascism in the 1930s, see Bernard E. Doering, *Jacques Maritain and the French Catholic Intellectuals* (Notre Dame, IN: University of Notre Dame Press, 1983), chapter 1. For a broader contextualization of Maritain's work during this period, see James Chappel, *Catholic Modern: The Challenge of Totalitarianism and the Making of the Church* (Cambridge: Harvard University Press, 2018), 34–40, 108–143.

[16] This text is translated and reprinted as Jacques Maritain, "Integral Humanism: Temporal and Spiritual Problems of a New Christendom," in *Integral Humanism, Freedom in the Modern World, and a Letter on Independence*, ed. Otto Bird, trans. Otto Bird, Joseph Evans, and Richard O'Sullivan, vol. 11, Collected Works of Jacques Maritain (Notre Dame, IN: University of Notre Dame Press, 1996), 141–345. On Maritain's ideal of a "New Christendom," see especially 233–284.

increasingly began to describe his own project in terms of "personalist" or "integrally human democracy." With the publication of *Christianity and Democracy* in 1943, he offered a full articulation of his democratic vision.[17]

While Maritain was developing a new democratic philosophy, Alinsky was pioneering a new approach to democratic organizing. As a graduate student in sociology at The University of Chicago, he had gained experience working in urban neighborhoods and doing community-based research; he had also absorbed his Chicago mentors' commitment to philosophical pragmatism and the highly practical, and participatory, conception of democracy associated with it.[18] After abandoning graduate school in 1930 to work at Chicago's Institute for Juvenile Research, Alinsky eventually found his way, in 1938, to the Back of the Yards neighborhood, the city's most notorious slum, where his initial assignment was to develop a program for combating juvenile delinquency.[19] It was in Back of the Yards that Alinsky built his first community organization, the Back of the Yards Neighborhood Council (BYNC). The BYNC became the prototype for all of the subsequent "people's organizations" Alinsky developed across his career, and furnished many of the stories he recounted in his first book, *Reveille for Radicals* (1946). Alinsky's achievement in Back of the Yards was also what first brought him into contact with Maritain, upon whom it made quite an impression. For both reasons, it is worth reviewing Alinsky's original organizing project in some detail.

When Alinsky arrived in Back of the Yards, the neighborhood was already nationally infamous for its terrible living conditions. The real-life basis for Upton Sinclair's muckraking classic, *The Jungle* (1906), Back of the Yards was so called because it was adjacent to Chicago's industrial stockyards and meatpacking facilities; more precisely, it was where people who worked in those facilities lived.[20] The neighborhood was overwhelmingly composed of Catholic immigrants

---

[17] This text is translated and reprinted in *Christianity and Democracy* and *The Rights of Man and the Natural Law*, trans. Doris C. Anson (San Francisco: Ignatius, 2011), 1–62. Prior to his encounter with democracy in the US, Maritain was wary of the idea of "democracy," owing to its association, in the French context, with the aggressively secularist legacy of the French Revolution. In the US, however, he came to appreciate alternative ways of understanding and practicing the democratic ideal, some of which aligned closely with his own project of "New Christendom." For his own contrast of French and American democracy, see Jacques Maritain, *Scholasticism and Politics*, trans. Mortimer J. Adler (Providence, RI: Cluny Media, 2018 [1940]), 91–118.

[18] For an analysis of the "Chicago school's" influence on Alinsky's approach to community organizing, see Lawrence J. Engel, "Saul D. Alinsky and the Chicago School," *Journal of Speculative Philosophy* 16, no. 1 (2002): 50–66, www.jstor.org/stable/25670402.

[19] On this period in Alinsky's life, see Horwitt, *Let Them Call Me Rebel*, 10–76.

[20] Horwitt, *Let Them Call Me Rebel*, 56–57.

of diverse ethnicities and languages: in addition to the Polish majority, it was home to Irish, Lithuanian, Slovak, German, and Mexican Catholics, all of whom gathered in separate national parishes and social institutions. Within each group, the native—and generally quite conservative—Catholic priests enjoyed a primacy of moral and communal authority, which they not infrequently used to reinforce inter-ethnic tensions.[21] In his initial analysis of Back of the Yards, Alinsky gleaned that both its ethnic divisions and powerful priests had proved fatal obstacles to all prior efforts to unionize the meatpackers, with the result that neighborhood conditions had seen little improvement for decades. To many priests, and the laity who deferred to them, any attempt to organize labor or promote cross-ethnic solidarity smacked of communism, which was decidedly beyond the pale.[22]

Compelled by the prospect of finally organizing a union in Back of the Yards, and concerned by the rise of fascism (domestically and worldwide), Alinsky sought to succeed where others had failed.[23] He recognized that to do so, however, he would need to find some way of uniting most, if not all, of the neighborhood's Catholic parishes behind the cause, and overcome their deep suspicion of organized labor and each other. Alinsky accordingly began to comb the neighborhood for "native leaders" who had roots in its institutions yet also an interest in collaborating to organize a union. Gradually consolidating those he found into a core team, he worked out a new strategy with them. Rather than trying to directly recruit neighborhood members into a union, Alinsky's group would instead invite the neighborhood's parishes and other social institutions to form a "neighborhood council": a federation of key neighborhood institutions whose purpose would be to identify, agree upon, and then take action to address the most pressing problems facing Back of the Yards.[24] This council would give neighborhood residents the opportunity to democratically decide for themselves what those problems were, and determine which solutions should be adopted in response to them. Whether labor unionization was the best solution or not would be left up to their choice.

---

[21] Horwitt, *Let Them Call Me Rebel*, 61.
[22] Horwitt, *Let Them Call Me Rebel*, 60.
[23] During the 1930s, Alinsky's passionate hatred of fascism and general sympathy with the democratic Left led him to identify with the "Popular Front," which brought non-communist liberals, democrats, and socialists into collaboration with communists against fascism. Like many within the Popular Front, however, Alinsky himself was never a communist and, in fact, quite repulsed by what he saw as the "totalitarian" character of Soviet Communism. See Horwitt, *Let Them Call Me Rebel*, 37–41.
[24] Finks, *The Radical Vision of Saul Alinsky*, 16.

Having settled on this strategy, Alinsky's team began holding meetings with other leaders from across the neighborhood. Starting from a place of listening, they would first ask those they met with to share what they saw as the primary problems afflicting their own community. Only after an individual leader had done so would Alinsky or his collaborators invite him to consider joining the proposed neighborhood council, by highlighting how it might serve the concrete "self-interest" of the leader and his community members.[25]

The strategy was a success. On July 14, 1939, the Back of the Yards Neighborhood Council held its founding meeting, with representatives from over 100 of the neighborhood's major institutions, including many churches, in attendance. At that meeting, after collective deliberation, the representatives democratically agreed upon a "people's program" to guide the BYNC's future work; the program included formal endorsement of the Congress of Industrial Organization's (CIO) new effort to unionize meatpacking workers, whose avowedly communist lead organizer was himself present at the assembly. Shortly thereafter, with the robust support of the neighborhood's Catholic churches, the residents won their first union contract from the meatpackers.[26] And that was only the beginning of the BYNC's wins. Within the first months of its founding, in accord with its self-formulated program, the fledgling organization opened a baby clinic, established a credit union, brought new jobs to the neighborhood, and secured funds from the state and federal government to start a hot lunch program for schoolchildren.[27]

Unsurprisingly, given the major role played by the Catholic church in the neighborhood, Alinsky's organizing in Back of the Yards brought him into contact with a number of prominent Catholics. One of these was Chicago's popular and nationally renowned auxiliary bishop, Bernard Sheil, who became a pivotal supporter of Alinsky's efforts.[28] Another was John O'Grady, the legendary director of

---

[25] The experience left a lasting impression on Alinsky, who continued to stress the importance of connecting to community members' "self-interest" throughout his career. "If they [the neighborhood leaders] had been originally asked to join on grounds of pure idealism they would unquestionably have rejected the invitation," the organizer reflected. "Similarly, if the approach had been made on the basis of co-operative work, they would have denounced it as radical" (Saul Alinsky, *Reveille for Radicals* [New York: Vintage, 1989], 98).

[26] On the BYNC's founding meeting, and the subsequent union victory, see Horwitt, *Let Them Call Me Rebel*, 71–76.

[27] Finks, *The Radical Vision of Saul Alinsky*, 21; see Horwitt, *Let Them Call Me Rebel*, 156–158.

[28] In addition to his pastoral role in Chicago, Sheil also oversaw the national Catholic Youth Organization. In 1940, he became one of the founding board members for Alinsky's Industrial Areas Foundation. On Sheil, see Horwitt, *Let Them Call Me Rebel*, 69–70, 74–75, 84–87.

Catholic Charities, and Alinsky's chief collaborator throughout the 1950s.[29] A third was Jacques Maritain. The illustrious philosopher was likely introduced to Alinsky during a visit to The University of Chicago, one of several academic institutions with which he was affiliated during his wartime exile, and subsequent sojourn, in the United States.[30]

That Alinsky and Maritain felt profound affinity for each other is apparent from Alinsky's first letter to the latter which, though undated, seems to have been written shortly after they met. In the letter, the ordinarily irreverent Alinsky was uncharacteristically reverential, and self-conscious for being so. Confessing his admiration for Maritain as one of those very "rare persons—actual real Christians," he proceeded to ask him for a personal photograph to set on his desk; the philosopher's image, Alinsky hoped, would counteract his temptation toward "straight cynicism and materialism" and remind him there were other ways to look at the world.[31] "This is most difficult to write," the hardboiled organizer continued, "because I have an aversion towards sentimentality and a horror of idols, hero worshipers, etc. But what I am trying to say is that a picture of you with some personal statement on it would be one of my most cherished possessions." In his postscript, Alinsky added that having a photo of Maritain would also "serve as a constant reminder to finish the book"—with "the book" in question being *Reveille for Radicals*.

Maritain's first extant letter to Alinsky, meanwhile, is dated August 20, 1945. The philosopher wrote it shortly after reading Alinsky's manuscript, which he received rapturously. "As I cabled to you," Maritain enthused, "this book is epoch-making. It reveals a new way for *real* democracy, the only way in which man's thirst for social communion can develop and be satisfied, through freedom and not through totalitarianism in our disintegrated times. You seem at first glance over optimistic [*sic*], in reality your method starting with self-interest and egotistic concerns in order to transform them shows how sound is your knowledge of human nature."[32] Maritain even went so far as to proclaim that his friend was "a Thomist, dear Saul, a practical Thomist!"

Subsequently, in his review of *Reveille* for the *New York Post,* Maritain described the book in nearly identical terms, while

---

[29] Finks, *The Radical Vision of Saul Alinsky*, 74.
[30] Finks, *The Radical Vision of Saul Alinsky*, 30.
[31] Letter I, in Doering, *The Philosopher and the Provocateur*, 3.
[32] Letter VI, in Doering, *The Philosopher and the Provocateur*, 11. Both Maritain and Alinsky, following the conventions of their time, frequently used "man" to refer to all human persons. I retain their original language in quoting them, but adopt more inclusive language in my paraphrasing.

elaborating his meaning more fully. "I think that this book will be epoch-making," he began.

> It was born not of theory only, but of experience, concrete human knowledge and love for the people. In my opinion the achievements of The Back of the Yards Movement open a new road to real democracy, and show us the only way in which that deep need for communion which today stirs up men threatened by technocratic civilization, can be satisfied in freedom and through freedom, in and through genuine respect for the human person, in and through actual and living trust in the people. No totalitarianism can worm its way into a democracy built on such basic communal activities and the principles involved. At the same time, we see the manner in which one of our great problems—how real leaders can emerge from and be chosen by real people—is to be solved.[33]

Later in the review, Maritain announced his intention to have *Reveille* translated and published in France. "I am convinced," he wrote, "that the same effort, adapted to different historical conditions, should be undertaken in European democracies."[34]

Evidently Maritain saw in Alinsky's organizing a remarkable, even unique, embodiment of the "personalist democracy" he had envisioned theoretically. But what was personalist democracy? And how, concretely, was it reflected in the comparatively humble achievements of the BYNC? Let me now turn to considering these questions directly.

Persons in Community: The Vision of Personalist Democracy

By the time Alinsky published *Reveille for Radicals* in 1946, he and Maritain had converged on a common political vision, which I think is best named by Maritain's term "personalist democracy." Not much interested in philosophical theorizing, Alinsky never explicitly used that term, typically speaking simply of "democracy." Nevertheless, in substance, the vision of personalist democracy Maritain elaborated theoretically corresponded closely to the democratic ideals informing Alinsky's organizing practice—as Maritain himself recognized.[35] Both the philosopher and organizer

---

[33] The review is reprinted in Doering, *The Philosopher and the Provocateur*, 18–20.
[34] Doering, *The Philosopher and the Provocateur*, 19.
[35] As already noted (see n. 14), it is difficult to assess the degree to which Maritain actually influenced Alinsky's understanding of democracy. Given the limited sources available, the best one can do is speculate, and speculation has led scholars to conflicting conclusions. On the one hand Sanford Horwitt submits that "in his relationship with Maritain . . . one has the impression that it was Maritain who believed he had learned something important from Alinsky, but not the reverse." On the other hand, Luke Bretherton claims it was through his connection with "the

would remain committed to the project of personalist democracy for the rest of their lives.

As Maritain and Alinsky conceived it, "democracy" was not primarily a form of government or set of institutional procedures, but an *ethical* ideal, which underwrote an entire philosophy and way of life. In *Christianity and Democracy*, Maritain accordingly defined "integrally human democracy" as a "general philosophy of human and political life and a state of mind," going on to specify that "respect for human dignity and the rights of the person" were its "essential bases."[36] Analogously, in *Reveille,* Alinsky breathlessly characterized democracy as "a way of life . . . a process—a vibrant, living sweep of hope and progress . . . the search for truth, justice, and the dignity of man."[37] Both thinkers thus understood democracy as a "telic" concept, to employ a recent term from Charles Taylor; that is, democracy was a "matter of purposes and ideals, not merely conditions or causal relations."[38] It was an ethical end, more or less perfectly actualized in history, as well as the dynamic process of striving toward that end.

Further, for these figures, the "dignity of the person" was the fundamental principle that defined "democracy" as ideal, philosophy, and project. Maritain, the Thomistic philosopher, understood human dignity in explicitly theistic terms. By virtue of her creation in the *imago dei,* he argued in *The Rights of Man and the Natural Law* (1942), each person constituted a free and unique subject, who enjoyed "direct relationship with the Absolute" and was called to communion with it; as such, she possessed absolute value in her own right.[39] Consequently, a truly democratic society would be one that respected the dignity of each person. This meant, first, never violating or instrumentalizing the dignity of persons for the sake of other, lesser goods (state power, national glory, or the accumulation of wealth), and second, actively promoting the dignity of all of society's members.

---

emerging expression of Christian Democracy and Roman Catholic social teaching, most notably through his relationships with Bishop Sheil and Jacques Maritain, that Alinsky found a political vision to complement and help him articulate his own" (Horwitt, *Let Them Call Me Rebel*, 197; Bretherton, *Resurrecting Democracy*, 37). In my view, Bretherton's case is more persuasive. Alinsky sounds much more "personalist" in *Reveille* (and subsequent works) than in his earlier writings, suggesting that his dialogue with Catholics like Sheil and Maritain may well have given him a new language, and perhaps a new framework, to articulate his own democratic values.

[36] Maritain, *Christianity and Democracy*, 19.
[37] Alinsky, *Reveille for Radicals*, 47.
[38] Calhoun, Gaonkar, and Taylor, *Degenerations of Democracy*, 19.
[39] This text is translated and reprinted as Jacques Maritain, "The Rights of Man and the Natural Law," in *Christianity and Democracy* and *The Rights of Man and the Natural Law,* trans. Doris C. Anson (San Francisco: Ignatius, 2011), 63–141. Quoted text at 67.

Such, indeed, was the very *raison d'être* of human social life itself.[40] Alinsky, the agnostic organizer, offered no comparably developed account of human dignity. Yet he did insist, to the end of his life, that human dignity was the foundational "sacred" value of democracy, and the organizer's "constant guiding star"; democracy itself was "not an end but the best means" toward promoting human dignity. Furthermore, like his friend Maritain, Alinsky saw the dignity of the person as a value derived historically from the living traditions of "Judeo-Christianity," still sustained by them in the modern age.[41]

Because Maritain and Alinsky premised their democratic vision on the dignity of the person, they viewed the defense and promotion of human rights, comprehensively understood, as essential to the democratic project. As Maritain conceived them, human rights articulated the "things which are owed to man because of the very fact that he is man"—that is, a person, endowed with dignity.[42] On Maritain's expansive account, such rights encompassed not only the civil and political liberties central to the classical liberal tradition (freedom of speech, religion, and association, for example), but also the social and economic rights—rights to work, decent living conditions, healthcare, and so on—more typically stressed by socialist traditions, as well as cultural rights to education and participation in the vital traditions of one's own people.[43] Though Alinsky did not theorize about human rights, he shared Maritain's belief in their paramount importance, and likewise insisted that persons had not only political rights, but economic and social rights too. "The radical places human rights far above property rights," he wrote, and "want[s] to see the established political rights or political freedom of the common man be augmented by economic freedom."[44]

Although Maritain and Alinsky considered human rights to be necessary foundations for a democratic society, they did not believe they were sufficient. On their account, in addition to possessing freedom and dignity, human persons were also essentially *social* and *political* creatures, who could only achieve self-realization through *participation* in community with others. Again, Maritain presented a theological rationale for this claim, famously arguing in *The Person and the Common Good* (1946) that "personality tends by nature to

---

[40] See Maritain, "The Rights of Man and the Natural Law," 66–67, for further elaboration of these points.
[41] See Alinsky, *Reveille for Radicals*, xiv, 175; Alinsky, *Rules for Radicals*, 122.
[42] Maritain, "The Rights of Man and the Natural Law," 107.
[43] For Maritain's exposition of these rights, see "The Rights of Man and the Natural Law," 112–136. He offers a summary list on 136–138.
[44] Alinsky, *Reveille for Radicals*, 16, 26. In the former passage, Alinsky enumerates a number of specific rights, including rights to a "high standard of food, housing, and health," to "universal free public education," and "local control"; he also acknowledges that the last of these rights may come into conflict with the others.

communion."[45] The God in whose image human persons are made, Maritain held, was a Triune God, a communion of divine Persons who were only "themselves" through their perfected relations of mutual knowledge and love with the other Persons. Insofar as human persons were analogues—albeit radically imperfect ones—of the divine Persons, we could likewise only become ourselves, and attain our own fulfillment, through participation in relationships of communion with other persons, both human and divine.[46] Alinsky, of course, did not share Maritain's Trinitarian theology. But he very much shared his friend's richly social conception of the human person. "The complete man," Alinsky wrote in *Reveille*, "is one who is making a definite contribution to the general social welfare," "is a vital part of that community of interests, values, and purposes that makes life and people meaningful," and who, consequently, "can say to himself, 'What I do is important and has its place.'"[47]

This constitutively social conception of the person had definite implications for democracy, which both Alinsky and Maritain developed. First, it led both to stress the importance of human association, as well as the diversity of its forms. A personalist democracy, Maritain wrote, requires a *pluralist* body politic, because it "assumes that the development of the human person normally requires a plurality of autonomous communities which have their own rights, liberties, and authority."[48] Along similar lines, Alinsky conceived "democracy" as "a way of government in which we recognize that all normal individuals have a whole series of loyalties—loyalties to their churches, their labor unions, their fraternal organizations, their social groups, their nationality groups, their athletic groups, their political parties, and many others."[49] Life in a democratic society was accordingly incompatible with a "single, unqualified, primary loyalty to the state," which was not democracy, but "totalitarianism."[50] Both thinkers, in other words, considered a variety of associations beyond the state necessary for human persons to develop themselves, such that a democratic society entailed not only the protection of personal rights, but of associational rights as well. Beyond this, it required the promotion of a flourishing, pluralistic associational life, which provided persons with the institutional

---

[45] Jacques Maritain, *The Person and the Common Good*, trans. John J. Fitzgerald (Notre Dame, IN: University of Notre Dame Press, 1946), 47.
[46] Maritain, *The Person and the Common Good*, 56–62.
[47] Alinsky, *Reveille for Radicals*, 17.
[48] Maritain, *Christianity and Democracy* and *The Rights of Man and the Natural Law*, 78.
[49] Alinsky, *Reveille for Radicals*, 85–86.
[50] Alinsky, *Reveille for Radicals*, 86.

vehicles needed to sustain relationships with each other and meaningfully contribute to the common good.[51]

Second, the social conception of the person led both Maritain and Alinsky to conceive "the common good" itself along similar lines. More specifically, they saw the common good and human person as interdependent realities. The common good could only be achieved in a society that fully respected and promoted the dignity and rights of persons, which is to say a democratic one. Reciprocally, however, individual persons only fulfilled themselves through freely contributing to society and promoting its common good, such that the common good itself was only actualized insofar as all the members of society actively pursued and participated in it.

Thus, Maritain could define the "common good" as "the communion in good living" of the human persons who shared in it.[52] "Man finds himself by subordinating himself to the group," he summarized, "and the group attains its goal only by serving man and by realizing that man has secrets which escape the group and a vocation which the group does not encompass."[53] Alinsky nowhere attempted to define the common good, or elaborate upon its components. Yet he did explicitly characterize it as "the greatest personal value" of the radical, identifying democracy with "the ongoing pursuit of the common good by *all* of the people."[54]

Third, and consequently, both Maritain and Alinsky considered *participation* just as essential to personalist democracy as human rights; indeed, the two could not be divorced from each other. This meant that the democratic ideal could only be made a reality through the free, ongoing, participatory action of *"the people"* themselves. "The people," as Maritain defined them in *Man and the State* (1951), comprised "the multitude of human persons who, united under just laws, by mutual friendship, and for the common good of their human existence, constitute a political society or body politic."[55] As such, he continued, they represented "the very substance, the living and free substance, of the body politic"; the state existed for the sake of the people, rather than the other way around. Furthermore, Maritain emphasized, it followed from the dignity of the person, and the primacy of the people, that "the program of the people should not be offered from above to the people, and then accepted by them; it should

---

[51] Maritain elaborates this point more systematically in *Man and the State* (Washington, DC: The Catholic University of America Press, 1951), 1–27.
[52] Maritain, *The Person and the Common Good*, 50–51.
[53] Maritain, *The Person and the Common Good*, 66.
[54] Alinsky, *Reveille for Radicals*, 15; Alinsky, *Rules for Radicals*, xxv, emphasis in original.
[55] Maritain, *Man and the State*, 26. In the course of defining "the people," Maritain also deemed it the "highest and noblest" of political philosophy's basic concepts.

be the work of the people." To substantiate the point, he cited *Reveille for Radicals*.[56]

The reference was apt, for if Alinsky's book had a single, overarching thrust, it was that "the people themselves" were the true protagonists of democracy. The *"real democratic program,"* Alinsky recurrently insisted,

> *is a democratically minded people*—a healthy, active, participating, interested, self-confident people who, through their participation and interest, become informed, educated, and above all develop faith in themselves, their fellow men, and the future. The people themselves are the future. The people themselves will solve each problem that will arise out of a changing world. They will if they, the people, have the opportunity and power to make and enforce the decision instead of seeing that power vested in just a few. No clique, or caste, power group, or benevolent administration can have the people's interest at heart as much as the people themselves.[57]

Such was the essence of what Alinsky called "democratic faith."

At the same time, both Alinsky and Maritain were painfully aware that democracy as it actually existed scarcely approximated their ideal of a government "of the people, by the people, and for the people." "In our modern urban civilization," Alinsky lamented, "multitudes of our people have been condemned to urban anonymity. . . . They find themselves isolated from the life of their community and their nation, driven by social forces beyond their control into little individual worlds in which their own individual objectives have become paramount to the collective good." As a result, he went on, "social objectives, social welfare, the good of the nation, the democratic way of life—all these have become nebulous, meaningless, sterile phrases."[58] Maritain agreed, adding that the contemporary problems Alinsky identified were compounded by human nature's perpetual tendency toward inertia. "People as a rule prefer to sleep," he wrote. "Awakenings are always bitter. Insofar as their daily interests are involved, what people would like is business as usual: everyday misery and humiliation as usual. People would like not to know that they are *the* people."[59]

The philosopher and organizer further agreed that to understand the serious challenges facing democracy in their day it was not enough to focus on structural problems alone. "If . . . we confine our entire

---

[56] Maritain, *Man and the State*, 68.
[57] Alinsky, *Reveille for Radicals*, 55, emphasis in original. Maritain cites the whole of chapter 4, "The Program" (53–63), from which this passage comes.
[58] Alinsky, *Reveille for Radicals*, 43–44.
[59] Maritain, *Man and the State*, 142.

attention to the problem of structure," Alinsky contended, "we will revert to the ancient fallacy of assuming that laws make men rather than that men make laws."[60] Though structural problems—perverse inequalities of power and wealth, institutionally entrenched racism, social atomization, and an unaccountable state and corporate elite, to name but a few—were both very real and grave, they remained unredressed in significant part because the people had not democratically organized themselves to combat them. A lack of collective agency and responsibility on the part of the people was perhaps the most fundamental problem afflicting contemporary democracies.

For this reason, Alinsky and Maritain charged, proposals for democratic reform that did not prioritize the agency of the people themselves were fundamentally flawed, on both moral and practical grounds. "The world is deluged with panaceas, formulas, proposed laws, machineries, ways out, and myriads of solutions" to democracy's problems, Alinsky observed in *Reveille*. "It is significant and tragic that almost every one of these proposed plans and alleged solutions deals with the structure of society, but none concerns the substance itself—the people." Yet "in the last analysis of our democratic faith," Alinsky submitted, "the answer to all of the issues facing us will be found in the masses of people themselves, *and nowhere else*."[61] In the course of criticizing overly state-centric solutions, Maritain drove home the same point. It was necessary, he wrote, "that the people have the will, and the means, to assert their own control over the State."[62]

What, exactly, did this mean in practice? How were the people to be roused from their sleep, and moved to assume responsibility for enacting the ideals of personalist democracy—and their own common good? For both Maritain and Alinsky, the answer may be encapsulated in a single word: "organization."

FORMING THE PEOPLE: THE ORGANIZATION OF PERSONALIST DEMOCRACY

If Maritain and Alinsky are considered in isolation from each other, it is easy to overlook the significance of organization to the vision of personalist democracy they both shared. Maritain, the philosopher, is best known for his rich accounts of the ideals and principles that ought to guide human political life, as well as his visionary flights of imagination; he is not usually regarded as a thinker with much to say about something so mundane and practical as "organization." By

---

[60] Alinsky, *Reveille for Radicals*, 41.
[61] Alinsky, *Reveille for Radicals*, 40, emphasis in original.
[62] Maritain, *Man and the State*, 27.

contrast, Alinsky was a theorist and practitioner of organization par excellence, whose books (*Reveille* and *Rules for Radicals*) have gained canonical status as "how-to" guides for subsequent generations of community organizers. Yet for this very reason, what is often missed in Alinsky's organizing approach is the larger, ultimately moral vision of democracy that informed every aspect of his practice. When Maritain and Alinsky are read in dialogue with each other, however, organization emerges as the focal point at which the theory and practice of personalist democracy converged. To both, it was the privileged process for translating their democratic ideals into reality.

Prior to meeting Alinsky, Maritain grasped the significance of organization theoretically, yet had only a vague idea of what it might look like in practice. In *Integral Humanism,* he perceived the need to somehow mobilize "the people" around what he called the "common task" of building a New Christendom. Recognizing that it was the institutionalized party organizations of fascism and communism that made them such woefully powerful political movements, Maritain advocated that lay Christians respond in kind, by forming what he called "organized political fraternities."[63] These fraternities, as Maritain envisioned them, would be like secular analogues of the Catholic religious orders, insofar as they would draw together Christians who shared a deep commitment to practicing the virtues and pursuing a disciplined and distinctive way of life together. Unlike the religious orders, however, the political fraternities would be formally independent of the church hierarchy, while also retaining their independence from the state and its parliamentary parties. Meanwhile, they would differ emphatically from their communist and fascist counterparts not only in the principles they upheld, but also in their internal organization and methods, which would be "founded on freedom" and "pluralism." Nevertheless, in *Integral Humanism,* Maritain offered scarcely any concrete details, to say nothing of actual examples, of how such political fraternities would work, or how they might bring about the transformation of society.[64]

When Maritain encountered Alinsky and the BYNC, he found a real approximation of the political organizations which, to that point, he had largely only imagined.[65] This was why he could write so enthusiastically, in the *New York Post,* that the "Back of the Yards Movement" opened "a new road to real democracy." Meanwhile, it was Maritain's repeated prompting, and perhaps his inspiration, that moved Alinsky to articulate, in *Reveille,* not only the practical

---

[63] Maritain, *Integral Humanism,* 260.
[64] For Maritain's fuller exposition of his idea of Christian political fraternities, see *Integral Humanism,* 259–261, 322–326.
[65] Doering, *The Philosopher and the Provocateur,* xxvii.

methods for building organizations like the BYNC, but the larger democratic vision and philosophy undergirding them. As Alinsky himself stressed, his practical methods were not extricable from the democratic ends they were meant to serve. "They can be utilized," the organizer wrote, "only to a limited extent by those whose main interest is manipulation either for the sake of manipulation or for undemocratic objectives. In the last analysis the use of these tactics for evil or selfish purposes will defeat the tactician's own objectives."[66]

Analogously, the "people's organization"—the distinctive institutional form Alinsky may justly be said to have invented—was specifically designed to serve the larger democratic ends he and Maritain shared.[67] In *Reveille,* using the BYNC as a prototype, Alinsky offered a detailed account of the nature and purposes of people's organizations. Like the BYNC, they were to be neighborhood-based "organizations of organizations," drawing together all the institutions central to the life of the people in that neighborhood: churches, fraternal organizations, labor groups, block clubs, and so on.[68] As Alinsky initially described them, such people's organizations had two principal functions. First, they existed to provide an institutional structure for democratic deliberation and collaboration, enabling diverse individuals and communities within a neighborhood to identify common interests and, on the basis of those interests, agree upon a "people's program." Second, through the very solidarity they created within the community, people's organizations functioned to "generate power," which could then be "controlled and applied for the attainment of the program."[69]

For Alinsky, "organization" was thus not only a process for bringing people together around common interests, but also, simultaneously, a way of building and exercising the collective power needed to achieve those interests.[70] In one form or another, organization was what the powerful few within society—the moneyed interests, politicians, and leaders of elite institutions—nearly always had, and what most ordinary, non-elite people nearly always lacked. Yet by the same token, Alinsky believed, through forming people's organizations, pooling what resources they had, and deploying those

---

[66] Alinsky, *Reveille for Radicals,* 130.
[67] Organizer and Alinsky scholar Mike Miller stresses Alinsky's invention of the democratic people's organization—a "new social form"—as counting among his most important contributions. See Aaron Schutz and Mike Miller, eds., *People Power: The Community Organizing Tradition of Saul Alinsky* (Nashville, TN: Vanderbilt University Press, 2015), 312.
[68] Alinsky, *Reveille for Radicals,* 86.
[69] Alinsky, *Reveille for Radicals,* 54.
[70] For Alinsky, "power" was simply the "ability to act," the capacity to achieve one's ends. As such, there was nothing inherently bad or oppressive about it; what mattered was who had it, and to what ends they used it (*Rules for Radicals,* 50).

resources in strategic ways, individuals and communities who lacked power on their own could develop significant collective power, and even defeat more conventionally powerful opponents in political conflict.[71] Indeed, today Alinsky is perhaps most famous, or notorious, for the highly creative and confrontational "conflict tactics" he developed for use by people's organizations, which he elaborated at length in both *Reveille* and (especially) *Rules*.[72]

Although people's organizations certainly were "power organizations," they were also much more than that. Ultimately, the purpose of people's organizations, and the organizing process as a whole, was to *form the people*, in a moral as well as a political sense. They did so, first, by bringing people together across differences of culture, race, class, religion, and ideology that might otherwise divide them, and giving them practical experience of collaborating with others different from themselves for the sake of a common goal. "Once people get to know each other as human beings," Alinsky wrote in a 1946 paper, "rather than as impersonal symbols representing diverse philosophies and organizations, then a new set of relationships composed of a genuine understanding and real sympathy will arise."[73] He knew of what he spoke: in Back of the Yards, Alinsky had actually seen this happen.

Second, Alinsky believed, through the process of acting together for a common good, and successfully achieving tangible goals they set for themselves, the members of the people's organization would experience their own agency in a new and transformative way. They would come to recognize that their individual "good" as persons did not exist in isolation from that of others, but subsisted in a common good, shared with those others. As these two shifts took place, the people participating in the organizing process would discover their own goodness and dignity as persons, and more fully actualize them. "Not only must the dignity of the individual be restored but in that process man must begin to see the good in other men," Alinsky

---

[71] "The building of a People's Organization," Alinsky summarized, "is the building of a new power group" (*Reveille for Radicals*, 132).

[72] Alinsky, *Reveille for Radicals*, 132–154; Alinsky, *Rules for Radicals*, 125–183. Alinsky's penchant for describing political conflict in bombastic, military terms—for example, as a "war" in which "there are no rules of fair play" (*Reveille*, 133)—has led many readers to misunderstand the character of his conflict tactics, which were actually quite principled in practice. For one, while Alinsky-style conflict tactics could be highly confrontational, they were always nonviolent and within the formal bounds of the law. For another, the purpose of such tactics was not to harm or destroy an opponent, but to compel them to the bargaining table, with the ultimate aim of achieving compromise. To the organizer, Alinsky insisted, "compromise is a key and beautiful word" (*Rules for Radicals*, 59).

[73] Quoted in Horwitt, *Let Them Call Me Rebel*, 106.

insisted. "*He cannot see the good in others unless he has some of it himself.*"[74] It was this aspect of Alinsky's organizing that most moved Maritain, who arguably articulated the ethical significance of Alinsky's work better than Alinsky himself. "The manner in which, starting from selfish interests, [Alinsky's methods] succeed in giving rise to the sense of solidarity and finally to an unselfish devotion to the common task, conveys an invaluable teaching to us," he wrote in his review of *Reveille*. It revealed that "in the very bosom of the humblest, most material needs of a community of men, an internal moral awakening is linked with the awakening to the elementary requirements of true political life."[75]

In the same review, Maritain also highlighted a third way in which people's organizations "formed" those who participated in them. Such organizations, he observed, not only awakened the moral consciousness of persons to the common good they shared with their immediate neighbors but could also expand their moral horizon to more encompassing common goods. It was accordingly one of Alinsky's great achievements to explain how "a small community, thus organized from within as a living whole, becomes definitely aware of its power of initiative and its common good, [and] naturally develops into concrete awareness of the common good of the nation and the common good of the international community."[76]

As Alinsky himself elaborated in *Reveille*, beyond their immediate local organizing, each people's organization had an additional role to play in providing "popular education" to its members, to help them learn of "the functional relationship between the community, the city, the state, the nation, and the world as a whole."[77] But this popular education had to be practical in bent, he emphasized: the people in the organization had to discover these "functional relationships" for themselves, through the process of investigating how the immediate problems they sought to solve at the local level were symptoms of the various anti-democratic social structures that organized society. Only in this way could ordinary, non-elite people come to understand how those social structures—which would otherwise remain distant or meaningless abstractions—shaped their own reality, while gaining the sense of agency and motivation to change them. This, too, Alinsky had seen happen in the BYNC. Through their participation in the organization, and their own conduct of social analysis, its members became "intensely interested in subjects which had hitherto never been

---

[74] Alinsky, *Reveille for Radicals*, 92, emphasis in original.
[75] Doering, *The Philosopher and the Provocateur*, 20.
[76] Doering, *The Philosopher and the Provocateur*, 19.
[77] Alinsky, *Reveille for Radicals*, 169.

thought of, let alone regarded as having any relationship to the people's lives and experiences."[78]

Correlatively, Alinsky insisted that to be truly effective as vehicles of social change, people's organizations had to work together to take on the many larger problems that could not be addressed at the local level. He accordingly called for a national movement of people's organizations, claiming that "the development of other People's Organizations throughout the nation" ought to be a principal objective of every individual organization.[79] Nevertheless, any such large-scale movement would have to remain institutionally anchored at the local level, where the most formative experiences of personal agency, solidarity, and participation were possible. As Maritain wrote in *Man and the State,* for "the program" of democracy to truly come from the people, "the interest and initiative of the people in civic matters" had to "begin with an awakening of common consciousness in the smallest local communities, and remain constantly at work there."[80]

In sum, for Alinsky and Maritain, people's organizations were not merely deliberative bodies or power groups: they were the institutional incarnations of personalist democracy. People's organizations were the democratic vehicles through which solidarity could be built across difference, communities could pursue their common good, and persons could realize their dignity as human beings. Likewise, the organizing process such organizations made possible was what formed that motley body of persons into *the people,* a continually reconstituted collective subject capable of freely assuming responsibility and taking action for the common good. By becoming "the people," human persons could progressively discover the truth of personalist democracy for themselves. Its high ideals would no longer be the "meaningless, sterile" abstractions Alinsky feared they so often were. Through the process of organization, they would take on flesh and blood, and become real, in the persons and institutions who embodied them.

---

[78] Alinsky, *Reveille for Radicals,* 169.
[79] Alinsky, *Reveille for Radicals,* 62. Far from being a naïve partisan of the local, as he is sometimes portrayed, Alinsky contended it was a basic "fallacy" of community organization to believe all, or even most, problems afflicting local communities could be solved at the local level. A second basic fallacy was considering individual social problems in isolation from others: for example, by trying to combat crime without addressing the poverty, social breakdown, and political powerlessness that often drive it. Alinsky discusses both of these fallacies in *Reveille for Radicals,* 56–63.
[80] Maritain, *Man and the State,* 67–68.

Conclusion: Rekindling the Democratic Faith Today

What became of Maritain and Alinsky's dream of personalist democracy? In their own lifetimes, the two visionaries had but limited success in realizing it. Though Maritain's ideas proved widely influential across the Atlantic world, inspiring movements for "Christian Democracy" throughout Europe and Latin America, Maritain himself regarded most of the political Christian Democratic parties with disappointment. With the notable exception of Eduardo Frei's Christian Democrats in Chile, he found many of them neither especially "Christian" nor particularly democratic, at least when measured against his own, decidedly more radical vision of democracy.[81] By contrast, to the end, Maritain continued to see Alinsky as the truest exemplar of the democratic project to which they were both committed. Yet though Alinsky built several remarkable people's organizations over the course of his life, his efforts to launch a larger movement out of them never really got off the ground in the US, to say nothing of Europe.[82] Still more discouragingly for Alinsky, the BYNC—for years his flagship organization—turned segregationist in the 1950s, partly as a consequence of its own success at bringing its immigrant constituents into the "white" middle class. In a painful irony, by the 1960s, Alinsky's organizing with African Americans in Chicago led him to oppose the very organization he and Maritain had seen as a beacon of hope in the 1940s.[83]

Nevertheless, for all these disappointments, neither Alinsky nor Maritain lost "the democratic faith," as Alinsky always called it. The organizer ended his last book, *Rules for Radicals,* with a chastened yet unwavering profession of that faith. "When Americans can no longer see the stars," he wrote, "the times are tragic. We must believe that it is the darkness before the dawn of a beautiful new world; we will see it when we believe it."[84] Not long after, in his last extant letter to Alinsky, Maritain proclaimed *Rules* "a great book, admirably free, absolutely fearless, *radically revolutionary.*" Rightly seeing through the book's performative cynicism and overblown "realist" rhetoric, which has led many since to fundamentally misunderstand Alinsky, Maritain celebrated his friend for what he was: "an incurable idealist"

---

[81] Chappel, *Catholic Modern,* 180–181.

[82] On some of the reasons why, see, e.g., Finks, *The Radical Vision of Saul Alinsky,* 51–60, 117–119, 254.

[83] Mark R. Warren, *Dry Bones Rattling: Community Building to Revitalize American Democracy* (Princeton, NJ: Princeton University Press, 2001), 45–47. As Warren goes on to recount, however, later generations of Alinsky's students would learn from the cautionary tale of the BYNC, and eventually have much more success building truly cross-racial organizations.

[84] Alinsky, *Rules for Radicals,* 196.

and "heroic witness of Judaeo-Christian tradition and true democracy."[85] The description could just as well have applied to Maritain himself. "You know that I am with you with all my heart and soul," he confided to Alinsky at the letter's end.[86]

Was Maritain and Alinsky's "democratic faith" misplaced? The disappointments they experienced in their own lifetime, and the sorry state of democracies around the world today, certainly give the skeptic reasons to think it might have been. Yet I would argue that one of the most important lessons these figures from the past have to teach us in the present is that commitment to the democratic project is precisely what Alinsky said it was: a faith. Though reality and reason alike may challenge it, whether we abandon the democratic faith is ultimately a choice, an act of morally responsible agency. It is a testimony to the strength of Maritain and Alinsky's faith in democracy that they never did abandon it, even when they had ample reason to do so. In fact, they first found their faith in the 1930s, at precisely the moment when many were abandoning it—for fascism, communism, nostalgia, or despair. In that respect, our own moment may not be so distinct from theirs, even though the historical conditions under which we live are in other ways, of course, notably different. When faith in democracy is flagging, it is perhaps most important of all to remember that democracy lives by faith.

Not only by faith, however. If we are to have faith in democracy, we must also have some orienting conception of the object of our faith. In this respect, too, Maritain and Alinsky may yet have much to teach us. They recognized that democracy was not simply a form of government or a set of procedures, but a moral vision, way of life, and project. As such, it must be founded upon certain ideas or principles. To morally anchor the project of democracy, both Maritain and Alinsky looked to a certain understanding of the person, according to which she is a free being, possessed of dignity, yet also called to realize herself through participatory relationships of communion. From that simple starting point, they arrived at conclusions Alinsky was right to call "radical," and Maritain "revolutionary."

At a time when various thinkers, religious and secular, are reminding us that democracy is a "telic" concept, and calling for a recovery of its moral foundations, the vision of "personalist democracy" offers one promising starting point from which to

---

[85] Letter LXXIV (September 19, 1971), in Doering, *The Philosopher and the Provocateur*, 111.

[86] Letter LXXIV (September 19, 1971), in Doering, *The Philosopher and the Provocateur*, 112.

proceed.[87] For those of the Catholic faith, of course, it happens to align quite closely with the doctrinal principles of Catholic social teaching, which is no coincidence, given Maritain's historical influence upon the latter.[88] Yet both Maritain and Alinsky understood personalist democracy primarily as a *humanistic* project, culturally and historically anchored in Judaism and Christianity (today one might add Islam, the third Abrahamic faith, as well), yet compelling to persons of diverse religious professions and none. Just how compelling the democratic project actually is, however, can only be determined through ongoing dialogue, and actual democratic practice—a conclusion with which both thinkers would emphatically agree.

Indeed, it was a further, fundamental insight of Alinsky and Maritain that democracy could only be incarnated through organization. "The people," in theory, are the protagonists of democracy, yet in practice this is all too rarely the case. This is because, to fulfill their true vocation of pursuing the common good, the diffuse, often conflicting, and invariably imperfect human persons who comprise "the people" must be properly formed, and skillfully organized.[89] Though democracy may live by faith and be guided by ideals, it is made real only through institutions, and the relationships, practices, and moral formation those institutions make possible. And while Maritain and Alinsky themselves met only limited success in building the institutions they envisioned, the organizers who inherited their legacy have learned much since, creating highly diverse local organizations and national or even trans-national networks whose scale and power far transcend anything Alinsky himself created.[90] Today, when many of democracy's traditional institutions are in

---

[87] See, e.g., Calhoun, Gaonkar, and Taylor, *Degenerations of Democracy*. A complementary argument is made by James T. Kloppenberg, *Toward Democracy: The Struggle for Self-Rule in European and American Thought* (Oxford: Oxford University Press, 2016).

[88] Though many midcentury Catholic theologians and bishops drew inspiration from Maritain's ideas, he was especially influential upon Pope Paul VI, who presided over the second half of Vatican II and promulgated *Populorum Progressio* (1967). See Allan Figueroa Deck, "Commentary on *Populorum Progressio*," in *Modern Catholic Social Teaching: Commentaries & Interpretations*, ed. Kenneth R. Himes, Lisa S. Cahill, Charles E. Curran, David Hollenbach, and Thomas A. Shannon (Washington, DC: Georgetown University Press, 2005), 298–299.

[89] Though I cannot elaborate it here, it is worth noting that there is a striking similarity between the democratic vision of Alinsky and Maritain and the Argentine *teología del pueblo* embraced by Pope Francis, which likewise prioritizes "organizing the people." On the latter, see Rafael Luciani, *Pope Francis and the Theology of the People* (Maryknoll, NY: Orbis Books, 2017).

[90] On the development of "the Alinsky tradition" after Alinsky see, e.g., Schutz and Miller, *People Power: The Community Organizing Tradition of Saul Alinsky*; Richard L. Wood and Brad R. Fulton, *A Shared Future: Faith-Based Organizing for Ethical Democracy* (Chicago, IL: The University of Chicago Press, 2015).

serious crisis, the moment is ripe, and the need urgent, for building new "people's organizations" and reimagining old ones. To this task, the philosophers and organizers of democracy each have something vital to contribute. They will contribute best, however, if they dialogue with each other.

This speaks to the final respect in which Maritain and Alinsky may still have something to teach us today. Their friendship itself, sustained over decades, was an embodiment of the very democratic solidarity across difference in which both so fervently believed. The devout, French Catholic philosopher, enamored of ideas, and the irreverent Jewish-American organizer, insistent upon action, were profoundly different people. Yet in their shared democratic faith, they found not only a basis for friendship, but a wellspring of grace. The life and work of each was much the richer for it. By learning from their example, our own may be as well. 🅼

Nicholas Hayes-Mota, PhD, is Assistant Director of the Clough Center for the Study of Constitutional Democracy at Boston College, as well as the Center's inaugural Postdoctoral Research Fellow. He earned his doctorate in Theological Ethics from Boston College. In Fall 2024, he will join the faculty at Santa Clara University as Assistant Professor of Social Ethics.

Community Organizing for Democratic Renewal: The Significance of Jacques Maritain's Support for Saul Alinsky and His Methods

Brian Stiltner

Abstract: Jacques Maritain's ideas about democratic renewal remain as important and inspirational as ever. A less well-known element of Maritain's political thinking is his support for grassroots community organizing. This support, peppered throughout his writings, comes into stark relief when examining his longtime friendship and correspondence with Saul Alinsky, the dean of community organizing in the US. This article argues, first, that we must understand Maritain and Alinsky's friendship to properly appreciate the legacy of Maritain's political thought and, second, that understanding the complementarity of their approaches allows us to see that together these two friends present a powerful strategy for democratic renewal. After surveying their friendship, the article presents two insights from their work about community organizing as the pursuit of democratic justice and addresses an objection about Alinsky's methods. The article concludes with the case study of an interfaith community organization to show how it applies Alinsky's methods and embodies the political and ethical values Alinsky and Maritain supported in common.

Jacques Maritain's commitment to the cause of democracy received robust expression in the teachings of Pope John XXIII, Pope Paul VI, and the Second Vatican Council. After Maritain died in 1973, his ideas, though never forgotten, became less prominent and influential in Catholic social theory and action. Yet to read his political writings today, fifty years after his death, is to be reminded of his trenchant diagnoses of the ills besetting modern democracies. Many readers will be impressed that his ideas—about the content of the common good, the need for political heroism from both leaders and ordinary citizens, and the indispensable role of Christian action in the renewal of community—remain as important and inspirational as ever.

Maritain's ongoing relevance in this regard can be made clear by attending to a less well-known element of his political thinking: his support for grassroots community organizing. Maritain's masterworks of political philosophy—*The Rights of Man and Natural Law* (French, 1942; English, 1943), *Christianity and Democracy* (French, 1943; English 1944), *The Person and the Common Good* (French and English, 1947), and *Man and the State* (English, 1951)—are pitched at a high level: he is addressing the worldwide clash of ideologies, the general principles upon which national and international governance should be based, and the reasons Christian philosophy supports pluralist democracy. While he addresses specific political problems and applications throughout his writings, his task was never to lay out the practical methods by which politicians, citizens, social activists, and churches were to enact social change. Maritain was a philosopher, and he left the applications to those with the expertise.

The person with such expertise in whom Maritain placed the greatest stock was his dear, longtime friend, Saul Alinsky. It might seem unlikely that the gentle, scholarly, French-born Catholic philosopher was friends with this confrontational, pragmatic, American secular Jewish activist. Nonetheless, the two men maintained a close relationship for thirty years through letters and occasional visits. They expressed admiration for each other's efforts for justice, championed each other's publications, and cited each other in their own books. In a newspaper review of Alinsky's 1946 book *Reveille for Radicals*, Maritain predicted that it would be "epoch-making," and wrote in a personal letter to Alinsky that he considered *Rules for Radicals* (1971) as "history-making."[1] Hence, one of the greatest Catholic political philosophers of the twentieth century had tremendous respect for Alinsky and his methods of community organizing. Similarly, Alinsky collaborated with Bernard James Sheil, a Catholic auxiliary bishop of Chicago, and others to establish the Industrial Areas Foundation in 1940. The Industrial Areas Foundation trained generations of faith-based community organizers—including Catholic activists such as Edward T. Chambers, Ernesto Cortes, Jr., Cesar Chavez, and Dolores Huerta—and spawned numerous networks of interfaith community organizations whose grassroots work for social justice continues to this day.

The argument that follows is twofold. First, we must understand the friendship of Maritain and Alinsky to properly appreciate the legacy of Maritain's political thought. Second, understanding the complementarity of their approaches—Maritain focused on theory, Alinsky on praxis—allows us to see that together these two friends

---

[1] Quoted in *The Philosopher and the Provocateur: The Correspondence of Jacques Maritain and Saul Alinsky*, ed. Bernard Doering (Notre Dame, IN: University of Notre Dame Press, 1994), 18, 110.

present a powerful strategy for democratic renewal in societies currently riven by political polarization. After surveying their friendship, this essay presents two insights from their work about community organizing as the pursuit of democratic justice and addresses an objection about Alinsky's methods. Finally, a case study illustrates how current interfaith community organizing manifests the insights of Maritain and Alinsky and shows promise for addressing the current crisis of participatory democracy.

The crisis is as follows: much social power is concentrated in the hands of political and economic elites, and those with power, including control of partisan mass and social media, effectively turn citizens against each other. Citizens become fragmented and angry, and fight over agendas shaped by culture warriors instead of making common cause over shared needs and interests.[2] Commonly termed "political polarization," this crisis is parasitic upon the imbalance of power between elites and ordinary citizens. Many countries around the world are experiencing political polarization and a related rise in populist nationalism, but the focus here will be on the US context. Elites left to their own devices have little interest in practicing a politics of the common good. Community organizations carry the promise of forcing them to do so. That activity—which in this essay I variously call "democratic renewal," "the pursuit of democratic justice," "democratic practices," or "democratic politics"—is what Maritain and Alinsky together show to be necessary and possible.

TWO MEN AND THEIR FRIENDSHIP

Readers of this essay likely possess a basic familiarity with the outline of Maritain's life, but it will be helpful to summarize Alinsky's work before he met the French philosopher.[3] Born in 1909, Alinsky has been called the "dean of community organizing" in the United States.[4] He organized the disenfranchised, usually but not exclusively in urban neighborhoods, to vigorously shame and relentlessly annoy the elites until they agreed to give protesters a share of their power.

---

[2] I am painting this summary with a very broad brush. Among recent books with sensible and accessible analyses of these matters, see Keith Payne, *The Broken Ladder: How Inequality Affects the Way We Think, Live, and Die* (New York: Penguin, 2018) and Peter T. Coleman, *The Way Out: How to Overcome Toxic Polarization* (New York: Columbia University Press, 2022).

[3] The definitive biography of Maritain and his wife is Jean-Luc Barré, *Jacques and Raïssa Maritain: Beggars for Heaven*, trans. Bernard E. Doering (Notre Dame, IN: University of Notre Dame Press, 2005). For Alinsky, it is Sanford D. Horwitt, *Let Them Call Me Rebel: Saul Alinsky, His Life and Legacy* (New York: Knopf, 1989).

[4] This epithet for Alinsky is found in many sources, but its origin is unclear; one foundational source is Harry C. Boyte, *Community Is Possible: Repairing America's Roots* (New York: Harper & Row, 1984), 39.

The fundamental goal of all community organizing is to develop enduring *power* in the community to make its own changes. As explained by veteran organizer Michael Gecan:

> It's all just talk—this use of the word "power," just like so many other rhetorical claims—unless it is reinforced by the habit and practice of organizing. That's why, when we are called by the neighborhood or religious leaders of a city, we tell them that we won't come to solve a housing problem or an education problem or a low-wage problem. No, we say we'll try to help them solve a more fundamental problem—a power problem. No matter how terrible the conditions may be and no matter how intense the current crisis, we will spend a year or two or three with them *not* addressing these immediate and important issues and concerns. We'll use that time to build the organization and to develop a firm base of power, so that the group will someday have the punch and impact needed to instigate and preserve lasting change.[5]

"Many Jewish sons of immigrants picked up radical politics with their mother's milk; not so with Alinsky," writes one commentator.[6] Alinsky picked up his interest in urban problems much later, when taking sociology courses at The University of Chicago. He did research on juvenile delinquency and organized crime under the direction of sociologists pioneering ethnographic methods. Alinsky said of his time studying crime, "I learned, among other things, the terrific importance of personal relationships."[7] The sociologist Clifford Shaw hired Alinsky to help put together the Chicago Area Project, which "unlike traditional settlement house efforts . . . placed trained professionals like Alinsky in support, not leadership, roles."[8] Alinsky worked in the now-famous Back of the Yards Neighborhood, near meat-packing plants. Because the Chicago Area Project avoided labor organizing and other politically contentious matters, Alinsky grew disenchanted. In response, in 1940 he cofounded the Industrial Areas Foundation to continue working in the Back of the Yards Neighborhood with his own methods.[9]

For Alinsky, community organizing meant connecting with and building up indigenous neighborhood institutions; that, in turn, required working with ethnic Catholics and parishes, as more than

---

[5] Michael Gecan, *Going Public: An Organizer's Guide to Citizen Action* (New York: Anchor, 2002), 9.
[6] John Clark, "Reveille for Alinsky," *Commonweal*, June 4, 1990, 360–361.
[7] Luke Bretherton, *Resurrecting Democracy: Faith, Citizenship, and the Politics of a Common Life* (New York: Cambridge University Press, 2015), 26.
[8] Clark, "Reveille for Alinsky," 360.
[9] Bretherton, *Resurrecting Democracy*, 30.

ninety percent of the neighborhood residents were Catholic.[10] Scholars widely agree that "critical to the success of Alinsky's first organization and all subsequent organizations was the foundational participation of the Catholic Church."[11] Although older priests in the neighborhood tended to be less supportive, younger priests were more enthusiastic. Several Chicago bishops lent strong support to the Industrial Areas Foundation over the years. Cardinal Joseph Bernardin, Monsignor George Higgins, and others who founded the Catholic Campaign for Human Development in 1969 were influenced by their collaborations with Alinsky and their familiarity with his methods, and they openly credited him.[12]

The legacy of Alinsky, who died in 1972, is not easily summed up or quantified, but both supporters and critics alike have paid tribute to his organizational genius. Perhaps one of the most telling tributes is that Alinsky's name continues to strike fear and loathing in the hearts of activists on the far right, even as some of them use his methods of face-to-face meetings and creative publicity-seeking. Alinsky published two books describing these methods, which serve as bookends for his life's work.[13] *Reveille for Radicals,* published in 1946, catapulted him to national attention. The book focuses on his philosophy of radicalism and its democratic roots. He tells stories about community organizing and lays out ambitious plans for the creation of People's Organizations, intended to connect all the civic, religious, and business institutions within a community. *Rules for Radicals* came out in 1971. Focusing less on an underlying philosophy, this later book conveys the strategies for which Alinsky is famous or infamous, such as "ridicule is man's most potent weapon" and "pick the target, freeze it, personalize it, and polarize it."[14] Critics focus more on *Rules* because the later-written book provides juicier sound bites. Yet to a fair-minded reader, the books are highly consistent in presenting Alinsky's philosophy and methods. One can

---

[10] Lawrence J. Engel, "The Influence of Saul Alinsky on the Campaign for Human Development," *Theological Studies* 59, no. 4 (1998): 637, n. 11, doi.org/10.1177/004056399805900403.

[11] Engel, "The Influence of Saul Alinsky," 637.

[12] Engel, "The Influence of Saul Alinsky," 641–643.

[13] Saul D. Alinsky, *Reveille for Radicals* (Chicago: The University of Chicago Press, 1946); paperback ed. with new afterword (New York: Vintage, 1969) and *Rules for Radicals: A Practical Primer for Realistic Radicals* (New York: Random House, 1971; paperback reissue, New York: Vintage, 1989). Alinsky's other published book was a biography of the longtime president of the United Mine Workers union, *John L. Lewis: An Unauthorized Biography* (New York: Putnam, 1949).

[14] Alinsky, *Rules for Radicals*, 128, 130.

often look to the earlier book to clarify what Alinsky most likely intended by his provocative statements in the later book.

Exiled in the United States during World War II, Jacques Maritain met Alinsky sometime in the early 1940s, "probably through George N. Schuster, former editor of *Commonweal* and later chair of the board of trustees of the Industrial Areas Foundation."[15] From the start, "the two men recognized their profound intellectual affinities. Whenever they met, they spent long hours exploring the democratic dream of people working out their own destiny," writes Bernard Doering, the Maritain scholar who collected the correspondence between the two in a 1994 book appropriately titled, *The Philosopher and the Provocateur*. Even though they managed to see each other in person only occasionally, their friendship was very significant to both of them. When Maritain was visiting the United States for the last time in 1966, in declining health, he insisted on visiting three friends, no matter what effort it took: John Howard Griffin, the author of *Black Like Me*, Thomas Merton, and Saul Alinsky. He was able to visit all three.[16]

In their correspondence, running from 1945 to 1971, Maritain and Alinsky show tender affection as well as support for each other through the challenges each encountered in their personal and professional lives. A particularly poignant moment is when Saul's first wife Helene died on September 2, 1947, in a drowning accident while saving her daughter and another child caught in an undertow on Lake Michigan. Less than two weeks later, Alinsky wrote to Maritain, "It is unbearable for me to discuss what has happened. . . . Helene and I were madly in love with each other for every minute of our 18 years together. . . . [How I will continue on] is one of those things that time will tell, and right now time is a terrible thing. There is nothing more to say. I send you and Raïssa what love there is left inside me."[17] Maritain wrote back:

> My beloved Saul, our hearts are full of your distress and agony, and what is our love capable of, unless suffering with you? Everything human is powerless in the face of such a tragedy, there is no help on earth. We pray for you.

---

[15] Doering, "Introduction," in *The Philosopher and the Provocateur*, xviii.
[16] Doering, "Introduction," in *The Philosopher and the Provocateur*, xxx; see also Barré, *Jacques and Raïssa Maritain*, 434–436.
[17] Alinsky to Maritain, 15 September 1947, in Doering, *The Philosopher and the Provocateur*, 32–33.

Saul, she died in love and by love. She saved the children. She accomplished at once what we are gropingly trying to learn: to die for those we love . . .

You cannot be consoled, every fiber of happiness in you has been struck by lightning. Dear Saul, the gift of yourself to others, the work to which you have been assigned, requires you now more than ever . . .

Saul, pardon my poor infirm words. I and Raïssa we love you, we embrace you.[18]

The collected correspondence of Maritain and Alinsky is a lovely testament to friendship across the miles and years, across differences in faith and personality, anchored by shared moral commitments, intellectual fervor, and deep respect for each other and other human beings as unique persons. Why the friendship between Maritain and Alinsky mattered to each—and should matter to those interested in social justice and democratic renewal—is well expressed by Patrisse Cullors, the cofounder of the Black Lives Matter Global Network, in her handbook for making social change: "Interpersonal relationships are important because they are how we build our communities, and healthy connections to other human beings build strong societies."[19] This quote is a contemporary expression of Aristotle's ancient insight that "friendship would seem to hold cities together."[20] Or, as Maritain might have put it, friendship is both the form of the common good and the path to it.

FIRST INSIGHT: HUMANE REGARD

As one digs into the two men's publications and correspondence, two insights about community organizing as the pursuit of democratic justice come to light. The first is that community organizers strive to practice *humane regard*, reminding us that all social activism for justice and democratic politics should be grounded in this core value. In *Making Space for Justice*, political philosopher Michele Moody-Adams argues that "what we learn from progressive social movements could be transformative for political theory as well as for political practice." She offers this insight:

> A central element of the moral knowledge generated by social movements is that justice is never simply a matter of "respect for persons"

---

[18] Maritain to Alinsky, 4 October 1947, in Doering, *The Philosopher and the Provocateur*, 34–35.
[19] Patrisse Cullors, *An Abolitionist's Handbook: 12 Steps to Changing Yourself and the World* (New York: St. Martin's, 2021), 233.
[20] Aristotle, *Nicomachean Ethics*, VIII.1, trans. Terence Irwin (Indianapolis, IN: Hackett, 1999), 119.

but also demands compassionate concern for others' vulnerability to suffering. The combination of respect and compassionate concern is what I call humane regard, and injustice consists in a society's failure to extend humane regard to all those to whom it is due.[21]

Moody-Adams's argument, developed throughout her book, is that social movements are lived forms of moral inquiry that deepen our insights about the requirements of justice and the shape of democratic cooperation. The praxis of movements extends and enriches the overly rational accounts of justice produced by John Rawls and other political philosophers.

Against right-wing portraits of Alinsky as a Marxist, atheistic thug who stoked class warfare,[22] a fair-minded reading of the organizer's words and deeds show him to be a practitioner of humane regard. Alinsky was seized with a passion to protect the people he called "the Have-Nots" as well as the "Have-a-Little, Want Mores."[23] Despite this use of group-based terminology, he expresses respect for *each* person and *all* groups in their particularity. The beginning of *Reveille for Radicals* illustrates this well. Alinsky opens, "The people of America live everywhere from Back Bay Boston to the Bottoms of Kansas City. From swank Highland Park, Illinois, to slum Harlem, New York."[24] He continues for a few pages, surveying the cultural, ethnic, religious, and linguistic diversity of Americans, as well as the fact that there have always been conservatives, liberals, and radicals. The clash of these identities and ideologies creates the story of American democracy.

Then Alinsky suddenly asks the reader: "How do you feel about people? Do you like people?" He bores into how Americans often answer these questions in their hearts:

> You are white, native-born and Protestant. Do you like people? You like your family, your friends, some of your business associates (not too many of them) and some of your neighbors. Do you like Catholics,

---

[21] Michele Moody-Adams, *Making Space for Justice: Social Movements, Collective Imagination, and Political Hope* (New York: Columbia University Press, 2022), 1, 7.
[22] For an overview and explanation of this vitriol, see Dylan Matthews, "Who is Saul Alinsky, and Why Does the Right Hate Him So Much?," *Vox*, July 19, 2016, www.vox.com/2014/10/6/6829675/saul-alinsky-explain-obama-hillary-clinton-rodham-organizing. Interestingly, in less polarized times, conservative theologian Richard John Neuhaus said that in both of his books, "Alinsky attempted to channel radical impulses toward the fulfillment of an essentially Madisonian view of American democracy" ("Briefly Noted," *First Things*, April 1990, 58).
[23] Alinsky, *Rules for Radicals*, chap. 1.
[24] Alinsky, *Reveille for Radicals*, 3.

Irish, Italians, Jews, Poles, Mexicans, Negroes, and Chinese? Do you regard them with the warm feeling of fellow human beings or with a cold contempt symbolized in Papists, Micks, . . . [other ethnic slurs follow]? If you are one of those who think of people in these derogatory terms, then you don't like people.

You may object to this and say that you do not fall into this classification. You don't call people by such names. You are broad-minded and respect other peoples if they *know their place*—and that place is not close to your own affections. You feel that you are really very tolerant. The chances are that you are an excellent representative of the great American class of MR. BUT.[25]

Alinsky explains that "Mr. But" is the kind of person you meet in respectable society who says things like, "Now nobody can say that I'm not a friend of the Mexicans or that I am prejudiced, BUT—. Nobody can say that I am anti-Semitic. Why, some of my best friends are Jews, BUT—. . . . Anybody knows that I would be the first to fight against this injustice, BUT—."[26]

This is a remarkable passage for a popular book written at the end of World War II. More remarkable, to my mind, is that Alinsky continues his litany, calling out the ways Irish Catholics, Jews, African-Americans, Mexicans, and Polish people are prone to make the same justifications. His point is that being a member of an oppressed group does not let you off the hook. The higher calling, the personal virtue, is to love other people in the sense of respecting them and trying to get along with them—to love in deed and not just in word. Yet, being realistic about human nature and not much of a moralizer, Alinsky is asking, at minimum, that people stop being hypocrites.

This, then, is Alinsky's moral core: respect for other individuals, which he associates with the verbs "love" and "like." In Christian teaching, this moral core is known as the love command. For Maritain, love underlies every authentic human action for justice and exerts a moral power that orients social activism to its proper end, the common good. Maritain saw this authentic power working in and through Alinsky, even at his most confrontational. He wrote in a letter to his friend: "All your fighting effort as an organizer is quickened *in reality* by *love for the human being, and for God*, though you refuse to admit it."[27] In another letter, Maritain wrote:

---

[25] Alinsky, *Reveille for Radicals*, 6–7.
[26] Alinsky, *Reveille for Radicals*, 7–8.
[27] Maritain to Alinsky, 14 September 1964, in Doering, *The Philosopher and the Provocateur*, 106.

You—being a Jew (whom I consider a Christian at heart, a better Christian perhaps than I am) committed to the quest of justice on earth—are giving priority to the first of love's requirements, and offering your life for the temporal salvation and emancipation of mankind.... You act and fight also ... for the recovery by man of his inner, moral dignity—that is to say, finally, even if you do not have such a purpose in your mind, for his spiritual redemption.[28]

Maritain was nearing the end of his life when Karl Rahner developed the concept of "anonymous Christian";[29] while Maritain may not have known the term, that is essentially what he is calling Alinsky in these letters. Alinsky did not demur; he always kindly accepted Maritain's expressions of prayers and blessings.

Maritain similarly affirms that Christians and the church have a moral responsibility "to exist with the people," as he put it in the title of a 1953 essay. "*To exist with* is an ethical category. It does not mean loving someone in the mere sense of wishing him well; it means loving someone in the sense of becoming one with him, of bearing his burdens, of living a common moral life with him, of feeling with him and suffering with him."[30] The people are "the mass of non-privileged ones ... that moral community which is centered on manual labor ... [with] a certain way of understanding and living out suffering, poverty, hardship, and especially work itself ... a certain way of being 'always the same ones who get killed.'"[31] Because the people, the poor, were those whom Christ loved, and because they are the "mass" in which the vital life of a new civilization takes root, the church and its members are bound to them.

Alinsky's community organizing and Maritain's ecclesiology center on the virtue and praxis of humane regard. For Alinsky, organizing achieves nothing permanent if activists and the citizens they inspire do not genuinely love all other people. For Maritain, the church is not the church if its members do not genuinely love all other people. Both men were impatient with the hypocrisy of Christians who do not exist with and serve the people. In *Rules for Radicals*, Alinsky cautions organizers that it may be difficult for them to appeal to the

---

[28] Maritain to Alinsky, 5 November 1962, in Doering, *The Philosopher and the Provocateur*, 94.
[29] One of Rahner's earliest articles about his concept was "Anonymous Christianity," in *Theological Investigations,* vol. 6, trans. Karl-Heinz and Boniface Kruger (New York: Longman & Todd, 1969), 390–398.
[30] Jacques Maritain, "To Exist with the People," in *The Range of Reason* (London: Geoffrey Bless, 1953), 121.
[31] Maritain, "To Exist with the People," 122. It is not clear what Maritain is quoting here; he may just be citing a popular phrase.

moral beliefs of Christians they organize, for "here is a Christian civilization where most people have gone to church and have mouthed various Christian doctrines, and yet this is really not part of their experience because they haven't lived it. Their church experience has been purely a ritualistic decoration."[32] Maritain understood and approved Alinsky's criticisms of religious hypocrisy and inaction; in fact, in *Rules*, Alinsky used a quote from Maritain's *Man and the State*: "The fear of soiling ourselves by entering the context of history is not virtue, but a way of escaping virtue."[33] As Maritain wrote elsewhere, "The faith must be an actual faith, practical and living. To believe in God must mean to live in such a manner that life could not possibly be lived if God did not exist. Then the earthly hope in the Gospel can become the quickening force of temporal history."[34]

SECOND INSIGHT: SUBSIDIARITY *AND* SOLIDARITY THROUGH COMPROMISE *AND* CONFLICT

A second insight that arises from the praxis of community organizing is that two polarities can be held together: local action by civic groups is complemented by systematic policy action by the government, and the conflict generated by grassroots activism paves the way toward negotiated agreements in which each side compromises. To start with the first polarity, critics have tried to tar Alinsky with the label of statism. At minimum, the criticism goes, his views violate Catholic teachings on subsidiarity and overemphasize government solutions; at worst, Alinsky is a subtle or not-so-subtle communist. However, Alinsky's philosophy is thoroughly democratic. *Reveille for Radicals* discusses democracy and democratic ideals explicitly on about one-third of its pages. Two representative quotes are these:

> The Radical is deeply interested in social planning but just as deeply suspicious of and antagonistic to any idea of plans which work from the top down. Democracy to him is working from the bottom up.[35]

> Democracy is that system of government and that economic and social organization in which the worth of the individual human being and the multiple loyalties of that individual are the most fully recognized and provided for . . . loyalties to their churches, their labor unions,

---

[32] Alinsky, *Rules for Radicals*, 87.
[33] Alinsky, *Rules for Radicals*, 25–26; see Jacques Maritain, *Man and the State* (Chicago: The University of Chicago Press, 1951), 63.
[34] Jacques Maritain, "The Meaning of Contemporary Atheism," in *The Range of Reason*, 117.
[35] Alinsky, *Reveille for Radicals*, 17.

their fraternal organizations, their social groups, their nationality groups, their athletic groups, their political parties, and many others. Democracy provides for the fulfillment of the hopes and loyalties of our people to all of the various institutions and groups of which they are a part.[36]

By contrast, in both *Reveille* and *Rules*, there are very few mentions of communism, socialism, and thinkers associated with these ideologies; such mentions are usually just descriptive, and sometimes they are critical. Alinsky once said in an interview, "I've never joined any organization—not even the ones I've organized myself. I prize my own independence too much. And philosophically, I could never accept any rigid dogma or ideology, whether it's Christianity or Marxism."[37]

There is plenty of evidence in Alinsky's writings and actions to show that even milder concerns about his supposed statism are misplaced. The just-quoted statements about democracy working from the bottom upward and providing for the fulfillment of people's group loyalties are consonant with Catholicism's principle of subsidiarity and its respect for mediating institutions. Like Catholic social theorists, Alinsky balances appeals to subsidiarity with appeals to solidarity; for instance: "The Radical . . . is that person to whom the common good is the greatest personal value. He is that person who genuinely and completely believes in mankind. The Radical is so completely identified with mankind that he personally shares the pain, the injustices, and the sufferings of all his fellow men."[38] Based on this philosophy, Alinsky spends a remarkable amount of space in *Reveille* criticizing labor organizations and leaders of his day for such flaws as practicing racial segregation, becoming inward-looking special interest groups, and failing to challenge the structures of state capitalism.

The center of gravity in community organizing is the grassroots. The work of organizing is building group solidarity through interpersonal relationships. The entire goal is to facilitate ordinary people's ability to forge grassroots solutions to their problems. Community organizing is a viable way of implementing the "see, judge, act" pastoral process as recommended by Catholic social thinkers. For Alinsky, as for Catholic social thought, the full promise of political and economic democracy will involve structural changes

---

[36] Alinsky, *Reveille for Radicals*, 85–86.
[37] Eric Norden, "Saul Alinsky: *Playboy* Interview (1972)," *Scraps from the Loft*, May 1, 2018, scrapsfromtheloft.com/comedy/saul-alinsky-playboy-interview-1972/.
[38] Alinsky, *Reveille for Radicals*, 15.

and social planning, but through initiatives that emerge from the bottom up. The bottom-up approach makes personal character and interpersonal relationships important for its success. A sense of responsibility to others and the ability to compromise are not mere tools for the success of a political program; they are the qualities we should want to characterize our social relationships. "A society devoid of compromise is totalitarian," Alinsky writes. "If I had to define a free and open society in one word, the word would be 'compromise.'"[39]

According to Luke Bretherton, in his ethnographic-ethical study of faith-based community organizations in the United Kingdom, Alinsky-style organizing supplements this civil conception of politics with a more conflictual conception. What kind of conflict? Not violence, for sure. Alinsky-style conflictual politics employs such methods as naming and shaming the entity that needs to change—such as a business or city council—through dramatic public actions and other forms of protest. The goal is to annoy, frustrate, cut into the profits of, and generate negative publicity about those in power, to make them implement the changes those with less power are seeking. In this way, those organizing and demonstrating are developing *relational power*. Relational power changes the dynamic from one where the wealthy have "power over" the poor, to one where citizens have "power with" each other and "to get things done collectively."[40]

This mix of conflict and compromise remains healthily democratic because it is ultimately directed toward the common good. Bretherton labels this understanding of political life as *consociational* or *confederal*. A consociational polity "is made up of a plurality of interdependent, self-organizing associations."[41] The common good of a consociational polity does not require angelic consensus and an absence of conflict. Maritain often points out that democracy is imperfect, since it is an association of imperfect human beings: "Democracy can be awkward, messy, clumsy, defective, open to the risk of betraying itself by yielding to instincts of cowardice, or of oppressive violence.... Yet democracy is the only way through which the progressive energies in human history do pass."[42] In *Reflections on America*, Maritain singled out the American system of democracy as "in my opinion the best conceived and the most efficient (at least in

---

[39] Alinsky, *Rules for Radicals*, 59.
[40] Bretherton, *Resurrecting Democracy*, 136.
[41] Luke Bretherton, *Christ and the Common Life: Political Theology and the Case for Democracy* (Grand Rapids, MI: Eerdmans, 2019), 168.
[42] Maritain, *Man and the State*, 60.

the long run) among all existing democratic regimes," in part because it was not made for perfect beings.[43]

Maritain understood that, when guided by a commitment to the common good, willingness to engage in conflict is a necessary and valuable path to democratic justice. That is why he praises Alinsky's organizing work in these same pages of *Reflections on America*; he does so not simply because Alinsky's methods secure benefits for the working classes and poor neighborhoods, but because Alinsky patiently worked to build up genuine community among people.[44] Elsewhere Maritain expressed how much he admired "the spirit of self-effacement and combative generosity which is required from those who start these people's organizations.... The manner in which, starting from selfish interests, they succeed in giving rise to the sense of solidarity and finally to an unselfish devotion to the common task, conveys an invaluable teaching to us."[45] Fighting for justice from a position of self-interest and group-preference as an interim step on the journey to the common good is appropriate, perhaps necessary, for Christians as well. In a statement suggestive of Rev. Martin Luther King, Jr. on the "creative tension" generated by nonviolent civil disobedience, Maritain wrote, all the way back in 1939, "The work the Christian has to do is to keep up and to increase in the world the internal tension and movement of slow and painful deliverance, a tension and movement due to the invisible powers of truth and justice, of goodness and love, acting on the mass which is opposed to them."[46]

ADDRESSING AN OBJECTION: THE PROBLEM OF MEANS

Although Maritain and Alinsky each accepted that grassroots action for justice is by turns conflictual and conciliatory, the friends

---

[43] Jacques Maritain, *Reflections on America* (New York: Charles Scribner's Sons, 1958), 170.
[44] Maritain, *Reflections on America*, 165.
[45] This quote is from a review of *Reveille for Radicals* Maritain published in the *New York Post* and sent to Alinsky in an October 9, 1945, letter. The review is reprinted in full in Doering, *The Philosopher and the Provocateur*, 18–20.
[46] Jacques Maritain, "Confession of Faith," in *The Social and Political Philosophy of Jacques Maritain*, ed. Joseph W. Evans and Leo R. Ward (London: Geoffrey Bles, 1956), 370. King wrote in his "Letter from Birmingham City Jail": "Nonviolent direct action seeks to create a crisis and establish such creative tension that a community that has constantly refused to negotiate is forced to confront the issue. It seeks so to dramatize the issue that it can no longer be ignored." King used this phrase here and there in his speeches and writings; one other direct discussion was when he was interviewed by *Playboy* magazine. For the "Letter" and the interview quotations, see James W. Washington, ed., *A Testament of Hope: The Essential Writings and Speeches of Martin Luther King, Jr.* (San Francisco: HarperSanFrancisco, 1986), 291, 514.

had very different ways of talking about that. Maritain was calm, rational, and systematic, while Alinsky was fiery, contrarian, and mercurial. The portrait of Alinsky as a class warrior certainly owes much to his provocative words. Conservative polemicists have taken those words out of context but, still, Alinsky gave them something to work with. Nowhere is this truer than on the topic of means and ends. Not only the polemicists, but also those with cooler heads, including Maritain himself, have concerns with how Alinsky addressed the relationship of means and ends. That Alinsky recommends an amoral or excessively consequentialist approach is an objection that must be addressed.

Alinsky's harshest critics all cite heavily from chapter 2 of *Rules for Radicals*. For instance, David Horowitz, the arch-conservative author, writes, "The most important chapter of Alinsky's manual is called '[Of] Means and Ends,' and is designed to address Alinsky's biggest problem: How to explain to radicals who think of themselves as creating a world of perfect justice and harmony, that the means they must use to get there are Machiavellian—deceitful, conniving, and ruthless?"[47] In my view, that is a wholly inaccurate description of Alinsky's intentions, even though this second chapter of *Rules* does sow confusion. It is the one part of the book that bothered Maritain, although he praised the book as a whole. In a long letter gratefully acknowledging his receipt of an inscribed copy as a gift, Maritain spends several pages pushing back on Alinsky's discussion of means and ends which, he says, makes him "jumpy."[48]

In the chapter in question, Alinsky frames the issue by stating, "That perennial question, 'Does the end justify the means?' is meaningless as it stands; the real and only question regarding the ethics of means and ends is, and always has been, 'Does this *particular* end justify this *particular* means?'"[49] The chapter as a whole names and illustrates eleven "rules" for the ethics of means and ends. The chapter is maddening because it is never clear when Alinsky is speaking normatively and when he is speaking descriptively. Often he is describing the way human social nature works, such as in his second rule, "The judgment of the ethics of means is dependent upon the political position of those sitting in judgment."[50] The point here is that those in power will claim moral superiority for what they do,

---

[47] David Horowitz, *Barack Obama's Rules for Revolution: The Alinsky Model* (Sherman Oaks, CA: David Horowitz Freedom Center, 2009), 44.
[48] Maritain to Alinsky, 19 September 1971, in Doering, *The Philosopher and the Provocateur*, 111.
[49] Alinsky, *Rules for Radicals*, 24.
[50] Alinsky, *Rules for Radicals*, 26.

regardless. At other times, Alinsky is prudentially stating how the means have to be rhetorically framed to be effective, as in his tenth rule, "You do what you can with what you have and clothe it with moral garments."[51] At yet other times he is speaking normatively, as when he says, in conjunction with the fifth rule, "To me ethics is doing what is best for the most."[52] These are my interpretations of when Alinsky is speaking descriptively, prudentially, and normatively, as he does not signal his interpretations or when he might be shifting the discourse.

Maritain reads the chapter similarly. In his letter, he reminds Alinsky that there are two different truths involved in this matter. The first is a philosophical truth that some means, such as torture or killing the innocent, cannot be justified by any end. The second is a truth of human experience that "moral justifications . . . are, in an immense number of cases, but a mask used to hide . . . often the vilest motivations." Maritain continues, "The second truth you see with such keenness, and you emphasize it so strongly that it seems sometimes to be the only one compatible with a realistic approach."[53] Maritain believes his old friend is not truly saying that, in principle, any and all means could be justified, but rather calling out hypocrisy with his characteristic frankness. According to one interpreter, Jacques is essentially saying here, "You know better than that, Saul."[54]

Some years before, in *Man and the State*, Maritain had devoted the entire second chapter to "the problem of means" which, he said, "is a basic, *the* basic problem in political philosophy."[55] He lays out in careful detail the distinction he wrote about to Alinsky, which allowed him to feel comfortable with the book. In fact, Maritain articulates several distinctions and identifies different situations in which the problem of means appears, each with its own nuances. One situation is that of pressure groups. Maritain discusses their tactics of pressure and agitation in the context of how people in a free society assert their control over the state. Pressure methods exist alongside methods such as voting and political speech. Pressure tactics are "normal" but "questionable" as a means of *standard* popular control; rather, they are "the flesh-and-blood means of political warfare" used "in certain

---

[51] Alinsky, *Rules for Radicals*, 36.
[52] Alinsky, *Rules for Radicals*, 33.
[53] Maritain to Alinsky, 19 September 1971, in Doering, *The Philosopher and the Provocateur*, 111–112.
[54] C. J. Wolfe, "Lessons from the Friendship of Jacques Maritain with Saul Alinsky," *Catholic Social Science Review* 16 (2011): 238, doi.org/10.5840/cssr20111620.
[55] Maritain, *Man and the State*, 54.

critical moments."[56] A bit later, Maritain praises "the means of spiritual warfare" such as those practiced by Gandhi. Anticipating how Dr. King and the Civil Rights Movement would take up these means, Maritain says they are the way Christians "transform society by making it actually Christian, actually inspired by the Gospel."[57]

Maritain was supportive of King's nonviolent methods of civil disobedience and recommended them in a letter to Alinsky as congenial to his own methods.[58] Alinsky was somewhat cool to King's methods, finding them not feisty enough, at least for the contexts in which he was working; he was likely also somewhat jealous of King's popularity.[59] Alinsky never advocated violence; he simply was willing to use methods of shaming and ridicule against business leaders and politicians if milder methods were not availing. It is important to note as well that Alinsky devotes a whole chapter of *Rules* to communication as a two-way process of talking and listening and never getting ahead of where the people are, and he says that the door always has to be open for compromise with the opponent.[60] This latter stance is expressed in one of the mantras of community organizing: "No permanent enemies, no permanent friends, just permanent interests." Community organizers should be focused on the interests of the people in order to improve their lives and should be flexible in making new alliances with those willing to help the people achieve their goals.

MARITAIN'S AND ALINSKY'S INSIGHTS AND COMMUNITY ORGANIZING TODAY

This final section gives an example of a community organization to show how it practices Alinsky's methods and embodies the political and ethical values Alinsky and Maritain supported in common. Congregations Organized for a New Connecticut (CONECT) is one of three major interfaith community organizations in Connecticut, based in the south-central region of the state. In keeping with the Catholic focus of this journal and Maritain's philosophy, I will highlight how

---

[56] Maritain, *Man and the State*, 66.
[57] Maritain, *Man and the State*, 70.
[58] Maritain to Alinsky, 14 September 1964, in Doering, *The Philosopher and the Provocateur*, 105–107.
[59] Such was the opinion of Alinsky's associate Ralph Helstein, who met periodically with King and often tried to get Alinsky to partner with him. See Horwitt, *Let Them Call Me Rebel*, 470–471.
[60] Alinsky, *Rules for Radicals*, 59, 81–97.

CONECT's history and current activities are intertwined with the history and activities of the local Catholic Church.[61]

Founded in 2011, CONECT grew out of an earlier network, Elm City Congregations Organized, dating back to the 1990s. Peter Rosazza, now emeritus auxiliary bishop of the Archdiocese of Hartford, was a central figure in the birth of Elm City Congregations Organized and has strongly supported CONECT over the years. CONECT was an IAF organization[62] having received funding from the local and national Catholic Campaign for Human Development. Among its current thirty-nine member institutions—mostly congregations comprising Catholic, Protestant, Muslim, Jewish, Sikh, Friends, and Unitarian communities—are four Catholic parishes and the Office of the Auxiliary Bishop of the Archdiocese of Hartford.[63] Five of the nineteen members of the combined executive and strategy team are Catholic.[64]

Like other Alinsky-style organizations, CONECT builds power through "organized people and organized money," to cite one of its mantras; the latter part of the phrase refers to institutional dues. CONECT also strengthens its power through building relationships within and among congregations, training emerging congregational leaders, collaborating with allied organizations, and developing relationships of mutual accountability with elected officials. CONECT organizers develop solidarity by engaging people in face-to-face conversations to learn about what social concerns these people face—what problems "keep them up at night," a phrase the organizers often use. CONECT congregational leaders conduct house campaigns at the start of a roughly two-year organizing cycle, to gather and filter these concerns into larger, cross-congregational forums at which public policy objectives or other concrete goals are formulated. To ensure that their policy aims are effective and achievable, CONECT has two standing task forces—one on health and mental health issues and one on criminal justice reform—to research problems and solutions. CONECT then holds large assemblies of several hundred members to which elected officials are invited; during election

---

[61] CONECT member organizations are largely located in New Haven county and Fairfield county. The Archdiocese of Hartford covers New Haven, Hartford, and Litchfield counties, and the Diocese of Bridgeport covers Fairfield county. Thus, CONECT straddles two dioceses, but its relationship to the Archdiocese of Hartford is stronger and more direct.
[62] Until just recently; now it is independent.
[63] CONECT, "Who We Are," weconect.org/about/.
[64] CONECT, *Celebrating 10 Years of Impact*, November 2021, 7, weconect.org/wp-content/uploads/2021/11/CONECT-10year-FINAL-Digital.pdf.

seasons, they hold candidate forums. In either case, on every specific issue, a CONECT member will present powerful personal testimony to the politicians, state the specific policy goal of the organization, and ask politicians to clearly state "yes or no" as to their support for the policy, with a limited amount of time to explain their answer.

Through this method, CONECT has won policy changes that benefit all citizens, including their member churches, lifting poor and marginalized citizens to participate more fully in society. Their two most recent policy victories, in 2021, were (1) the passage of a state bill to provide for the standardized collection of Race, Ethnicity, and Language (REaL) data on healthcare, to identify and address racial inequities across healthcare in Connecticut; and (2) the passage of "Clean Slate" legislation, which issues the automatic erasure of criminal records for certain convictions after a set period of time for individuals who remain free of the criminal justice system upon release from custody. This commonsense reform in the justice system allows citizens who have successfully returned to society to have improved opportunities for employment and housing. The governor signed this bill into law on June 10, 2021, making Connecticut only the fourth state in the nation to adopt a Clean Slate law. Over the past decade, CONECT has also played a key role in supporting the national "Do Not Stand Idly By" campaign for reducing gun violence; holding down health insurance rate increases; achieving measures to help immigrants safely integrate into local communities; promoting environmental protection; and passing legislation to protect minority and autistic students from excessive restraints.[65]

CONECT has shown itself to be motivated by humane regard, and it practices a strategy of grassroots solidarity to achieve public policy wins for the good of all people in the civic community. To recall, humane regard means unifying compassionate concern for others' vulnerability with larger, more abstract appeals for justice. CONECT builds its issues-agenda out of the lived experience of its members in their communities; throughout its work to win change, the organization highlights the personal stories beneath the issues. For instance, at a CONECT forum with candidates for statewide office in October, 2018, Kristin Song, the mother of Ethan Song, who died by a discharge from an unsecured handgun at a friend's house, told the story of her terrible loss and then put the candidates on record as to whether they supported the passage of Ethan's Law. This law, requiring citizens to safely secure guns in their homes, was signed into

---

[65] See CONECT, *Celebrating 10 Years*, for more on these and other achievements.

effect by the governor in June 2019.[66] As another example, the opportunity to listen to people affected by the lingering effects of misdemeanors strongly motivated CONECT members to work for passing the Clean Slate law.

Through grassroots organizing, CONECT identifies issues that affect the lives of ordinary people in the pews and the community. It advances issues having broad-based support its diverse members can endorse even if they disagree on other issues that tend to be divisive in culture wars. CONECT is thereby facilitating politics as a civic and civil activity, an expression of politics that is consociational and constructive. On the opposite side of the spectrum from this form of politics is what political scientist Eitan Hersh calls "political hobbyism."[67] Political hobbyism means following political news, websites, and podcasts and then complaining about issues to family and friends and in online forums. Hersh conducted a survey that found that one-third of Americans say they spend at least two hours a day involved in "politics," but for four-fifths of this group, this involvement consists solely of political hobby activities. Such activity is not real politics, argues Hersh—hobbyism does not serve others concretely, build coalitions, win votes, or convince other people to join a cause. All it does is make people angry in ways that are unhealthy for themselves and their local communities.

These examples demonstrate that CONECT's community organizing reflects the two insights of the Maritain-Alinsky alliance—humane regard and consociational politics. Its work also displays an ethical use of means. Like other Alinsky-style organizations, CONECT is transparent about its policy goals; it works with whoever is in office, regardless of party; it advocates for issues, not candidates; and it employs confrontational methods only when dialogue and collaboration are blocked by those in power. CONECT's two most confrontational activities have been challenging a local police department on its use of racial profiling and demonstrating against a restaurant that had been the site of repeated gun violence, eventually leading to the closure of the establishment when its liquor license was not renewed.[68]

---

[66] Joseph De Avila, "Ethan's Law in Connecticut Tightens Gun-Storage Requirements," *Wall Street Journal*, June 13, 2019, www.wsj.com/articles/ethans-law-in-connecticut-tightens-gun-storage-requirements-11560460960.

[67] Eitan Hersh, *Politics Is for Power: How to Move Beyond Political Hobbyism, Take Action, and Make Real Change* (New York: Scribner, 2020).

[68] See CONECT, *Celebrating 10 Years*, 10, 15; Mary O'Leary, "The Rev. James Manship of St. Rose of Lima in New Haven Reassigned to Meriden Parish," *New Haven Register*, May 14, 2017,

All CONECT's issue-based activities require some impingement on the interests of others. Often these impacts are quite minor and spread out, requiring the redirection of some public spending, the collection of data at the governmental level, or the practice of greater responsibility by citizens, as in the case of Ethan's Law. Such impingements are justified by the value of policy change for the common good. In the police profiling and unsafe restaurant cases, the violations of justice by certain actors were clear, and facts supported the need for accountability. CONECT used nonviolent methods to draw public attention to the injustices and mount public support for remediating problems through democratic avenues.

CONCLUSION

Charles Curran argued in a 1985 essay that Alinsky's community organizing method is a praxis for social justice originally distinctive to the United States and that it merited theoretical attention of theologians and ethicists similar to the attention they gave to the praxis of Latin American liberation theology. "Unfortunately," Curran claimed, "the theological and the ethical communities in Roman Catholicism have not reflected on this phenomenon."[69] Curran's article was attempting to give a platform for Alinsky's methods at a time when Maritain's endorsements were being forgotten and when Alinsky and community-organizing were not yet enjoying much scholarly attention in any discipline.

The paucity of reflection remained the case for roughly two decades, but fortunately, the new millennium has seen sociologists of religion and Christian ethicists paying more and more attention to community organizing. Many of those who write about community organizing are or have been active in the practice themselves. Sociologists, such as Richard L. Wood, have conducted ethnographic studies of faith-based community organizations and their practices of citizenship.[70] The work of Bretherton, straddling ethnography and theological ethics, has been noted above. In 2010, Jeffrey Stout published *Blessed Are the Organized*, which had a galvanizing effect

---

www.nhregister.com/connecticut/article/The-Rev-James-Manship-of-St-Rose-of-Lima-in-New-11313803.php.

[69] Charles E. Curran, "Saul D. Alinsky, Catholic Social Practice, and Catholic Theory," in *Directions in Catholic Social Ethics* (Notre Dame, IN: University of Notre Dame Press, 1985), 147.

[70] Richard L. Wood, *Faith in Action: Religion, Race, and Democratic Organizing in America* (Chicago: The University of Chicago Press, 2002) and, with Brad R. Fulton, *A Shared Future: Faith-Based Organizing for Racial Equity and Ethical Democracy* (Chicago: The University of Chicago Press, 2015).

on the religious study of community organizing.[71] Trained by ethicists such as Luke Bretherton, Gary Dorrien, and Stephen Pope, a younger generation of Christian ethicists are now devoting their research to community organizations.[72] In Catholic ethics, this generation includes Nicholas Hayes-Mota, whose complementary article on the Maritain-Alinsky alliance appears in this issue. Hayes-Mota has also argued that methods of relational accountability, used in broad-based community organizing, should be applied to the crisis of trust in the Catholic Church in the wake of the child sex abuse scandal.[73]

The only difference between Curran's wish in the mid-1980s and the recent burgeoning scholarly interest in community organizing is that there is not a large, explicitly Catholic subgenre in this literature. But that situation is fine, even preferable. Community organizing in the Alinsky style is interfaith, broad-based (involving many ethnic, racial, and social groups), and cross-institutional. The healthiest scholarly approach, then, is for thinkers from many religious traditions to articulate why their own tradition has a stake and role to play in pluralist democratic practices, and to encourage their coreligionists to become committed to collaborating with others in civic efforts. Such is the approach Maritain recommended when explaining why people intellectually divided by their fundamental beliefs nonetheless could and should support international human rights documents and UN peacebuilding efforts.[74]

Maritain and Alinsky reached outward from their own perspectives and learned from each other. From their dialogue we can take lessons. Alinsky's outlook can be appreciated as congenial to Catholic social thought, while providing challenges and corrections to its residual status-quo-ism. On the other side, Maritain's common good philosophy provides a guiding star to keep Alinsky-style organizing focused beyond the group's interests and directed to its stated higher civic goals. What Maritain saw in his friend's outlook was not class

---

[71] Jeffrey Stout, *Blessed Are the Organized: Grassroots Democracy in America* (Princeton, NJ: Princeton University Press, 2010).

[72] One of them is Aaron Stauffer; see "The Relational Meeting as a Political and Religious Practice," *Political Theology* 23, nos. 1–2 (2022): 167–173, doi.org/10.1080/1462317X.2021.1899704, and "Radical Democracy and Sacred Values: John Dewey's Ethical Democracy, Sheldon Wolin's Fugitive Democracy and Politics of Tending, and Cornel West's Revolutionary Christianity," *American Journal of Theology & Philosophy* 42, no. 2 (2021): 72–92, doi.org/10.5406/21564795.42.2.02.

[73] Nicholas Hayes-Mota, "An Accountable Church? Broad-Based Community Organizing and Ecclesial Ethics," *Journal of the Society of Christian Ethics* 43, no. 1 (2023): 111–128, doi.org/10.5840/jsce202342183.

[74] Jacques Maritain, "The Possibilities for Co-operation in a Divided World," in *The Range of Reason*, 172–184.

warfare or militant secularism, but a quest for justice animated by love of neighbor and, implicitly, love of God. Maritain offers an apologia for Alinsky, which should challenge some American Catholics' too-easy dismissal of Alinsky and his legacy as expressed in contemporary activist movements.

Moreover, all those who care about the fate of democracy have something to learn. In *Blessed Are the Organized*, Stout concludes that "the imbalance of power between ruling elites and ordinary citizens is the principal cause of democracy's current ills. . . . It can be set straight only if broad-based organizing is scaled up significantly, only if it extends its reach much more widely throughout American society than it has to date."[75] Edward Chambers, Alinsky's Catholic protégé who built enduring community organizations around the US, concludes his *Roots for Radicals* in a similar vein: "The traditional political parties will not work for the twenty-first century. . . . This century's refounders must create new instruments for public life based not on technology or science but on communal habits of the heart. New radical, nonpartisan, international assemblies must be created and fostered as countervailing institutions."[76] Will such scaling up happen? Of that, neither Stout nor Chambers is sure. But we can confidently conclude, with Maritain, that the messy practice of grassroots democracy "is the only way through which the progressive energies in human history do pass."[77] M

Brian Stiltner, PhD, is Professor of Theology and Religious Studies at Sacred Heart University, where he co-directs the Hersher Institute for Applied Ethics. He is author of *Toward Thriving Communities: Virtue Ethics as Social Ethics* (Anselm Academic, 2016). He is working on an ethnographic study about community bonding within churches and how this bonding affects local civic communities.

---

[75] Stout, *Blessed Are the Organized*, 286.
[76] Edward T. Chambers and Michael A. Cohen, *Roots for Radicals: Organizing for Power, Action, and Justice* (New York: Continuum, 2010), 137.
[77] Maritain, *Man and the State*, 60.

A Common World is Possible: Maritain, Pope Francis, and the Future of Global Governance

Kevin Ahern

Abstract: From planetary climate change to the COVID pandemic, the human family is faced with urgent challenges that transcend the borders of the traditional nation state. Here, the Catholic moral tradition, as embodied in different ways by the writings of Jacques Maritain and Pope Francis, offers constructive insights as to how the global political landscape should be organized. In the wake of the Second World War and the advent of the nuclear age, Jacques Maritain proposed a political philosophy for the creation of a future world state. Six decades later, Pope Francis offers a more pastoral argument for a more just, equitable, and fraternal world order. This paper examines the visions of global governance advocated by both Maritain and Pope Francis. Drawing from both figures, this paper identifies five key values that might guide the mobilization of the Catholic community as it works for a more just and common world order: a universal solidaristic vision centered on the human person that affirms the value of pluralism, a multi-layered structure of global governance, and bottom-up change through participation. Together, these values offer ethical guideposts as the international community considers how to reform the present system of global governance, including the United Nations system.

On February 23, 2022, Ambassador Vassily Nebenzi of the Russian Federation presided over the United Nations (UN) Security Council as his government launched a new military offensive against Ukraine. During the session, Ukraine's ambassador, Sergiy Kyslytsya, demanded that Nebenzi relinquish the rotating position of president and "pass these responsibilities onto a legitimate member of the Security Council, a member that is respectful of the charter."[1] Over the next few hours and

---

[1] Zoe Zaczek, "Ukraine's Representative to the United Nations Blasts Russia's Ambassador, Says It Is 'Too Late' for de-Escalation," *Sky News Australia*, February 24, 2022, www.skynews.com.au/world-news/ukraines-representative-to-the-united-nations-blasts-russias-ambassador-says-it-is-too-late-for-deescalation/news-story/70f75f01b1775a913d651b5909ce8cde.

months, the world watched in near helplessness as Russia intensified the conflict, threatening global grain and energy supplies, unleashing a humanitarian disaster, and eroding trust in the Security Council (UNSC) and wider UN system. A year later, after the brutal terrorist attacks by Hamas on October 7, 2023, and the beginning of Israel's highly criticized military response in Gaza, the UNSC again appeared unable to offer an adequate and timely response to an escalating regional conflict that resulted in a record number of deaths of UN aid workers. Efforts to address humanitarian concerns in the International Court of Justice and human rights bodies also failed to stop the conflict.

These latest spectacles at UN Headquarters come as the world confronts a growing number of what Kofi Annan once described as "problems without passports" that threaten the stability and security of people and the planet.[2] These transnational challenges include the COVID-19 pandemic, climate change, terrorist groups, and a fragile, unregulated global economy.

In the midst of this hyper-globalization, what might the Catholic moral tradition have to offer? Writing in two very different contexts, both Jacques Maritain and Pope Francis make compelling cases for greater global integration in the creation of a new just and peaceful world order. Both point to possibilities and moral priorities that can guide the development of a more just and virtuous way of organizing our common home. For Maritain, who experienced both the horrors of the Second World War and the hopeful creation of the UN, the answer, albeit a long-term goal, is a world state. Six decades later, Pope Francis offers a more immediate and pastoral vision. Unlike the French philosopher, Francis does not call for the creation of a world state—in the singular. Rather, he looks at how the systems of global governance can be strengthened, and power distributed more justly.

This paper explores these visions of global governance in four sections. Part one briefly outlines the present need for reforms to bridge gaps in the present multilateral infrastructure. The second and third parts consider the approaches proposed by Maritain and the current pope. The final section identifies five guiding principles at the convergence of both figures that might guide the mobilization of the Catholic community as it works for a more just and common world order, namely: a universal solidaristic vision centered on the human person that affirms the value of pluralism, a multi-layered structure of global governance, and bottom-up change through participation. Taken together, these values offer ethical guideposts for discernment among Catholics and other people of good will as the international community engages in new discussions over the reform and future of

---

[2] Kofi A. Annan, "Problems Without Passports," *Foreign Policy*, no. 132 (2002): 30, doi.org/10.2307/3183446.

global governance, including the United Nations system. But first, what is global governance?

GOVERNING GLOBALIZATION

The term "global governance" emerged in scholarly circles at the end of the Cold War and gained policy attention with the Commission on Global Governance (1992–1995). One early definition offered by Robert Cox describes it as "the procedures and practices which exist at the world (or regional) level for the management of political, economic, and social affairs."[3] These procedures and practices, like the proposals made to reform them, take different shapes, including models of centralized power in a world state, decentralized federations or unions of states, and systems based on looser multilateral coordination networks.

In considering global governance, two dimensions are often overlooked. First, while the term may be relatively new, efforts to envision "procedures and practices" to organize the world at a macro level are not. Medieval empires and European mercantilism, for instance, had their own models of how to manage affairs beyond the local level. Second, global governance has always incorporated input from non-state actors; as one analytical report put it: "government, though important, is not the totality of governance, let alone human experience."[4] Thus, the term "global governance," as Thomas Weiss and Rorden Wilkinson argue, serves as a useful analytical tool that invites a wider and more comprehensive look at the dynamic interplay of power and authority across time and space, and involving a range of actors.[5]

The normative and juridical perspectives that dominate the present approach to global governance, however, remain largely rooted in (or perhaps even constrained by) a post-Westphalian outlook that centers power in sovereign states. This can be seen, for example, in the *United Nations Charter*, which Robert Drinan described as "a compromise

---

[3] Robert W. Cox, "Introduction," in *The New Realism: Perspectives on Multilateralism and World Order* (Tokyo: United Nations University Press, 1997), xvi, www.catdir.loc.gov/catdir/description/hol055/96017550.html.

[4] Commission on Global Security, Justice, and Governance, *Confronting the Crisis of Global Governance* (The Hague: The Hague Institute for Global Justice, 2015), 13.

[5] Thomas G. Weiss and Rorden Wilkinson, eds., "Making Sense of Global Governance Futures," in *Global Governance Futures* (London: Routledge, 2021), 7–8. See also Timothy J. Sinclair, *Global Governance: Key Concepts* (Cambridge: Polity, 2012).

solution among nations too jealous of their own sovereignty to form a union of nations with real juridical enforceability."[6]

Increasingly, however, this system and the idea of state sovereignty are under pressure. There is a growing awareness of the power of agents that go beyond the state, including transnational corporations, nongovernmental organizations (NGOs), social media, and international criminal networks. "We are," as Maryann Cusimano Love argues, "in a period of transition." While it is unlikely that the sovereign state will soon disappear as the building block of planetary order, it remains unclear if it "can be retrofitted to weather the storms" as some corporations and media elites wield more power and wealth than many governments."[7]

Indeed, the tempests brought about by Russia's invasion of Ukraine, the pandemic, and climate change all reveal cracks in the current infrastructure. Even a cursory inspection exposes structural defects, or what Weiss has described as various kinds of gaps. First, there are *knowledge gaps*, evident in the failure to communicate information on the nature of transnational problems. The inability and/or unwillingness to share data on COVID infection rates or greenhouse gas emission levels, for instance, can have real impacts on the lives of peoples on the other side of the planet.

For Weiss, effective global governance is further hindered by *normative gaps*, which surface in the absence of agreed-upon values regarding global problems such as climate change. Action to address a global issue is nearly impossible without consensus on fundamental guiding values. Thirdly, even when there are adequate information about a problem and a shared set of values, there is *policy gaps* which inhibit the international community from agreeing on concrete principles, goals, and the steps needed to achieve them.[8] The failure to reach consensus on policies is linked to a fourth gap, the *institutional gap*, or the absence of effective and properly funded mechanisms to implement and assess selected policies.[9] Finally, all of this is exacerbated by *compliance gaps*. Constrained by absolute notions of state sovereignty, the present system relies on the voluntary will of states to comply with international norms, policies, and agreements. Ultimately, as Pope Benedict XVI points out, this means that the system often lacks "real teeth" (*Caritas in Veritate*, no. 67). Thus, if states, especially powerful states with veto power in the United

---

[6] Robert F. Drinan, "Pius XII's Legacy to World Federalism," *Catholic Lawyer* 6, no. 1 (1960): 14.

[7] Maryann Cusimano Love, ed., *Beyond Sovereignty: Issues for a Global Agenda*, 3rd ed. (Belmont, CA: Thomson Wadsworth, 2007), 339.

[8] Thomas G. Weiss, *Global Governance: Why? What? Whither?* (Malden, MA: Polity, 2013), 51.

[9] Weiss, *Global Governance*, 15.

Nations Security Council, choose to violate agreed upon norms, there is often little that can be done beyond naming and shaming.

Given the fragility and instability of the present infrastructure, what role can the Catholic tradition play? Strengthening global governance is not welcome in all sectors of the church. Some, especially those inspired by Christian realism, are concerned that governance structures are at far too much danger of being corrupted by human sinfulness and the interplay of power and self-interest at collective levels. Christian populists and Christian nationalists, for their part, oppose efforts that might limit the power and privileges of their own countries (e.g., America First). Sometimes these may coincide with widespread, and often antisemitic, conspiracy theories concerning global elites and the creation of a new world order. Still others, including strands of Catholic anarchism (e.g., Catholic Worker), oppose strengthening global governance out of a distrust for large scale governmental solutions.

Overall, however, the Catholic Church has proven to be a vocal supporter of more robust forms of global governance, and is engaged with these systems of governance on at least three levels. At the grassroots level, the Catholic Church has a wide global reach, with educational institutions and charitable networks in nearly every country. Here, it has enormous potential to both mobilize and educate citizens in support of systemic reforms and cooperate with the structures of global governance on the ground (e.g., humanitarian relief). Second, the Catholic Church has a long tradition of operating at the highest levels of policy development through the diplomatic work of the Holy See. Today, the Holy See maintains bilateral diplomatic relations with over 183 states, and multilateral relations with over forty intergovernmental organizations.[10] Finally, operating in a space between the grassroots and the Holy See are a range of international Catholic organizations and religious congregations, many with formal relations with the UN system.[11] Given the increasing pressures facing people and the planet today, how might this "Catholic potential" be mobilized to bridge some of the governance gaps enumerated above?

---

[10] "Bilateral and Multilateral Relations of the Holy See," The Holy See, October 22, 2009, www.vatican.va/roman_curia/secretariat_state/documents/rc_seg-st_20010123_holy-see-relations_en.html.

[11] See Kevin Ahern, "Mediating the Global Common Good: Catholic NGOs and the Future of Global Governance," in *Public Theology and the Global Common Good: The Contribution of David Hollenbach*, ed. Kevin Ahern, Meghan J. Clark, Kristin Heyer, and Laurie Johnston (Maryknoll, NY: Orbis Books, 2016), 14–25.

MARITAIN: FROM THE NEW CHRISTENDOM TO THE WORLD STATE

One potential source of guidance comes from Jacques Maritain (1882–1973), a figure uniquely positioned to develop a political philosophy of global governance. Maritain saw firsthand the dark side of humanity as he faced totalitarian and fascist governments in Europe, regimes that forced him and Raïssa, his Jewish-Catholic wife, into exile. Not content to remain a detached philosopher, he became involved directly in the efforts to reconstruct Europe and articulate new legal instruments on human rights and education, as Ambassador of France to the Holy See (1944–1948) and as head of the French delegation to the Second General Conference of the United Nations Educational, Scientific, and Cultural Organization (UNESCO). In this space of straddling philosophy and diplomacy, Maritain also contributed to the committee of philosophers who gave comments on the draft of the *Universal Declaration of Human Rights* (1948).

Influenced by Thomistic political philosophy, Maritain advanced a positive view of the government's role in the growing horizon of the common good. Before the Second World War, he looked beyond the borders of the nation state in his proposals for a "new Christendom." In *Humanisme intégral* (1936), Maritain proposes a (Eurocentric) path to democratically unite peoples across the continent based on shared Christian values and heritage.[12] In a series of articles in *Commonweal* magazine in 1940, the exiled philosopher widens this proposal. Assuming an Allied victory, Maritain endorses the idea of a federation of nations in Europe: "Truly our times require a complete recasting of the modern idea of the State and of the relations between States."[13] Such a federated entity, emerging from the ashes of destruction, he believed, would be the only way to preserve a lasting peace. As with *Humanisme intégral,* the *Commonweal* articles argue that a European federation would be possible given the shared (Christian) common past and "common spirit of civilization."[14] Importantly, in these articles, written more than a year before the Japanese attack on Pearl Harbor, he is less optimistic about anything larger than a European system: "It would also be illusory to suppose that at the end of the war the entire planet could enter into a federal régime which would forever guarantee universal peace. Those who spread such ideas . . . will be

---

[12] Jacques Maritain, *Integral Humanism, Freedom in the Modern World*, and *A Letter on Independence*, ed. and trans. Otto Bird (Notre Dame, IN: University of Notre Dame Press, 2012), 255. See also Jacques Maritain, *The Things That Are Not Caesar's* (New York: Charles Scribner's Sons, 1931).

[13] Jacques Maritain, "Europe and the Federal Idea (Part I)," *Commonweal*, April 19, 1940, 547; See also Jacques Maritain, "Europe and the Federal Idea (Part II)," *Commonweal*, April 26, 1940.

[14] Maritain, "Europe and the Federal Idea (Part I)," 545.

disappointed."[15] Within a decade, Maritain would become one of those evangelists.

Following his exile in the more pluralistic context of the United States and his post-war experiences working directly with diplomats and philosophers from dozens of countries and cultures, Maritain expands his earlier work with *Man and the State* (1951) in two significant ways. First, rather than focusing only on Europe, the philosopher employs a wider perspective in the wake of the devastation of the war, a disaster for humanity marked by both the Holocaust and the advent of nuclear weapons. Second, he moves away from the term "new Christendom" and exclusive appeals to a common Christian heritage. Instead, with nods to his Thomistic natural law framework, he looks to a shared understanding of human rights as a common unifying base. Already in 1941, Maritain expressed a more optimistic understanding of how people of different faiths could cooperate based on the "primordial ethical value of the law of brotherly love."[16] There are indeed, as he famously points out in acknowledging the universality of human rights, common bases among all peoples of different cultures and religions, so long as you don't ask "why?"[17] A decade later, he argues that people "belonging to very different philosophical or religious creeds and lineages could and should co-operate in the common task and for the common welfare of the earthly community."[18] In such a pluralist society, the Christian tradition would still have an important role to play, not as the unifying skeleton or imposed framework but as a "leaven" for justice.[19]

Maritain's progressive vision toward a worldwide political society is framed by important distinctions between the community, society, nation, state, and body politic. Briefly, the *community* is a fact, a product of reality as opposed to a *society*, which is an entity created by reason for a specific task. Thus, societies are created and shaped by the "voluntary determination of human persons" and can often lead to the creation of communities and community sentiments.[20] One of the most important societies for the creation of a nation is the *body politic*, a political society "required by nature and achieved by reason."[21] By

---

[15] Maritain, "Europe and the Federal Idea (Part I)," 545.
[16] Jacques Maritain, "The Achievement of Co-Operation among Men of Different Creeds," *Journal of Religion* 21, no. 4 (1941): 366.
[17] Jacques Maritain, *Man and the State* (Washington, DC: Catholic University of America Press, 1998; originally published in 1951), 77.
[18] Jacques Maritain, "The Pluralist Principle in Democracy," in *The Range of Reason* (New York: Charles Scribner's Sons, 1952), 166.
[19] Maritain, "The Pluralist Principle in Democracy," 170.
[20] Maritain, *Man and the State*, 4.
[21] Maritain, *Man and the State*, 10.

their very nature, Maritain argues, human persons need to come together to form such societies for the achievement of common tasks and the common good. The experience of working together and achieving concrete tasks solidifies a sense of shared meaning and can engender a wider sense of community.

Like Aquinas, Maritain sees the perfect society as one based on both justice and friendship, with an eye to the common good. The *state* is the instrumental part of the political society, specifically "concerned with the maintenance of law, the promotion of the common welfare and public order, and the administration of public affairs."[22] Importantly, the state has an instrumental role; it is not an end in itself, it is not the totality of public life, and it can change over time.

In this analysis, Maritain points to the United States as an example where the people of thirteen separate colonies consented to the common task of creating a common political society (body politic), to be served by institutional structures (the federal state). After years of struggle, joint enterprises and a civil war, the United States were able to form a nation. Similar developments took place in the development of modern European states, such as France or Germany, and some states emerging out of colonialization, including Tanzania. In these examples, communities of nations have come together in political societies for a specific task which has then resulted in the creation of multinational nations.[23] This, as history also reveals, is not always easy or possible.

For Maritain, a difference between the successful development of a body politic and an unsuccessful effort lies in the *people*, "the multitude of human persons who, united under just laws, by mutual friendship, and for the common good of their human existence, constitute a political society or a body politic."[24] As a society, the body politic must be willed by the people in order to take proper shape. In other words, if the people do not wish the creation of a body politic, then efforts to create institutions such as the state cannot be successful. Echoing Aquinas, a "political perversion" occurs when persons are put at the service of the state.[25] If persons form the political society and if the state is the instrument of that society, then the state should be at the service of persons and the common good, not the other way around.

These considerations lead him to envision the creation of larger and larger political societies, served by corresponding structures to appropriately tackle more complex problems. Indeed, *Man and the State* suggests an almost natural widening or growth in the

---

[22] Maritain, *Man and the State*, 12.
[23] Maritain, *Man and the State*, 8.
[24] Maritain, *Man and the State*, 26.
[25] Maritain, *Man and the State*, 13.

development of the body politic from smaller geographic units toward a more universal dimension, where the end result is a political society with a global scale and the creation of a world state.[26]

Not surprisingly, this proposal for something far more ambitious than the UN system was met with criticism by some philosophers and theologians. One of the earliest critiques, for example, came from the Jewish Hungarian philosopher Aurel Kolnai in a 1951 review of *Man and the State*. For Kolnai, unconvinced by Maritain's appeals to pluralism and democracy, the idea of creating a world state dangerously invites "the despotic rule of one massive totalitarian power."[27] Replacing the state with a world government, Kolnai worries, would "conjure up the specter of an infinitely worse Caesar."[28]

Writing almost seventy years later, Emily Butler Finley echoes Kolnai's concerns about totalitarianism and argues that Maritain's utopic vision downplays "the darker side of humanity that was taken seriously by earlier Christian political thought."[29] This overly optimistic proposal, she argues, underestimates the reality of sin, and contributes to what she identifies as Catholicism's turn "away from beliefs previously deemed central to the faith."[30] Ultimately, this romantic utopia, she contends, is "dangerous in the same way that other political ideologies are to the body politic."[31]

While critics are right to worry about the risk of totalitarianism in proposals for a world state, Maritain's proposal attends to the importance of keeping the instruments of the state in check. Drawing on his distinctions between state and body politic, Maritain is insistent that a world state can only ever come about following the creation of a corresponding political society. This, in other words, is a longer-term proposal with built in democratic checks and balances.

Here, the French philosopher takes inspiration from the work of the Committee to Frame a World Constitution, a group of scholars founded in 1945 at The University of Chicago, which included Maritain's friends Mortimer Adler and Chancellor Robert Hutchins. Like Maritain's articles in *Commonweal*, the Committee proposed a

---

[26] One could even apply Maritain's view to some fictional accounts of the future where the planet enters wider governmental systems with other worlds (e.g., the United Federation of Planets in the popular *Star Trek* series, Galactic Republic in *Star Wars*).

[27] Aurel Kolnai, "Between Christ and the Idols of Modernity," in *Privilege and Liberty and Other Essays in Political Philosophy*, ed. Daniel J. Mahoney (Lanham, MD: Lexington, 1999), 179.

[28] Kolnai, "Between Christ and the Idols of Modernity," 179.

[29] Emily Butler Finley, "Catholicism and Democratism: The Case of Jacques Maritain," *Journal of Church and State* 61, no. 3 (2019): 467, doi.org/10.1093/jcs/csy081.

[30] Butler Finley, "Catholicism and Democratism," 471.

[31] Butler Finley, "Catholicism and Democratism," 470.

federalist model of organizing a world state and released a *Preliminary Draft of a World Constitution* in 1948.[32] While Maritain was not among the authors of this draft, members of the committee were in dialogue with his work and Catholic Thomistic philosophy as they proposed the creation of a world state.

In 1949, Hutchins delivered the Aquinas Lecture at Marquette University on *St. Thomas and the World State*. In the lecture, he cites Maritain and argues that "according to the mind of St. Thomas, only the world state can now be the perfect community."[33] The creation of such a community, equipped with the power and enforceability of positive law, becomes even more urgent given the threats posed by nuclear weapons: "As war is inevitable in a world of sovereigns uncontrolled by positive law, so the destruction of civilization is inevitable if war breaks out after more than one nation has atomic weapons."[34] Though not Catholic, Hutchins summarizes the church's teachings and support for the idea of a global state and the tradition's resistance to notions of absolute state sovereignty. "The Catholic tradition," he argues, "points clearly toward the necessity of a world government. . . . Catholics . . . have always known that the society of nations can never be maintained in order and peace without the institution of positive law, giving determination, authority, and coercive power to the rule of natural law."[35]

In the last chapter of *Man and the State*, Maritain is clear that he is offering a "political philosophy" in dialogue with the committee, and cites Hutchins's text. Here, Maritain suggests two reasons for the development of a worldwide political society. The first is the growing economic interdependence of markets and the dangers such a system presents when deprived of a corresponding political society to regulate the international economy.[36] A second reason concerns the necessity to avert global warfare. With the advent of nuclear weapons, wars are no longer localized problems. Wars now have the ability to impact people around the world and can threaten humanity's very existence. The choice, as he suggests, is *"either a lasting peace or a serious risk of total destruction."*[37] This risk calls for the creation of spaces to meditate and resolve conflicts before they descend into war.

To help bring about this long-term project, Maritain proposes the creation of a "super-national advisory council."[38] This expert body or

---

[32] Committee to Frame a World Constitution, *Preliminary Draft of a World Constitution* (Chicago: The University of Chicago Press, 1948).
[33] Robert Maynard Hutchins, *St. Thomas and the World State* (Milwaukee, WI: Marquette University Press, 1949), 44.
[34] Hutchins, *St. Thomas and the World State*, 17.
[35] Hutchins, *St. Thomas and the World State*, 40.
[36] Maritain, *Man and the State*, 189.
[37] Maritain, *Man and the State*, 191.
[38] Maritain, *Man and the State*, 213.

think-tank would be separate from any existing structure, including the UN, and would not have any power, except "unquestionable moral authority."[39] According to Maritain, this group could be nominated by institutions and governments and elected by the peoples of the world. The members of the council would give up their national citizenship so as to be free from the interests of their own state.[40]

Such a body would need to confront both sovereignty and Machiavellianism. For Maritain, the notion of state sovereignty is "intrinsically wrong" as it turns the instrument of the political society into a kind of person and end in itself.[41] This, he argues, is a perversion with negative repercussions both internally and externally. Internally, if the state is perceived as a sovereign being, there is the risk that the rights of citizens will be suppressed by totalitarianism. In democratic societies, these extremes are ideally checked by opposition parties, the press, and popular associations. Externally, in international relations, however:

> there is nothing to check the trend of the modern States—to the extent to which they are infected with the Hegelian virus—toward supreme domination and supreme amorality, nothing except the opposite force of the other states. For there is no more powerful control, no organized international public opinion, to which these States can be submitted.[42]

Ultimately, absolute sovereignty places the state governments above both international law and the body politic. This concept allows for states to do what they want in international relations to protect their own self-interest (e.g., preventive war, torture) and avoid taking responsibility for humanitarian crises (e.g., Rwanda, Darfur). Ultimately, institutions grounded in this principle, such as the UN, are insufficient because they "cannot touch the root of the evil, and remain inevitably precarious and subsidiary, from the very fact that such institutions are organs created and put into action by the sovereign States, whose decisions they can only register."[43]

Maritain's sharp assessment of the dangers of absolute state sovereignty is linked to his concerns about Machiavellianism in international politics, where power and conquest are seen as the principal ends of politics. Such a conception, tied to false notions of sovereignty, can only lead to competitive and dangerous relations in

---

[39] Maritain, *Man and the State*, 213.
[40] In some ways, the group of "Elders" founded by Nelson Mandela in 2007 has demonstrated the potential of such a group to address some of the key problems facing the planet. See "Who We Are," The Elders, www.theelders.org/who-we-are.
[41] Maritain, *Man and the State*, 29.
[42] Maritain, *Man and the State*, 193.
[43] Maritain, *Man and the State*, 193.

the world. In this model, ethics, morality, and justice can, and should be put aside in favor of the accumulation of power. Even in its less radical form of Realpolitik, Machiavellianism also leads to a "radical pessimism regarding human nature" and the distrust of others who might be trying to take power from you.[44]

With *Man and the State*, Maritain develops and expands his previous political vision to offer a thoughtful political philosophy that would endorse the creation of a democratic and pluralistic world state. Building on the proposals made by his colleagues at The University of Chicago and the experience of the post-war context, he offers another model for organizing the world going beyond the temptation to Machiavellianism and appeals to absolute state sovereignty: a model that looks at politics with a more positive, justice-informed conception of the person. For him the end of politics is not power, as Machiavelli would argue, but "the common good of a united people; which end is essentially something concretely human, therefore something ethical."[45] To be effectively promoted and protected, this common good demands a more robust worldwide political society to be served by corresponding institutional structures, such as a world state.

While he remains grounded in Catholic Thomistic philosophy, Maritain eventually arrives at a universalistic approach that is a considerable development from the earlier European and Christian-centric models he proposed in the pages of *Commonweal*. In light of this development, how does his vision align with contemporary Catholic social teaching and the church's engagement as a transnational entity directly involved in multilateral debates on the future of global governance?

POPE FRANCIS AND THE GLOBALIZATION OF GOVERNANCE

Like Maritain, Pope Francis takes issue with modern conceptions of sovereignty, particularly as expressed in prevailing conceptions of borders. Unlike Maritain, however, Francis does not go as far as envisioning a world state in the singular. Rather, he advocates for more effective and equitable structures of global governance. This call for more robust forms of global governance appears in various ways throughout his pontificate, in formal encyclicals, World Day of Peace Messages, and meetings with governmental leaders. Whereas Maritain relies on a natural law foundation, Francis uses a more robustly scriptural basis with a key focus on universal siblinghood (fraternity/sorority). Here, he follows more than sixty years of Catholic social doctrine on the question of global governance. Around the same time as the publication of *Man and the State*, Pope Pius XII

---

[44] Jacques Maritain, "The End of Machiavellianism," in *The Range of Reason*, 136.
[45] Maritain, "The End of Machiavellianism," 142.

signaled his support for the UN and a more ambitious "world political organization . . . federal in form" as being in "harmony with the principles of social and political life so firmly founded and sustained by the church."[46] Subsequent popes developed this teaching in their social encyclicals and speeches to the UN. In *Pacem in Terris,* for example, Pope John XXIII argues for the creation of a "public authority with power, organization, and means" to address, promote, and protect the "universal common good" (nos. 135 and 137). This was followed by similar calls to support an empowered universal public authority in *Gaudium et Spes* (no. 84), *Populorum Progressio* (no. 78) and *Sollicitudo Rei Socialis* (no. 43).

In their visits to the UN General Assembly, Paul VI, John Paul II, and Benedict XVI offered, as Paul VI put it, "a solemn moral ratification of the work of the UN."[47] In 2008, for example, Benedict XVI explicitly calls for the strengthening of the UN and endorses the emerging framework of the Responsibility to Protect, a humanitarian framework that offers an important challenge to absolute state sovereignty. Citing this address, in *Caritas in Veritate* Benedict is more explicit than his predecessors in supporting UN reform so that "the concept of the family of nations can acquire real teeth" (no. 67). Such a change would entail *"giving poorer nations an effective voice in shared decision-making"* and strengthening the UN's "authority to ensure compliance with its decisions from all parties, and also with the coordinated measures adopted in various international forums" (no. 67). Absent such power, there is a risk that international law becomes "conditioned by the balance of power among the strongest nations" (no. 67).

In 2011, the Pontifical Council for Justice and Peace expanded on *Caritas in Veritate* with an official note calling for a reform of international financial systems. The text echoes many of the ideas developed by Maritain, making a compelling case for the need for an authority over globalization. "The time has come," it reads, "to conceive of institutions with universal competence. . . . The conditions exist for going definitively beyond a 'Westphalian' international order in which States feel the need for cooperation but do not seize the opportunity to integrate their respective sovereignties for the common good of peoples."[48] Rather than proposing the creation of a singular

---

[46] Quoted in Drinan, "Pius XII's Legacy to World Federalism," 11. See also Emile Guerry, *The Popes and World Government* (Baltimore, MD: Helicon, 1966).

[47] Paul VI, "Address to United Nations General Assembly," October 4, 1965, w2.vatican.va/content/paul-vi/en/speeches/1965/documents/hf_p-vi_spe_19651004_united-nations.html.

[48] Pontifical Council of Justice and Peace, *Towards Reforming the International Financial and Monetary Systems*, 2011, www.vatican.va/roman_curia/pontifical_councils/justpeace/documents/rc_pc_justpeace_doc_20111024_nota_en.html.

world state immediately, the text calls for several "sensible and realistic" steps, including taxes on international financial transactions, conditional recapitalization of national banks, and efforts to regulate and control the so-called shadow markets. The note concludes with a brief theological reflection on the Tower of Babel and its antithesis in the Pentecost experience, which should inspire Christians to go beyond division and "conceive of a new world with the creation of a world public Authority at the service of the common good."[49]

Since the beginning of his papacy in 2013, Pope Francis, like his predecessors, has drawn attention to the need for more legitimate and authoritative structures to address the cross-border challenges that threaten the human family. His magisterial teachings frequently reference the need to welcome migrants and refugees, abolish nuclear weapons, build bridges across ethnic, national, and religious groups, and develop concerted strategies to respond to global challenges.

Unlike Maritain, however, Francis's starting point is more scriptural and pastoral than philosophical. Since his visit to Lampedusa in 2013, the pope has appealed to the account of Cain and Abel to affirm the belief that all of us are brothers and sisters and have a solidaristic responsibility to each other regardless of nationality.[50] In 2015, he used St. Francis's *Canticle of the Creatures* to extend this biblical notion of siblinghood to "Sister, Mother Earth" (no. 1).[51] Released in the preparatory phase to both the 2015 UN Sustainable Development Summit and the Paris Climate Conference, *Laudato Si'* addresses questions of global climate governance.[52] While chapter six calls for personal ecological conversion through ecological education and spirituality, chapter five focuses on the structural and political changes needed to address the crisis. Here, the text takes stock of many positive developments, including the 1992 Earth Summit in Rio de Janeiro, and reads almost like a memo to those involved in climate diplomacy.

Commenting on the difficulty of mobilizing change, Francis, like Benedict before him, speaks of the need to bolster the authority of legally binding instruments to ensure action and not only words. A voluntary system with few or no consequences for sovereign states that fails to live up to promises cannot adequately address the related

---

[49] Pontifical Council of Justice and Peace, *Towards Reforming the International Financial and Monetary Systems*.
[50] Pope Francis, "Homily on the Visit to Lampedusa," July 8, 2013, www.vatican.va/content/francesco/en/homilies/2013/documents/papa-francesco_20130708_omelia-lampedusa.html.
[51] Pope Francis, *Laudato Si', Encyclical Letter on Care for our Common Home,* May 24, 2015, nos. 1–2, www.vatican.va/content/francesco/en/encyclicals/documents/papa-francesco_20150524_enciclica-laudato-si.html.
[52] Sean McDonagh, *On Care for Our Common Home: The Encyclical of Pope Francis on the Environment, Laudato Si'* (Maryknoll, NY: Orbis Books, 2016), xvii–xix.

crises of poverty and climate change. "Enforceable international agreements," he writes, "are urgently needed, since local authorities are not always capable of effective intervention. Relations between states must be respectful of each other's sovereignty but must also lay down mutually agreed means of averting regional disasters which would eventually affect everyone" (no. 173).

Several weeks later, Francis reiterated this call to action at the World Meeting of Popular Movements in Bolivia. "There exists," he stressed, "a clear, definite, and pressing ethical imperative to implement what has not yet been done. We cannot allow certain interests—interests which are global but not universal—to take over, to dominate states and international organizations, and to continue destroying creation."[53] Importantly, Francis does not see the necessary change coming from the top-down, but rather issues a call to action for peoples, especially marginalized groups, to organize and hold political structures accountable.

Speaking to a very different audience, Francis followed this up in his address to the Sustainable Development Summit at the United Nations in September. The fourth pope to speak in the UN General Assembly Hall, Francis both praised the historic contribution of the organization and identified areas for reform. Like Benedict XVI, Francis is particularly concerned with the disproportionate power held by some states and conversely, the lack of power by other, less economically powerful nations. "All countries, without exception," he insists, with a nod to the debates on reforming the UN Security Council, are entitled "a share in, and a genuine and equitable influence on, decision-making processes."[54]

Just as UN member states were readying to adopt the *2030 Agenda for Sustainable Development,* Francis's address to the UN decried a "declarationist nominalism," whereby countries make solemn commitments but fail to take concrete action. "Our world," he stresses, "demands of all government leaders a will which is effective, practical, and constant." Achieving this, however, requires that states and political leaders "set aside partisan and ideological interests, and sincerely strive to serve the common good."[55]

---

[53] Pope Francis, "Address to the World Meeting of Popular Movements," July 9, 2015, www.vatican.va/content/francesco/en/speeches/2015/july/documents/papa-francesco_20150709_bolivia-movimenti-popolari.html.
[54] Pope Francis, "Address to the Members of the General Assembly of the United Nations Organization," UN Headquarters, New York, September 25, 2015, w2.vatican.va/content/francesco/en/speeches/2015/september/documents/papa-francesco_20150925_onu-visita.html.
[55] Pope Francis, "Address to the Members of the General Assembly of the United Nations Organization."

Five years later, amid the COVID pandemic, Francis again addressed the UN General Assembly, this time in a video message. Reflecting on the growing awareness of the interconnectedness and fragility of the human family exposed by COVID, he offers a call to action: "Solidarity must not be an empty word or promise."[56] What is needed is a "change of direction." The pope laments the lack of action on climate change and reiterates his warning concerning a "declarationist nominalism." Instead, he urges a "a frank and coherent dialogue aimed at strengthening multilateralism and cooperation between states. The present crisis has further demonstrated the limits of our self-sufficiency as well as our common vulnerability. It has forced us to think clearly about how we want to emerge from this: either better or worse."[57]

Not surprisingly, these same themes appear in *Fratelli Tutti*, his encyclical on fraternity and social friendship, released a few weeks after the video message.[58] The text again uplifts the notion of universal siblinghood, but this time uses the parable of the Good Samaritan to understand the universal obligations to others beyond borders. In chapter five, Francis echoes both the 2011 note and *Laudato Si'* (no. 189), bemoaning the failure of the international community to effectively and ethically respond to the economic crisis of 2007–2008. Rather than developing "new ways of regulating speculative financial practices and virtual wealth," the response of the international community "fostered greater individualism, less integration, and increased freedom for the truly powerful, who always find a way to escape unscathed" (no. 170).

Citing *Caritas in Veritate* and Francis's 2015 UN address, *Fratelli Tutti* critiques the unjust distribution of power in international relations (nos. 171 and 173). The authority of individual nation-states, especially poorer countries, is eroding in the face of powerful transnational interests. What is needed, according to the encyclical, is a "stronger and more efficiently organized" structure of global governance "equipped with the power to provide for the global common good, the elimination of hunger and poverty, and the sure defense of fundamental human rights" (no. 172).

---

[56] Pope Francis, "Video Message to the Seventy-Fifth Meeting of the General Assembly of the United Nations," September 25, 2020, www.vatican.va/content/francesco/en/messages/pont-messages/2020/documents/papa-francesco_20200925_videomessaggio-onu.html.

[57] Pope Francis, "Video Message to the Seventy-Fifth Meeting of the General Assembly of the United Nations."

[58] Pope Francis, *Fratelli Tutti, Encyclical letter on Fraternity and Social Friendship*, October 3, 2020, www.vatican.va/content/francesco/en/encyclicals/documents/papa-francesco_20201003_enciclica-fratelli-tutti.html.

These themes appear again in 2023, with *Laudate Deum,* Francis's 2023 follow-up to *Laudato Si'*.[59] The exhortation, released before UN's Climate Conference in Dubai, offers a bold critique of the failures of the present system of global governance. "Our responses," he laments, "have not been adequate, while the world in which we live is collapsing and may be nearing the breaking point" (no. 2). The previous models of governance, which he terms "old multilateralism" or "old diplomacy," have failed to generate an approach "capable of responding to the new configuration of the world" (no. 41). The infrastructure and norms which emerged following the Second World War, based on the sovereign state as the prime agent, must be reconfigured and recreated to take "into account the new world situation" (no. 37).

For Francis, this means supporting a more expansive and equitable order, built not from national capitals or the United Nations headquarters, but the bottom-up, a "multilateralism 'from below'" (no. 38). Without abandoning the structures of the state and intergovernmental bodies, Francis here points to the need for mobilizing and supporting civil society groups to be involved in "a sort of increased 'democratization' in the global context, so that various situations can be expressed and included. It is no longer helpful for us to support institutions in order to preserve the rights of the more powerful without caring for those of all" (no. 43).

But just how is the world supposed to achieve this? As with Maritain, the pope could be criticized for being imprecise and not offering specific policy proposals to strengthen the system (e.g., what to do about the UNSC veto powers). As Anna Rowlands points out, however, the pope is "less interested in the careful demarcation of activities proper to the state, market, and society and more in tracing the wide human tendencies that are replicated across these arenas."[60] While not offering a clear-cut policy roadmap, Pope Francis and Jacques Maritain do offer several guiding values that have the potential to bridge some of the gaps in global governance today.

BRIDGING THE GAPS

In many ways, the two figures considered in this paper represent complementary strands. Rooted in Thomistic political philosophy and informed by the experience of post-war reconstruction, Maritain offers

---

[59] Pope Francis, *Laudate Deum, Apostolic Exhortation to All People of Good Will on the Climate Crisis,* October 4, 2023, www.vatican.va/content/francesco/en/apost_exhortations/documents/20231004-laudate-deum.html.

[60] Anna Rowlands, *Towards a Politics of Communion: Catholic Social Teaching in Dark Times* (London: T&T Clark, 2022), 211.

a long-term vision with a world state as a goal. Meanwhile, Pope Francis, the first pope from Latin America, approaches the question from a more immediate, pastoral perspective. While he nods to longer term possibilities, Francis looks more to what needs to happen in the present to address the pressing realities facing real people. These two strands, the philosophical and the pastoral, converge to illuminate five values that frame a Catholic approach to global governance. These values, if promoted by the Catholic Church, have the potential to mobilize efforts to heal some of the gaps in global governance today.[61]

First, *both Maritain and Francis highlight the universal solidaristic vision embedded in the "catholic" political worldview.* This normative principle, whether rooted in Maritain's claims of the universality of human rights or Francis's appeal to shared siblinghood, looks towards a horizon wider than any one state or region. Like many forms of cosmopolitanism, this solidaristic value rejects appeals to absolute state sovereignty.

In order to make the UN system fit for purpose, the issue of sovereignty, which undergirds the declarationist nominalism that Francis decries, must be addressed. Both the emerging doctrine of the Responsibility to Protect and the development of the International Criminal Court, in different ways, reframe sovereignty more positively (as responsibility rather than strict non-intervention). Each of these efforts are however impeded by the lack of support by key nations, including the United States.

One of the most fundamental challenges, as Francis noted in 2015, is the inequity of power in the UN Security Council. Several unsuccessful attempts and proposals have been made, including limiting the veto power of the Permanent Five (P5) and introducing new permanent members from Latin America, Africa, and South Asia. Absent a global movement to reform the structures, it will be difficult to imagine the five victors of the Second World War giving up their power, even if such reforms, as former ambassador Kishore Mahbubani points out, would be in their best interest. The absence of reform, Mahbubani argues, will ultimately entail for the body a progressive loss of credibility.[62] Recently, in the context of seeking more support from African countries to counteract the influence of

---

[61] See also *Global Governance: Our Responsibility to Make Globalisation an Opportunity for All* (Commission of the Bishops' Conferences of the European Community, 2001), www.comece.eu/wp-content/uploads/sites/2/2022/03/20010901-COMECE-Report-on-Global-Governance-22Our-responsibility-to-make-globalisation-an-opportunity-for-all22.pdf; and Kevin Ahern, *An Introduction to Global Governance through the Lens of Catholic Social Teaching* (Brussels: CIDSE and Caritas Internationalis, 2007), www.cidse.org/index.php?option=com_k2&Itemid=195&id=200_1d9500e121d2d35633b125dc0ca6f9aa&lang=en&task=download&view=item.

[62] Kishore Mahbubani, "Civilizations: Fusion or Clash?," in *Global Governance Futures*, 76–77.

Russia in the region, President Joseph Biden has indicated renewed support to reform both the UN Security Council and G20 network "to include permanent representation for Africa," something slated for consideration by the UN in 2024.[63] While this would be a step in the right direction, how this will take shape and other countries/regions who have asked for greater representation (e.g., Brazil and India) will be included remains unclear.

Reframing sovereignty also demands a reappraisal of the role of borders, something increasingly urgent given the complexities posed by contemporary flows of refugees and migrants. A universal perspective on global migration governance looks at those crossing borders as siblings, and adopts a wider analysis to consider the complex mix of push and pull factors involved. This does not mean the elimination of borders, something neither Maritain nor Francis calls for, but rather a refocusing of the question on the vulnerability of those on the move, the root reasons for their displacement, and the responsibility of states to abide by the established norms of humanitarian law.

Addressing the crisis of global displacement, theologian David Hollenbach draws on the work of Daniel Philpott to suggest the beginning of a "third revolution in sovereignty." Developments in humanitarian and human rights movements, he argues, have established norms that "imply that states not only have the responsibility to protect the dignity of their own citizens but also have transborder duties to respect the human rights of the citizens of other countries."[64] So while there remain institutional and compliance gaps, there is a growing consensus on the importance of established humanitarian principles.

Here, the church's responsibility to bridge doctrinal gaps between what it formally teaches and what individual members hear is particularly important in those countries with more political power. The church in the United States, United Kingdom, and France, the three P5 members with significant Catholic populations, has a particular responsibility to call for and support efforts for equitable and just reforms. Among other things, this includes strengthening monitoring and enforcement mechanisms related to already agreed

---

[63] The White House, "Remarks by President Biden at the US-Africa Summit Leaders Session on Partnering on the African Union's Agenda 2063," The White House, December 15, 2022, www.whitehouse.gov/briefing-room/speeches-remarks/2022/12/15/remarks-by-president-biden-at-the-u-s-africa-summit-leaders-session-on-partnering-on-the-african-unions-agenda-2063/.

[64] David Hollenbach, *Humanity in Crisis: Ethical and Religious Response to Refugees* (Washington, DC: Georgetown University Press, 2019), 66–67. See also Daniel Philpott, *Revolutions in Sovereignty: How Ideas Shaped Modern International Relations* (Princeton, NJ: Princeton University Press, 2010).

upon human rights and humanitarian law, strengthening support and funding for the United Nations and UN agencies, supporting efforts to reform the composition and privileges enjoyed by the P5, and resisting appeals to country-first nationalisms. The reflective disposition to universality at the heart of the Catholic tradition must continuously be integrated into church life, as the Second Vatican Council teaches (*Gaudium et Spes*, no. 90).

Second, *both Maritain and Francis affirm the value of pluralism.* While it took Maritain time to arrive at possibilities for uniting groups with different religious and cultural heritages and going beyond a new European Christendom, his experiences after the war revealed the possibility of convening different groups for common tasks. Francis shares Maritain's optimism on the promise of pluralism and has deepened his predecessors' work on fostering ecumenical and inter-religious dialogue, including the 2019 Abu Dhabi Declaration, *Human Fraternity for World Peace and Living Together.* Co-signed with Sheikh Ahmed el-Tayeb, the Grand Imam of Al-Azhar, the text rejects religiously-based violence and calls for action to advance fraternity and dialogue. In *Fratelli Tutti*, a whole chapter is dedicated to this project.

At the same time, Pope Francis has facilitated unprecedented ecumenical and inter-religious cooperation in addressing key issues on the global governance agenda. For example, ahead of the 26th Conference of Parties (COP26) meeting in Scotland in 2021, the Holy See, along with the governments of Italy and the United Kingdom, convened a conference at the Vatican on "Faith and Science: Towards COP26." The meeting included representatives of more than nine religious traditions and UN officials and followed an earlier joint message on the protection of creation by Pope Francis, Justin Welby, the Archbishop of Canterbury, and Bartholomew, the Orthodox Ecumenical Patriarch.[65]

Third, *for both Francis and Maritain, the structures of global governance should be multilayered, something the Catholic tradition describes with the language of subsidiarity.* Though occasionally framed through an anti-government libertarian lens, subsidiarity is not a principle against governmental intervention, but rather one that prioritizes the most appropriate and proximate level of governmental response. While the local level is often privileged, Catholic social teaching affirms that "when there is serious need at a greater distance or when a local community is not responding to the needs of its members, larger regional communities or the international community

---

[65] Philip Pullella, "Pope, Other Religious Leaders Issue Pre-COP26 Appeal on Climate Change," *Reuters*, October 4, 2021, www.reuters.com/world/europe/pope-world-religious-leaders-issue-pre-cop26-appeal-climate-change-2021-10-04/.

as a whole can have a duty to respond."[66] This call for different levels of government is evident in a remarkable way in the various efforts toward post-war European integration, a project which, as Anna Rowlands argues, had "solidarity and subsidiarity at its heart."[67] Today, subsidiarity remains a key principle for the vision of Europe, appearing even in the unratified *European Constitution*.

Beyond the layers of local, national, regional, and global organizations, a range of other informal structures and networks have been created, including what Anne-Marie Slaughter describes as "horizontal networks," such as the G20.[68] However, while promising in some respects, these evolving networks often have their own challenges in relation to participation, power distribution, and transparency. Though more flexible than some existing policies and institutions, the emergence of these networks alone cannot bridge the urgent institutional and policy gaps. Addressing these ruptures will demand a multipronged approach, or what Hollenbach describes as "a polycentric understanding of responsibility" where "no one community, country, or agency bears the responsibility to act all on its own. As polycentric and network-based, the responsibility is shared among local, regional, and global actors. When responsibility is seen as shared, the needed action becomes more likely."[69]

Fourth, *both Francis and Maritain look for change from the bottom up through participation.* Like pluralism and subsidiarity, participation offers an important check to corruption, abuse of power or, in extreme cases, Machiavellian totalitarianism. For both figures, global structural change must "spring up from peoples."[70] For Maritain, the future world order must be "fully political."[71] In other words, a unified state structure can only come about once a general sense of a worldwide body politic is developed. Like his critics, Maritain knows that to impose something as significant as a world state from above would be an invitation to conflict. The formation of a body politic, of a worldwide political society, happens in a particular way as people join together in concrete common tasks with a shared sense of belonging.

In a similar way, the pope points to the need for people to join together to organize the necessary structural change. As Lisa Sowle Cahill acknowledges, it is almost revolutionary for Catholic social

---

[66] Hollenbach, *Humanity in Crisis*, 73.
[67] Rowlands, *Towards a Politics of Communion*, 219.
[68] Anne-Marie Slaughter, *A New World Order* (Princeton, NJ: Princeton University Press, 2004).
[69] Hollenbach, *Humanity in Crisis*, 78.
[70] Pope Francis, "Address to the World Meeting of Popular Movements."
[71] Maritain, *Man and the State*, 202.

teaching to arrive at the understanding "that effective political action must be broad-based and multi-layered, gathering energy and strength among affected populations," and not primarily focused on the elites.[72] Using the successful example of the campaign against landmines as an example, *Laudate Deum* calls for a process that attends to the voices of citizens "that rise up from below throughout the world," and "not simply one determined by the elites of power" (no. 38.) Accordingly, the structures of global governance must involve and engage a range of actors from grassroots popular movements and large non-governmental organizations to scholars, media platforms, religious leaders, transnational corporations, and governments. As Rowlands notes, Francis understands that the "best route out" of the present crisis "is to begin with a politics of attention from below: hearing the cry of the earth and the cry of the poor. This is a political imperative for the sake of a common people in a common home."[73]

Since the foundation of the UN system, Catholics have sought to do this bottom-up engagement by participating in global governance in ways that circumvent their national capitals through the creation of organized groups, movements, and networks in civil society. Significantly, the *UN Charter* recognized the demands of some groups and made provisions for granting consultative status to some non-governmental organizations (NGOs). Over the past eight decades, thousands of NGOs, including many Catholic groups, have contributed to the development of the present global governance system.

As *Fratelli Tutti* rightly points out, collectives within civil society, like these NGOs, "help to compensate for the shortcomings of the international community, its lack of coordination in complex situations" (no. 175). But the voices and experiences of those "globally governed" remain under-appreciated and far too often sidelined.[74] A new approach is needed with more accessible mechanisms and lines of communication to address this democratic deficit and foster a more participatory world order. Several proposals have advanced more ambitious forms of participatory structures, from the creation of a global parliament akin to the European Parliament to a new body within the UN system comprised of the mayors of major world cities. These and other proposals have the potential to help bridge the information and normative gaps afflicting the present world

---

[72] Lisa Sowle Cahill, "Social Justice and the Common Good: Improving the Catholic Social Teaching Framework," in *Ethical Challenges in Global Public Health: Climate Change, Pollution, and the Health of the Poor*, ed. Philip J. Landrigan and Andrea Vicini, SJ, CTEWC Book Series 1 (2021): 112.

[73] Rowlands, *Towards a Politics of Communion*, 211.

[74] Thomas G. Weiss and Rorden Wilkinson, "The Globally Governed—Everyday Global Governance," *Global Governance* 24, no. 2 (2018): 193–210, doi.org/10.1163/19426720-02402003.

order.[75] Ultimately, however, participation will require the interest and ability of an informed population, with particular option for the poor, for those people most vulnerable to the decisions made by higher levels of government.

If Francis is correct that the future of humanity depends on the ability of people to organize from the bottom up, then the Church needs to invest more time and resources into supporting the work of participatory structures such as social movements, NGOs, and community groups.[76] In the United States, the work of the Catholic Campaign for Human Development (CCHD) has had enormous success in funding community organizing groups around the country.[77] An international fund for NGOs and movements that work on issues of global governance, akin to the work of CCHD, could go a long way to mobilize bottom-up participation.

Finally, *the Catholic moral vision shared by Jacques Maritain and Pope Francis remains centered on the human person.* In Maritain's personalist philosophy, the human person in all its integrated elements must be at the root of any legitimate form of governance. Important to Maritain's personalist democracy is his belief that the proper end of each person is God, not the state or the individual. For Maritain, the human being is much more than just the individual and the rights or material goods he or she possesses. The person has important spiritual and social dimensions which gives us a holistic understanding of human dignity and compels us to work and, if necessary, sacrifice for the common good.[78]

Francis consistently echoes the centrality of putting actual people first. In his 2015 address to the UN, he called states to engage in "an examination of conscience" that would consider the real experiences of living human beings: "In wars and conflicts there are individual persons, our brothers and sisters, men and women, young and old, boys and girls who weep, suffer, and die. Human beings who are easily discarded when our response is simply to draw up lists of problems, strategies, and disagreements."[79] In addressing migration during his 2016 visit to the border with the United States in Ciudad Juarez,

---

[75] Daniel Pejic and Michele Acuto, "Cities: Understanding Global Urban Governance," in *Global Governance Futures*, 107. See also Simon Curtis, *Global Cities and Global Order* (Oxford: Oxford University Press, 2017).

[76] Pope Francis, "Address to the World Meeting of Popular Movements."

[77] See Jeffry Odell Korgen, *Beyond Empowerment: A Pilgrimage with the Catholic Campaign for Human Development* (Maryknoll, NY: Orbis Books, 2015).

[78] Jacques Maritain, *The Rights of Man and Natural Law*, in *Christianity and Democracy* and *The Rights of Man and Natural Law*, trans. Doris C. Anson (San Francisco, CA: Ignatius, 1986), 88.

[79] Pope Francis, "Address to the Members of the General Assembly of the United Nations Organization."

Mexico, Francis made a similar point: "This crisis, which can be measured in numbers and statistics, we want instead to measure with names, stories, families."[80] As *Laudate Deum* points out, centering the global debate on the "primacy of the human person," can engender an approach to multilateralism ensuring that "ethics will prevail over local or contingent interests" (no. 39). Here, again, is an area where the Catholic community can contribute by going beyond numbers to promoting a holistic vision that prioritizes the dignity of each human being.

As the largest faith-based educational provider on the planet, the Catholic Church has an enormous potential to influence public opinion to bridge some of the gaps inhibiting the present global governance infrastructure. The church, however, must contend with its own gaps, especially what might be described as a doctrinal gap between the official social doctrine and what is understood by its members and leaders. Catholics are not immune from temptations to various kinds of nationalisms. Education about the UN system and the church's teaching on global governance ought to be integrated more clearly and intentionally into Catholic educational systems, seminary formation, and public outreach. Some places already do this by integrating official UN days into institutional and liturgical calendars, hosting Model UN clubs in schools, and educating students or parishioners about international campaigns, such as the Sustainable Development Goals.

While they intentionally do not offer a detailed road map for reconfiguring the present world order, Pope Francis and Jacques Maritain provide a set of values and principles that can assist collective discernment by the community of nations as they seek to address the existential threats facing people and the planet. At a time when humanity is confronted by both challenges that demand new forms of multilateralism and renewed expressions of nationalisms that oppose meaningful global cooperation, the values proposed by these two figures can offer timely guideposts to inspire action.

CONCLUSION: NO OTHER ALTERNATIVE

At the beginning of the final chapter of *Man and the State*, Jacques Maritain quotes Mortimer Adler to lay out two possible paths ahead for the planet and its people: "either lasting peace or a serious risk of total destruction."[81] Nearly seventy years later, during the COVID-19

---

[80] Pope Francis, "Homily" (Ciudad Juárez, February 17, 2016), www.vatican.va/content/francesco/en/homilies/2016/documents/papa-francesco_20160217_omelia-messico-ciudad-jaurez.html.
[81] Maritain, *Man and the State*, 189.

pandemic, Pope Francis made a similar point in his 2020 address to the UN General Assembly:

> We are faced, then, with a choice between two possible paths. One path leads to the consolidation of multilateralism as the expression of a renewed sense of global co-responsibility, a solidarity grounded in justice and the attainment of peace and unity within the human family, which is God's plan for our world. The other path emphasizes self-sufficiency, nationalism, protectionism, individualism, and isolation; it excludes the poor, the vulnerable, and those dwelling on the peripheries of life. That path would certainly be detrimental to the whole community, causing self-inflicted wounds on everyone. It must not prevail.[82]

Ultimately, for both Jacques Maritain and Pope Francis, the answer is clear. We must resist nationalistic ideologies, strengthen existing mechanisms for multilateralism, and work towards the longer-term goal of creating a more robust, equitable and authoritative system of global governance. Contrary to what the critics of both figures allege, this is not a utopic vision, but rather a necessary step for our common world because whether we like it or not, we are all "in the same boat" (*Fratelli Tutti*, no. 30). M

Kevin Glauber Ahern, PhD, is Professor of Religious Studies and Director of the Dorothy Day Center at Manhattan College, where he has also directed the Peace and Justice Studies and Labor Studies programs. He is the author of *Structures of Grace: Catholic Organizations Serving the Global Common Good*. He has edited several books, including the award-winning *Visions of Hope: Emerging Theologians and the Future of the Church*, *The Radical Bible*, and the award-winning *Public Theology and the Global Common Good*. His most recent book is *God's Quad: Small Faith Communities on Campus and Beyond*. He serves as co-chair of the Dorothy Day Guild Advisory Committee, and has held leadership roles in the International Movement of Catholic Students as well as the International Catholic Movement for Intellectual and Cultural Affairs (ICMICA-Pax Romana), a global movement of intellectual and professionals committed to social action.

---

[82] Pope Francis, "Video Message to the Seventy-Fifth Meeting of the General Assembly of the United Nations."

Catholic Social Teaching: Toward a Decolonial Praxis

Alex Mikulich

Abstract: The claims to universality in the thought of Jacques Maritain and Catholic social teaching present a problem: they tend not to perceive their own entanglement in modernity and its hidden underside of colonial oppression. First, I explore this problem by drawing upon the scholarship of Catholic social ethicist Mary E. Hobgood to underscore the internal contradictions between three different social models in Catholic social teaching: feudal organic, liberal orthodox, and radical liberationist. I situate Maritain's work within these social models. Second, I utilize Sylvia Wynter's appropriation of Frantz Fanon's sociogenetic approach as a way of understanding how people and institutions are malformed by dominant modern epistemologies. I argue that the Roman Catholic Church lacks a coherent and credible praxis of transformation. Finally, I suggest three starting points to initiate shifts toward a decolonial ethic of Catholic social teaching.

This essay confronts a predicament in Catholic social teaching (CST): the Roman Catholic Church inaugurated a catastrophic metaphysical transformation of power, knowledge, and being in the 15th century that is nothing less than a counter scandal to the Gospel of Jesus Christ.[1] By "metaphysical catastrophe," I mean the ways the church divided the world, peoples, and diverse ways of thinking and being into "degrees of being human."[2] This concerns not only the violences inflicted upon peoples deemed less human; practitioners of CST should heed Aimé Césaire's admonition to "study how colonization works to *decivilize* the colonizer, to *brutalize* him in the true sense of the word, to degrade him, to awaken him to buried instincts, to covetousness, violence, race hatred, and moral

---

[1] I am deeply thankful to the reviewer who provided thorough and comprehensive comments on the initial draft of this essay.
[2] Nelson Maldonado-Torres, "Outline of Ten Theses on Coloniality and Decoloniality," Fondation Frantz Fanon (October 23, 2016), 13, fondation-frantzfanon.com/wp-content/uploads/2018/10/maldonado-torres_outline_of_ten_theses-10.23.16.pdf.

relativism."³ Utilizing the terms of decolonial praxis, I refer to the intersecting domains of global racial, class, gender, sex, and epistemic hierarchies as the colonial matrix of power (CMP).⁴ "We are all in the matrix," writes cultural anthropologist Walter Mignolo, and "each node is interconnected with all the rest, and the matrix cannot be observed and described by an observer located outside the matrix that cannot be observed—that observer would be the God of Christian theology or the Subject of secular Reason."⁵ The Roman Catholic Church and its social teaching are embedded in the epistemologies and structures of the colonial matrix of power, and the church tends to lack self-critical consciousness of its complicity in the CMP.

The Roman Catholic Church and its social teaching tend to operate in an hermetically sealed bubble of Western, Eurocentric epistemologies. Even when Jacques Maritain or particular enunciations of CST claim to critique modernity, they are not immune to Eurocentrism or the CMP. Not unlike modern social theory within Western thought, CST and Maritain seem blind to mythologies that perpetuate the violent predicament of our epoch, that is, the CMP. Theologian M. Shawn Copeland frames our epoch this way:

> Despite its reverence for Being and beings; despite its intense sacramental, and, therefore symbolic character; despite its intimate knowledge of, irrevocable relation to flesh—racialization of flesh has shaped Christianity, and thus Roman Catholicism, almost from its origins: women, Jews, people of color (especially, indigenous and black peoples) have undergone metaphysical violence.⁶

The epistemological claims to universality, as enunciated through the hierarchy's articulation of its social teaching, hide its complicity

---

[3] Aimé Césaire, *Discourse on Colonialism*, trans. Joan Pinkham (New York: Monthly Review, [1972], 2000), 35, emphasis in original. I do not update Césaire's language to maintain his clarity while acknowledging that patriarchal language is constitutive of the CMP.

[4] Anibal Quijano is credited with originating the term "patrón colonial de poder." See Aníbal Quijano, "Colonialidad y modernidad-racionalidad," *Los Conquistados: 1492 y la población indígena América*, ed. Heraclio Bonilla (Bogotá: Tercer Mundo/FLASCO, 1992), 437–447.

[5] Walter D. Mignolo, *The Darker Side of Western Modernity* (Durham, NC: Duke University Press, 2011), 16.

[6] M. Shawn Copeland, "Anti-Blackness and White Supremacy in the Making of American Catholicism," *American Catholic Studies* 127, no. 3 (Fall 2016): 6–7, doi.org/10.1353/acs.2016.0038. Copeland cites philosopher Gianni Vattimo for the phrase "metaphysical violence" as the attempt to master the real by force from "Towards an Ontology of Decline," in *Reading Metaphysics: The New Italian Philosophy*, ed. Giovanni Borradori (Evanston, IL: Northwestern University Press, 1988), 64.

in the origins of colonialism.⁷ Decolonial perspectives, however, interrogate the "locus of enunciation, that is, the geo-political and body political location of the subject that speaks."⁸ Too often, the church and CST tend to assert universal claims from its unspoken, Western perspective. The church has yet to sufficiently acknowledge its role in the CMP, much less enact an enduring decolonial shift in its ecclesial enunciations and praxis.

I proceed in three steps. First, drawing upon the scholarship of Catholic social ethicist Mary Elizabeth Hobgood, I underscore the internal contradictions between three different social models present in Catholic social teaching: feudal organic, orthodox economic, and radical liberationist. I situate Jacques Maritain's social philosophy within these conflicting paradigms. Second, drawing upon Frantz Fanon's sociogenetic analysis of Western coloniality, appropriated through Sylvia Wynter's hybrid account of humans as eusocial storytelling and biologically implemented living systems, I utilize sociogenesis as a way to interrogate the Roman Catholic origins of coloniality and the pathologies, especially white supremacist, from which it has yet to extricate itself. Finally, I conclude by suggesting three starting points to initiate shifts toward a decolonial ethic of CST and democracy.

This ethic is incommensurable with social change approaches that maintain or only seek to reform the colonial matrix of power.⁹ By incommensurable I mean that the church and white¹⁰ Catholic settlers must relinquish innocence, initiate processes of unlearning dominant modern epistemologies and pathologies, and take up the Gospel call that the first be last and the last first (Matt 20:16). The overturning of the dominant order is a "'way' of relinquishing what has failed (which we are likely to treasure) and *receiving* what God will give us."¹¹ This essay builds upon my *Unlearning White Supremacy: A Spirituality for*

---

⁷ Samuel Rayan, "Decolonization of Theology," *Jnanadeepa* nos. 1–2, (1998): 142, doi.org/10.5281/zenodo.4255241.

⁸ Ramón Grosfoguel, "The Epistemic Decolonial Turn: Beyond Political-Economy Paradigms," in *Globalization and the Decolonial Option*, ed. Walter D. Mignolo and Arturo Escobar (London: Routledge, 2013), 67.

⁹ Eve Tuck and K. Wayne Yang, "Decolonization is Not a Metaphor," *Decolonization: Indigeneity, Education, and Society* 1, no. 1 (2012): 1–40.

¹⁰ I am following the National Association of Black Journalists (NABJ) style guide for use of upper or lower case when referencing Black and White people and Indigenous communities. Not all Black people are African American so I use a person's preference or specific identity where possible. The NABJ does not use upper case "white" when referencing racist terms or actions, so, for example, I do not capitalize white supremacy or white settlers. I do not change upper or lower case where sources I quote use another style. The NABJ style guide is here: nabjonline.org/news-media-center/styleguide/.

¹¹ Walter Brueggemann, *The Prophetic Imagination*, 40th anniversary edition (Minneapolis, MN: Fortress, 2018), 132.

Racial Liberation where I argued that unlearning supremacy and all forms of domination entails "beginning the work of acknowledging, gaining consciousness of, and undoing the many ways we have been malformed and deformed by a society that idolizes whiteness."[12] A critical piece of the process of unlearning and undoing modernity/coloniality, I believe, are rituals of biblical lament.[13] Ultimately, that means creating conditions of possibility for relinquishing, and dying to, much of what the Roman Catholic Church and white settlers of faith value that perpetuates colonial dominations and pathologies, including relinquishing land, power, and privilege and initiating processes of reparation.[14]

CATHOLIC SOCIAL TEACHING: THREE CONFLICTING SOCIO-ECONOMIC MODELS

In her authoritative examination of three conflicting paradigms in Catholic social teaching, Mary Elizabeth Hobgood illuminates conflicts internal to the church's social teaching since Leo XIII's papacy. Hobgood's analysis unsettles assumptions that Catholic social teaching has progressed beyond premodern organic social theory and that the last century of social teaching represents a "neither liberal nor socialist" "third way."[15] I situate Jacques Maritain's Thomistic approach within Hobgood's analysis.

Hobgood identifies three conflicting economic paradigms in Catholic social teaching since the publication of *Rerum Novarum* in 1891.[16] These models are 1) premodern, feudal organic social theory;[17] 2) modern orthodox economic or liberal theory that "promotes the free agency of autonomous individuals who seek their financial self-

---

[12] Alex Mikulich, *Unlearning White Supremacy: A Spirituality for Racial Liberation* (Maryknoll, NY: Orbis Books, 2022), xix.

[13] Mikulich, *Unlearning White Supremacy*, 94–96 and 102–106.

[14] I suggest a set of practices to prepare for and enact repair in chapter five of *Unlearning White Supremacy*. The "p/reparations" I suggest include truthful remembering and listening, racial equity practice, Maafa, and embodying a "blues hope."

[15] See, for example, John A. Coleman, "Neither Liberal nor Socialist: The Originality of Catholic Social Teaching," in John A. Coleman, ed., *One Hundred Years of Catholic Social Thought: Celebration and Challenge* (Maryknoll, NY: Orbis Books, 1991), 25–42. Coleman wisely situates his interpretation of the church's social teaching within a broad spectrum of movements that claimed grounding in the tradition.

[16] Mary Elizabeth Hobgood, *Catholic Social Teaching and Economic Theory: Paradigms in Conflict* (Philadelphia, PA: Temple University Press, 1991).

[17] See also Joe Holland and Peter Henriot, *Social Analysis: Linking Faith and Justice*, revised and enlarged edition (Maryknoll, NY: Orbis Books and Dove Communications in collaboration with The Center of Concern, 1988), 32–34.

interest in a world presumed . . . to function in a rational and harmonious way"[18]; and 3) radical, liberationist theory.[19] There is no decolonial model in the magisterial body of CST. I sketch the use of the models by Leo XIII and Pius XI, John XXIII and Paul VI, John Paul II, and through Latin American, US, and Canadian episcopal statements.

The church's premodern organic social model is heavily indebted to Thomas Aquinas and European feudal relations. It is called "organic" because of the way Aquinas appropriates Aristotle's analogical continuum between the social and natural worlds.[20] Organic social theory compares society to the human body in which the whole body has priority over individual parts, so the good of society has priority over the needs of individual members. This theory stresses harmony in hierarchical relationships of feudal societies, including dualism between lord-serf, husband-wife, and rich-poor. This hierarchical understanding of feudal relationships applies dualism to the cosmos as well, meaning that the spiritual and eternal hold dominance over the material and historical.[21] Hobgood notices that organic social theory predisposed the church to critique the individualism of "economic man" in liberal theory, and yet, it also predisposed the church toward accepting the ways capitalism and liberal social theory support hierarchical arrangements.[22]

The church's appropriation of Aquinas's articulation of commutative and distributive justice affirmed his assumption that feudal social arrangements were divinely sanctioned and thereby good. Aquinas's interpretation of distributive justice assumes a natural inequality that maintains social ranking and the "obligation of privilege." The church "taught that endangering one's status disadvantaged the whole society."[23] This assumption, which maintains hierarchy and emphasizes paternalistic charity is, however, at odds with the patristic teaching of the Cappadocian fathers on property.[24]

---

[18] Hobgood, *Catholic Social Teaching and Economic Theory*, 5. Holland and Henriot refer to this model as "liberal" (*Social Analysis*, 34–37).
[19] Holland and Henriot also call this model "radical" (*Social Analysis*, 37–40).
[20] Hobgood, *Catholic Social Teaching and Economic Theory*, 98.
[21] Hobgood, *Catholic Social Teaching and Economic Theory*, 98.
[22] Hobgood, *Catholic Social Teaching and Economic Theory*, 98.
[23] Hobgood, *Catholic Social Teaching and Economic Theory*, 99. Hobgood cites Clement of Alexandria's treatise *The Rich Man's Salvation* arguing that wealth is not an obstacle to God as long as the "wealthy person is concerned with its paternalistic use." See note 13, 124.
[24] Brian E. Daley, "The Cappadocian Fathers and the Option for the Poor," in *The Option for the Poor in Christian Theology*, ed. Daniel G. Groody (Notre Dame, IN: University of Notre Dame Press, 2007), 77–88. The bishops known as the Cappadocian fathers—Basil of Caesarea, his brother Gregory of Nyssa, and their friend Gregory of Nazianzus—all took the view that "the goods of the world that

The organic sensibility of property relations in Catholic teaching "was, and still is, premodern."[25] An enduring assumption of Catholic social teaching, grounded in the feudal, organic model of society, is that the privileged are capable of benevolence. The organic model assumes the justness of male and class privilege in the patriarchal relations of the family, church, labor unions, and the state. Thus, it aims at preventing social equality because equality would violate the natural law and supposedly lead to anarchy.[26] From the perspective of the feudal, organic model, the church must be deeply troubled by Enlightenment liberalism or socialist movements that clamor for alternatives to capitalism.

Yet Leo XIII and Pius XI also offered structural analyses that reflect the radical model. They both acknowledged the relationship between economic power and political control that created conflict between the interests of capital and labor. Pius XI extended Leo's thought by connecting class conflict and war (*Quadragesimo Anno*, no. 108). Pius argued that charity was not enough to remedy structural exploitation within capitalism; changing structures was necessary for justice and peace (*Quadragesimo Anno*, no. 137). However, Leo XIII and Pius XI pursued social change strategies at odds with their radical analyses. They assumed that economic conflicts would erode if people accepted the universally valid teaching of the church (because it had access to eternal truth not mediated by the world).[27] Hobgood explains that their commitment to a premodern, organic social theory "allowed them to ignore their own analyses and assumed that Church teaching and a nonmilitant labor movement would be able to convince elites" to serve the common good.[28]

Hobgood finds in Pope John XXIII and Pope Paul VI a very similar dualism between their respective analyses and the model of social change they employ. Pope John XXIII and Paul VI both utilized elements of radical social theory, especially in their concern with global poverty and in qualifying the use and purpose of property. Returning more solidly to early church teaching and Aquinas, they argue that the destination of the earth's resources is first to serve the sustenance of human beings prior to the rights of private property (*Mater et Magistra*, no. 43; *Pacem in Terris*, no. 22; *Gaudium et Spes*, no. 69). Following Pius XI, Pope Paul VI closely links peace with

---

supply our needs are gifts of a beneficent creator, intended for the support of all creatures."

[25] Hobgood, *Catholic Social Teaching and Economic Theory*, 100.

[26] Hobgood, *Catholic Social Teaching and Economic Theory*, 101.

[27] Hobgood, *Catholic Social Teaching and Economic Theory*, 102. Hobgood cites *Quadragesimo Anno*, nos. 11 and 19.

[28] Hobgood, *Catholic Social Teaching and Economic Theory*, 229–230.

economic justice (*Populorum Progressio*, nos. 49, 55, 76, 83, 87). Paul VI and Vatican II also advocated worker ownership and control, and democratic control of production at every level of society (*Gaudium et Spes*, no. 68; *Populorum Progressio*, nos. 34, 65, and *Octogesima Adveniens*, no. 47). However, the change strategies of John XXIII and Paul VI were often in conflict with their radical prescriptions. Both consistently employed the "organic" assumption that governments, international agencies, and power elites were willing and "capable of voluntary responsibility for the domestic and global commonweal (*Mater et Magistra*, no. 54; *Pacem in Terris*, no. 98; *Gaudium et Spes*, nos. 65, 70, 71, 74, 83; *Populorum Progressio*, nos. 23, 61, 48–49; *Octogesima Adveniens*, nos. 18, 23; *Justice in the World*, nos. 68, 70)."[29]

Pope John Paul II's *On Social Concern* and the US Catholic bishops' *Economic Justice for All* acknowledge widespread injustice throughout the world. Both aspire to a strategy in which the majority of workers may be owners and/or managers of the instruments of production (*Laborem Exercens*, no. 14; *Economic Justice for All*, no. 300). Yet these documents reflect the prevailing orthodox or liberal economic paradigm "exclusively or almost exclusively." *On Social Concern*, Hobgood argues, "completely lacks any analysis that can be aligned with the radical model."[30] Similarly, the US bishops insisted that capitalist development was capable of eradicating poverty, and they advocated liberal methods of social change through regulatory and welfare agencies of the present system so that businesses and government could increase jobs, affirmative action, education, and investment policy (*Economic Justice for All*, nos. 92, 110, 163–166).

The radical model is most employed by Latin American and Canadian bishops drawing upon liberation theology. The Latin American conferences at Medellín in 1968 and Puebla in 1979 were the first to embrace an explicitly radical social model. These documents announced structural transformation of society as integral to the work of social justice, developed a theme of "integral liberation," and even called the church to take sides with the marginalized and divest from its privileges to become a converted church. However, Hobgood finds both the organic and orthodox economic models at work in these documents, in conflict with the predominant radical model.[31]

Among the hallmarks of Jacques Maritain's legacy, one must include his contribution to the development of Thomism prior to Vatican II, his influence on the development of the Universal Declaration of Human Rights, his unique articulation of integral

---

[29] Hobgood, *Catholic Social Teaching and Economic Theory*, 232.
[30] Hobgood, *Catholic Social Teaching and Economic Theory*, 233.
[31] Hobgood, *Catholic Social Teaching and Economic Theory*, 163–164.

humanism (particularly in the form that developed after Vatican II),[32] and his pragmatic advocacy of a Christian animated democracy. Gustavo Gutierrez, in his classic *A Theology of Liberation*, highlighted Maritain's enunciation of a "New Christendom" and his "distinction of planes."[33] While Gutierrez applauds Maritain's attempt to extricate the church from its medieval shackles, ultimately, Maritain's categories "were not able to shake off the traditional mentality, as we can better see with the help of hindsight."[34]

I draw upon Gustavo Gutierrez to emphasize both that Maritain's Thomistic categories helped modernize the church's moral theology and social teaching and, simultaneously, maintain a European organic social model. While Maritain's updating of Thomism, especially through his understanding of the relationship between the person and the common good, as well as his Christian-inspired democracy (critical of its bourgeois variant), move him distinctly away from a feudal order, he nonetheless maintains a distinctly Catholic, hierarchical, organic social model. Even if Maritain's approach makes significant strides beyond a feudal order, it still attempts to unify society from the basis of a Eurocentric, Catholic Christian vision of a harmonizing, hierarchical order of family, nation, and society. While his "open Thomism" contributes to the "liberal turn" at Vatican II, he writes that he feels compelled to be anti-modern "because of the spirit of all modern things that have proceeded from the anti-Christian revolution."[35] Being anti-modern, it must be noted, does not decolonize ontology or epistemology; does not shift the geopolitical or the geo-body politics of knowledge, to which I turn with the example of Frantz Fanon below. As decolonial anthropologist Walter Mignolo explains, "denunciation within the colonizer's society, while important, is not sufficient itself. It is necessary for dissenting actors to join projects of decolonization (political and epistemic) that are, at once, *articulated by the colonized yet not a project of the colonized elite.*"[36]

---

[32] Donal Dorr, *Option for the Poor: A Hundred Years of Vatican Social Teaching* (Dublin: Gill and MacMillan, 1983), 207–232.
[33] Gustavo Gutierrez, *A Theology of Liberation*, 15th Anniversary edition (Maryknoll, NY: Orbis Books, 1988), 34–38.
[34] Gutierrez, *A Theology of Liberation*, 35.
[35] Thomas F. O'Meara, *Thomas Aquinas: Theologian* (Notre Dame, IN: University of Notre Dame Press, 1997), 179. O'Meara quotes Maritain in *The Angelic Doctor*, trans. J. F. Scanlan (New York: Dial, 1931), xi–xii.
[36] Walter Mignolo, "The Rhetoric of Modernity, the Logic of Coloniality, and the Grammar of De-coloniality," in *Globalization and the Decolonial Option*, ed. Walter Mignolo and Arturo Escobar (New York: Routledge, 2013), 312, emphasis in the original.

James Baldwin points to the need to decolonize CST in his review of Maritain's *The Person and the Common Good*:

> The gin-soaked, Benzedrine-ridden children of our violent age are inclined—not without some reason—to hold philosophers in some doubt as being irritatingly serene watchers of a bloodbath; their rules and their conclusions may all be rather impressive, but of what relevance are they, how can these presumably hard-earned precepts do anything to make more bearable, the daily, urgent life?[37]

Baldwin found Maritain's argument "obscured by dogma," "circular," and concluded that it is "unhelpful to be assured of future angels when mysteries of the present flesh are so far from being solved."[38] Baldwin's review underscores the need for decolonizing CST. Hobgood demonstrates that as long as Catholic social teaching employs tripartite models of social analysis and "continues to employ social change strategies primarily within the orthodox model, its social analysis will be internally incoherent."[39] More importantly, in terms of living the Gospel, the church "seeks economic security, and racial and patriarchal privilege, and is more comfortable with the orthodox model that supports its own interests."[40] Instead, I now turn to a model of social analysis and transformation—the decolonial option—that does not yet exist in CST discourse.

FRANTZ FANON'S SOCIOGENETIC ACCOUNT OF COLONIALISM

A fundamental problem for CST is not constructing the most true and objective definition of "man" or clarifying "justice" but, rather, unveiling its own entanglement in coloniality. CST needs to unlearn coloniality and relearn from the perspectives of the *damnés*—the body politics of knowledge, so that the *damnés* may re-exist on their own terms. The body politics of knowledge is a critical epistemological dimension of decoloniality. Frantz Fanon describes his physical, bodily experience of recognizing that French society viewed him as less than human and that this dominant, racist view is inhuman. Viewed from a decolonial or Fanonian perspective, the lack of a body politics of knowledge in CST reveals its Eurocentric, white supremacist worldview.

---

[37] James Baldwin, "*The Person and the Common Good* by Jacques Maritain," in *The Cross of Redemption: Uncollected Writings*, ed. Randall Kenan (New York: Pantheon, 2010, originally published as "Present and Future," *New Leader*, March 13, 1948), 264.
[38] Baldwin, "*The Person and the Common Good*," 264–266.
[39] Hobgood, *Catholic Social Teaching and Economic Theory*, 243.
[40] Hobgood, *Catholic Social Teaching and Economic Theory*, 252.

I began to learn the body politics of knowledge when I was involved in a grassroots anti-poverty initiative in San Francisco in 1992. In the wake of the Rodney King verdict, I joined a group of African Americans protesting the April 29, 1992, acquittal of three police officers for their beating of Rodney King. At the corner of Golden Gate Avenue and Jones Street, then one of the poorest neighborhoods in the city, our group quickly found ourselves surrounded by police fully equipped with armor and weapons who, it seemed, were prepared to use deadly force against us. My Black American friends and colleagues let me know that the threat of violence I was experiencing was their daily existence. For me, it was only the beginning of bodily co-sensing how the US American democracy colonizes Black bodies and spaces.

This is when the Stanford University philosopher Sylvia Wynter wrote an open letter to her colleagues entitled "'No Humans Involved.'"[41] Wynter describes a radio news report she heard stating that "public officials in the judicial system of Los Angeles routinely use the acronym N.H.I. to refer to any case involving a breach of the rights of young Black males who belong to the jobless category of the inner city ghettos. N.H.I. means 'no humans involved.'"[42] Her letter begins with a discussion of how classification systems order human behavior. Everyone, including minorities, is equal in this classificatory schema, Wynter explains, "except in one category—that of peoples of African and Afro-mixed descent who, as Andrew Hacker points out in his recent book, are *the least equal of all.*"[43]

This raises the question: whence did this classification system come? How did these highly educated—college and law school educated—judicial professionals "conceive of what it means to be both *human* and *North American* in the *kinds of terms* (i.e., to be white, of Euroamerican culture and descent, middle class, college educated, and suburban) within whose logic, the jobless and usually school drop-out/push-out category of young Black males can be *perceived*, and *therefore behaved towards*, only as *Lack* of the human, the Conceptual Other to being North American?"[44] Undoubtedly, would not most, if not all, highly educated judicial professionals profess belief in universal human dignity?

This is an unsettling question for Roman Catholic social teaching. Even as the Roman Catholic hierarchy, Catholic social teaching

---

[41] Sylvia Wynter, "'No Humans Involved': An Open Letter to My Colleagues," in *Forum N.H.I.: Knowledge for the 21st Century* 1, no. 1 (Fall 1994): 1–17.
[42] Wynter, "'No Humans Involved,'" 1.
[43] Wynter, "'No Humans Involved,'" 1. She cites Andrew Hacker, *Two Nations: Black and White, Separate, Hostile, Unequal* (New York: Scribner's, 1992).
[44] Wynter, "'No Humans Involved,'" 1–2, emphasis in original.

advocates, and theologians may profess values of universal dignity and justice, that does not contend (by itself) with the ways in which all of us have been malformed by the colonial matrix of power (CMP). As theologian Jeannine Hill Fletcher reminds us, "It was in the academic spaces of theological training that ideas of Christian supremacy were manufactured as knowledge, to be put to the project of conquest, colonization, and conversion as they made their way from lecture hall to pulpit to legislative assemblies."[45]

How might we begin to take up the question "where did the system of classification that categorizes Black people as less than human originate?" Sylvia Wynter focuses attention on the Chilean biologists Humberto Maturana and Francisco Varela's work on autopoiesis, which defines living organisms "not as they are objects of observation and description, nor as interacting systems, but as self-contained unities whose only reference is to themselves."[46] The orthodox assumption in the 1960s was that the frog's *environment determined* what the frog could see. Maturana and Varela were thinking outside the orthodox paradigm. It is not coincidental, she notes, that Maturana and Varela were taking part in 1960s protests that helped them recognize how ignorant they were of social injustices.[47] Maturana and Varela revealed that, rather than the environment determining what the frog could see, the frog *specifies on its own* what is to be known in the environment; in other words, they discovered how biological organisms are "*autonomously functioning, living*," that is, autopoietic systems.[48]

Wynter is not suggesting that humans are biologically determined; she recognizes that systems like the beehive are "purely biological eusocial systems."[49] By contrast, human eusocial systems "are instead

---

[45] Jeannine Hill Fletcher, *The Sin of White Supremacy: Christianity, Racism, and Religious Diversity in America* (Maryknoll, NY: Orbis Books, 2017), 9. For a more in-depth examination of how the violence of colonialism has shaped US higher education, see Sharon Stein, *Unsettling the University: Confronting the Colonial Foundations of US Higher Education* (Baltimore, MD: Johns Hopkins University Press, 2022). See also Theresa Ambo and Theresa Rocha Beardall, "Performance or Progress? The Physical and Rhetorical Removal of Indigenous Peoples in Settler Land Acknowledgements at Land-Grab Universities," *American Educational Research Journal*, 60, no. 1 (2022): 103–140, doi.org/10.3102/00028312221141981.
[46] Robert S. Cohen and Marx W. Wartofsky, "Editorial Preface," in Humberto R. Maturana and Francisco J. Varela, *Autopoiesis and Cognition: The Realization of the Living* (Dordrecht: D. Reidel, 1980), v.
[47] Sylvia Wynter and Katherine McKittrick, "Unparalleled Catastrophe for Our Species? Or, to Give Humanness a Different Future: Conversations," in *Sylvia Wynter: On Being Human as a Praxis,* ed. Katherine McKittrick (Durham, NC: Duke University Press, 2015), 27–28. Wynter invites readers to notice and reflect on the ways social uprisings "have tremendous links to the transformation of knowledge."
[48] Wynter and McKittrick, "Unparalleled Catastrophe for Our Species?," 28.
[49] Wynter and McKittrick, "Unparalleled Catastrophe for Our Species?," 28.

hybrid languaging cum storytelling (if biologically implemented) living systems; but they function according to laws analogous to those regulatory laws of the supra-autopoietic system, which is the beehive."[50] Wynter thus refers to these laws of *hybrid human autospeciation* as autopoiesis.

Highlighting the dynamic interconnection between our genetic and non-genetic codes as "our first set of instructions" (the biological), Wynter interrelates "our second set of instructions" (what she refers to as our narrative mode of being) to the biological set. Her short terms for these instructions are *bios* and *mythoi*. The problem is: how do we become aware of the systems within which particular groups of people construct particular *genres* of the human? Wynter uses the term *genres*, as a play on gender, to highlight how humanness is not only *bios,* but also the stories we tell about our origins that also construct species-specific groupings of race, class, tribe, sexuality, etc.[51] Importantly, *genres* of the human are "enacted *outside* our conscious awareness—even though we ourselves have always rigorously and behaviorally adhered to them as indispensable to our genre-specific praxes of being hybridly human!"[52]

How do we become aware of our subjective sense of self and of the "referent-we" in which "we," for example—North American white settlers— reinscribe our sense of place and kin as a process of autopoiesis? Who is and is not included in specific use of the referent-we? The "abyssal line" is one way to sort out who is included or excluded. In his development of Fanon's description of *les damnés,* and the "zone of nonbeing" or subhumanity oppressed peoples inhabit, Boaventura de Sousa Santos describes the "abyssal line," as marking "the radical division between forms of metropolitan sociability and forms of colonial sociability that has characterized the Western world since the fifteenth century."[53]

White settlers on the colonial side of the abyssal line will likely be unable, on their own, to become self-reflective in response to the

---

[50] Wynter and McKittrick, "Unparalleled Catastrophe for Our Species?," 28, emphasis in original.
[51] Wynter and McKittrick, Unparalleled Catastrophe for Our Species?, 79, note 58. McKittrick explains that "Wynter put forward this hypothesis, revolving around 'gender' and 'genre,' in the paper 'Gender or the Genre of the Human?,' presented at a symposium held in honor of Sherley Anne Williams. A writer, poet, and professor of literature at UC San Diego, Williams first invited Wynter to join the faculty in the Department of Literature there."
[52] Wynter and McKittrick, "Unparalleled Catastrophe for Our Species?," 28.
[53] Boaventura de Sousa Santos, *The End of the Cognitive Empire: The Coming of Age of Epistemologies of the South* (Durham, NC: Duke University Press, 2018), 20.

question because of *where* and *how* we live.[54] Nonetheless, the question concerns the most pressing life and death predicaments today. There is an existential need to become aware of our origin myths in an epoch where, as "an already *postnuclear* cum post-cracking-the-code-of-our-genome species, we are now faced with an additional climate crisis situation in which it becomes even more imperative that these laws, for the first time in our species's history, be no longer allowed to function *outside our conscious awareness.*"[55]

Wynter draws heavily upon W. E. B. Du Bois and Frantz Fanon to reveal the geopolitical and paradoxical ways people socially-historically constructed as subhuman gain conscious bodily awareness of hybrid human auto-speciation or autopoiesis. I have drawn upon W. E. B. Du Bois's lived experience of double-consciousness in *Unlearning White Supremacy* as a gift[56] whereby white settler Christians might recognize, and begin to undo, a 500 year history of internalized supremacy and anti-Blackness. Here I draw upon Frantz Fanon, who described his own lived bodily experience of double consciousness within French colonialism that created an epistemological and ontological division between who counts and who does not count, as fully human. Wynter's reading of Fanon through Maturana and Varela informs my approach.

Fanon described his lived experience of an ontological division in *Les Damnés de la Terre*. Fanon wrote that "decolonization is the encounter between two congenitally antagonistic forces that in fact owe their singularity to the kind of reification secreted and nurtured by the colonial situation . . . continued at the point of the bayonet and under cannon fire."[57] Fanon responds directly to Roman Catholics when he argues that "by calling on humanity, on the belief in dignity, on love, on charity, it would be easy to prove, or to win the admission, that the black is the equal of the white. But my purpose is quite different: What I want to do is help the black man free himself from the arsenal of complexes that has been developed by the colonial environment."[58] The church has played a key role in establishing the

---

[54] Alex Mikulich, "White Habitus: The Ecosystem of Anti-Black White Supremacy," in *Unlearning White Supremacy,* chapter three.

[55] Wynter and McKittrick, "Unparalleled Catastrophe for Our Species?," 28. Original italics.

[56] In addition to Du Bois's gift of double-consciousness, I draw upon Fanon's appropriation of Martin Buber's "I-Thou" relationship to articulate a decolonial shift toward "co-sensing" reality and practicing receptive generosity in *Unlearning White Supremacy*, 82–90.

[57] Frantz Fanon, *The Wretched of the Earth,* trans. Richard Philcox (New York: Grove, 2004), 2.

[58] Frantz Fanon, *Black Skin, White Masks*, trans. Charles Lamm Markmann (New York: Grove, 1967), 30. Originally published in French as *Peau noire masques blancs* (Paris: Seuil, 1952).

pathology of white superiority and manipulation with which we must contend today.

Born in Martinique on July 20, 1925 and a decorated veteran of the Free French forces in World War II, Frantz Fanon attained his medical degree in psychiatry from the University of Lyons. He served a psychiatric hospital in Algeria before resigning and devoting his life to the decolonization of Algeria. He died of leukemia in 1961. Biographer David Macey enlists Lévi-Strauss's term *bricolage* to describe how Fanon wrote *Peau noire masques blancs,* eclectically integrating works by Jean-Paul Sartre, Maurice Merleau-Ponty, the emerging discourse of negritude,[59] and psychiatry.[60]

Fanon describes colonization as a "zone of nonbeing" because the black man "is the result of a series of aberrations of affect; he is rooted at the core of the universe from which he must be extricated." He continues to explain that he proposes "nothing short of the liberation of the man of color from himself. We shall go very slowly because there are two camps: the white and the black."[61] In the war between these two camps, "the black man wants to be white. The white man slaves to reach a human level. . . . The white man is sealed in his whiteness. The black in his blackness."[62]

The psychological inferiority complex is the result of a double process. This double process, he explains, is "primarily economic" and "subsequently, the internalization—or better, the epidermalization—of this inferiority." He continues to elaborate through an often quoted, critical paragraph:

> Reacting against the constitutionalist tendency of the late nineteenth century, Freud insisted that the individual factor be taken into account through psychoanalysis. He substituted for a phylogenetic theory the ontogenetic perspective. It will be seen that the black man's alienation is not an individual question. Beside phylogeny and ontogeny stands sociogeny . . . let us say this is a question of a sociodiagnostic.

What is the prognosis? "But society, unlike biochemical processes, cannot escape human influences. Man is what brings society into

---

[59] David Macey, *Frantz Fanon: A Life* (London: Granta, 2000), 181. The term negritude was implemented in the 1930s at a time when, as the Guyanese poet Leon-Gontras Damas explained, the Black man "wanted to become a historical and cultural actor, and not just an object of domination or a consumer of culture. . . . The word 'negritude' was coined in the most racist moment in history, and we accepted the word *nègre* as a challenge." Proponents included Aimé Césaire, Leopold Senghor, and Fanon, among others.
[60] Macey, *Frantz Fanon*, 162–163.
[61] Fanon, *Black Skin, White Masks*, 8.
[62] Fanon, *Black Skin, White Masks*, 9.

being. The prognosis is in the hands of those who are willing to get rid of the worm-eaten roots of the structure."[63] Sociogenesis reveals a geo-body political way to understand the social historical origins of race. Fanon opposes sociogenesis to *phylogeny*, the origins of species, and *ontogeny*, the development of an individual organism. Ontology does not help in understanding the origins of the double process because "Every ontology is made unattainable in a colonized and civilized society. . . . The black man has no ontological resistance in the eyes of the white man." Fanon goes on: "Overnight the Negro has been given two frames of reference within which he has had to place himself. His metaphysics, or, less pretentiously, his customs and sources on which they were based, were wiped out because they were in conflict with a civilization that he did not know and which imposed itself on him."[64] Fanon experiences bodily how Black people are simultaneously forced to see themselves through their own eyes, their "customs and sources," and through the eyes of white colonialists who "wiped out" Black people's customs and sources. He laments being unable to "make meaning for myself," because "it was the meaning already there, pre-existing, waiting for me."[65]

Both W. E. B. Du Bois and Fanon, who procured higher education and were inculturated into white bourgeois Western European institutions and languages, perceived what it is to be normal—to be perceived as a "Man"—and to be Black, that is, necessarily less than a man and abnormal. Fanon reveals this division through his experience of being a French *évolué*, one who evolved beyond his "native" Martinique through his fluency in French language and culture. Among his black fellows in Martinique, he experiences normality. This abruptly changes when contact occurs with the white "mother" nation.

As a French *évolué*, Fanon experienced the colonial curriculum which casts islands like Martinique as part of the extended French family yet, at the same time, teaches that Africans are primitive and savage. The slightest contact with the white world ensures "a certain sensitizing action takes place" in which "the black man stops acting as an *actional* person" and only can find self-esteem through the white Other.[66] Fanon becomes sensitized to a "corporeal schema," a "definitive structuring of the self and the world—definitive because it creates a real dialectic between my body and the world."[67] This corporeal schema begins to describe Fanon's experience of the body politics of knowledge.

---

[63] Fanon, *Black Skin, White Masks*, 13.
[64] Fanon, *Black Skin, White Masks*, 109–110.
[65] Fanon, *Black Skin, White Masks*, 134.
[66] Fanon, *Black Skin, White Masks*, 154.
[67] Fanon, *Black Skin, White Masks*, 111.

Echoing Maurice Merleau Ponty's *Phenomenology of Perception*, Fanon reflects on the example of all the movements he makes to begin smoking not out of habit but "implicit knowledge."[68] Mayra Rivera suggests that implicit knowledge is really "embodied knowledge."[69] In contrast to Merleau-Ponty's "open and dynamic, yet coherent structure of embodiment," Fanon "experiences constriction."[70] Perhaps the most famous example Fanon offers of his embodied experience of constriction is "the devastating experience" that "occurred on a cold day in Lyons when Fanon encountered a mother with her child."[71] Fanon tells his now famous story like this:

> "Look, a Negro!" It was an external stimulus that flicked over me as I passed by. I made a tight smile. Look, a Negro! It was true. It amused me. "Look, a Negro!" The circle was drawing tighter. I made no secret of my amusement. "Mama, see the Negro! I am frightened!" Frightened! Frightened! Now they were beginning to be afraid of me. I made up my mind to laugh myself to tears, but laughter had become impossible.[72]

Fanon's embodied knowledge leads him to discover a "historico-racial schema" that undergirds the imposed corporeal schema. It was no longer a question of experiencing his body in "the third person but in triple person. In the train I was given not one but two, three places . . . I existed triply: I occupied space. I moved toward the other . . . I was responsible at the same time for my body, for my race, for my ancestors. I subjected my body to objective examination; I discovered my blackness, my ethnic characteristics; and I was battered down by tom-toms, cannibalism, intellectual deficiency, fetishism, racial defects, slave ships, and above all else, above all: 'Sho' good eatin.'"[73] He concludes: "My body was given back to me sprawled out, distorted, recolored, clad in mourning, in that white winter day."[74] The "historico-racial schema" is composed of "white mythologies" and "produces objectification and fragmentation."[75]

White myths of innocence, as well as "an epistemology of ignorance" which, as Charles Mills explains, produces *"the ironic outcome that whites will in general be unable to understand the world*

---

[68] Fanon, *Black Skin, White Masks*, 111.
[69] Mayra Rivera, *Poetics of the Flesh* (Durham, NC: Duke University Press, 2015), 120.
[70] Rivera, *Poetics*, 121.
[71] Macey, *Frantz Fanon*, 115.
[72] Fanon, *Black Skin, White Masks*, 111–112.
[73] Fanon, *Black Skin, White Masks*, 112.
[74] Fanon, *Black Skin, White Masks*, 113.
[75] Rivera, *Poetics*, 121.

they have made,"⁷⁶ are dysfunctions that hide white violence: "The dominant, Fanon never stops reminding us, have a relation to their own violence, that of which they are the authors, which generally passes via mythologization, that is to say, a discursive derealization, a discourse cut out of history. The function of the myth is to make the victims responsible for the violence whose victims they are."⁷⁷ Fanon is clear that white colonial racism and objectification of Black people did not come out of nowhere, is not biological, natural, or transhistorical.⁷⁸ Racism in the form of anti-Blackness is a white colonial creation and endures because white society perpetuates mythologies that hide the violence within us. The white myth works, not only through an inverted epistemology (see Charles Mills in note 76), but also through a "bizarre emotional logic" in which racism operates as a way to defend "my lack" of something I want and, ultimately, my own insecurity.⁷⁹ The best way to "short circuit" my own self-realization that I am the source of racism is to project the other as the embodiment of evil and source of the threat.⁸⁰ White European society created Blackness, and especially Black men, as the "phobogenic object" with "all the attributes of malefic power.'"⁸¹ White society created a racist imagery of the "Negro as sexual object [that] is the equivalent of an aggressive and frightening object, capable of inflicting abuse and traumas on his victim."⁸² In the "twisted emotional logic of racism, I, the racist, hence become the victim of you, the 'racial other' who undermines and threatens my existence. You, on the other hand, become *my persecutor*, that which represents all that is threatening to me. Hence, I deserve protection against *you*, and *you*, on the other hand, *deserve punishment.*"⁸³ These psychological and political dynamics, as Fanon demonstrates, result in lynching and other forms of governmental regulation, policing, and vigilante violence that repeat, reiterate, and reinforce the sacramentalization of violence—necropolitics.⁸⁴ The church, CST, and its practitioners have yet to contend with the multiple ways sociopolitical and historical

---

⁷⁶ Charles Mills, *The Racial Contract* (Ithaca, NY: Cornell University Press, 1997), 18, emphasis in original.
⁷⁷ Achille Mbembe, *Necropolitics* (Durham, NC: Duke University Press, 2019), 137–138. [First published as *Politiques de l'inimitié* (Paris: La Découverte, 2016).]
⁷⁸ Derek Hook, "Fanon and the Psychoanalysis of Racism," in *Critical Psychology*, ed. Derek Hook (Lansdowne, South Africa: Juta Academic, 2004), 116. Mbembe, *Necropolitics,* 134.
⁷⁹ Hook, "Fanon and the Psychoanalysis of Racism," 134.
⁸⁰ Hook, "Fanon and the Psychoanalysis of Racism," 134.
⁸¹ Mbembe, *Necropolitics*, 134. Fanon, *Black Skin, White Masks*, 155.
⁸² Mbembe, *Necropolitics*, 134.
⁸³ Hook, "Fanon and the Psychoanalysis of Racism," 134, emphasis in original.
⁸⁴ Mbembe, *Necropolitics*, 137–138. See also Hook, "Fanon and the Psychoanalysis of Racism," 135.

circumstances of colonial domination interrelate with white pathological violence.

The historical racial schema reinscribes that Black people are perceived as abnormal and white people as normal and good. In other words, Fanon experiences in the Western colonial educational system that in order to be a normal human, an acceptable white bourgeois subject, he must also normally perceive Africans "as *savage, primitive, wicked*, and, as such, the predestined target villains, in French adventure stories, of a range of imperially civilizing French heroes!"[85]

Paradoxically, in their respective lived experiences of double-consciousness, both Du Bois in early twentieth century imperial America and Fanon in mid-twentieth century French colonial Algeria utilize a self-questioning heuristic of mistrust[86] of their own self-consciousness to discover both the causality of their predicament, a way to critique it and, ultimately, a way to extricate themselves and others from it. Fanon discovered, explains Wynter, "from today's hindsight . . . the hitherto unknown, unsuspected, yet law-likely functioning, non-physically, non-biologically *determined*, if itself biologically implemented, principle of causality. That principle alone . . . underwrites our *genre-specific* and hybridly instituted human orders of consciousness, together with their respective modes of mind/minding."[87]

Fanon observes how these dualistic dynamics are replicated in society. Childhood socialization, Fanon finds, is a case in point of this duality between being and nonbeing, man and not man, and "normal" and "abnormal." He discerns a close connection between the structure of the French family and the nation. In every European country or every "civilized and civilizing" country, Fanon argues, the "family is a miniature of the nation."[88] The child finds himself among the same laws, principles, and values and, as a "normal child that has grown up in a normal family will be a normal man. There is no disproportion between the life of the family and the life of the nation."[89]

Fanon's sociodiagnostic, comparative analysis of French socialization with the socialization of African Pygmies, reveals an ironic paradox. "Conversely," he wrote, "when one examines a closed society—that is, a society that has been protected from the flood of civilization—one encounters the same structures as those just

---

[85] Wynter and McKittrick, "Unparalleled Catastrophe for Our Species?," 55.
[86] Wynter and McKittrick, "Unparalleled Catastrophe for Our Species?," 52.
[87] Wynter and McKittrick, "Unparalleled Catastrophe for Our Species?," 52, emphasis in original.
[88] Fanon, *Black Skin, White Masks*, 142.
[89] Fanon, *Black Skin, White Masks*, 142.

described" of French society.⁹⁰ Drawing upon the scholarship of Father Trilles's *L'âme du Pygmée d'Afrique*, Fanon argues that despite Trilles's attempt to evangelize the Pygmies, Trilles describes conditions of worship, rites, and the survival of myths similar to the characteristics of French families. The characteristics of the family are projected onto the larger social environments in both the French and Pygmy families. If the family is the miniature of the nation in France, then the Pygmy family is a miniature of Pygmy society.

In terms of autopoiesis, Wynter explains that in both cases "they will come to subjectively experience themselves, reflexly in the respective terms of their own unquestioned, genre-specific, *normalcy of being human*."⁹¹ Simply put, the Pygmies view themselves as humanly normal—they have no experience of being Black or inferior. In both cases therefore, "*normalcy* underwrites their respective societal orders' status quo system of role allocations, as well as that of their also, always already autonomously invented, storytelling chartered and encoded, thereby auto-centered, genre-specific notions of the Self."⁹² Wynter unpacks an ironic reverse paradox in Fanon's comparative analysis. Fanon reveals that "in the everyday run of things—as in the transcosmogonic, transcultural cases of the auto-centered Pygmy and French bourgeois subjects—any questioning of their respective parts of their shared *reflexly subjectively experienced normalcy of being human* is law-likely foreclosed."⁹³ In other words, it is highly likely that the French bourgeois subjective response of racial phobia is not arbitrary; rather, it is collectively conventional. In contrast, Pygmies subjectively perceive themselves as human.

Returning to the present, Western epistemologies that created modernity/coloniality have developed over more than five hundred years. Some scholars trace the roots of the Roman Catholic Church's coloniality nearly back to early Christianity.⁹⁴ We must, at the very least, go back to the early 1400s.⁹⁵ After Columbus's so-called discovery of the "New World," Pope Alexander issued a series of bulls in 1493 that affirmed both Portugal's rights to Africa and Spain's rights to the lands and peoples of the "New World."⁹⁶ The Catholic partition of the world begins with the Treaty of Tordesillas in 1494,

---

⁹⁰ Fanon, *Black Skin, White Masks*, 142.
⁹¹ Wynter and McKittrick, "Unparalleled Catastrophe for Our Species?," 55.
⁹² Wynter and McKittrick, "Unparalleled Catastrophe for Our Species?," 55.
⁹³ Wynter and McKittrick, "Unparalleled Catastrophe for Our Species?," 56, emphasis in original.
⁹⁴ Aloysius Pieris, "The Option for the Poor and the Recovery of Christian Identity: Toward an Asian Theology of Religions Dictated by the Poor," in *The Option for the Poor in Christian Theology*, 271–289.
⁹⁵ Pius Onyemechi Adiele, *The Popes, the Catholic Church, and the Transatlantic Enslavement of Black Africans 1418–1839* (Hildesheim: Georg Olms, 2017).
⁹⁶ Adiele, *The Popes*, 349–354.

when the Pope draws a line that divides the north and south of the Atlantic ocean to settle a dispute between Portugal and Spain.[97] It is upon the basis of this treaty that Spanish administrators created a document in 1512–1513, named the Requisition, to "establish grounds of the legitimacy for the state's expropriation of lands, and the sovereignty of peoples of the indigenous cultural worlds of the Caribbean and the Americas."[98] Wynter draws the following quote from a report of the 16th century Centu Indians on the Requisition: "About the Pope being the Lord of all the universe in the place of God, and that he had given the lands of the Indies to the King of Castile, the Pope must have been drunk when he did it, for he gave what was not his . . . The king who asked for and received this gift must have been a madman for he asked to be given to him that which belonged to others."[99] The Requisition, Wynter explains, created a new world system that legitimated the "dynamic transfer of wealth and resources from the rest of the world to Western European enclaves . . . that made the 'real real' and the 'normal normal' for the invading European Christians."[100] The church and CST have yet to contend with this legacy of the "racialization of flesh" and "metaphysical violence."[101]

THREE SHIFTS TOWARD DECOLONIZING CATHOLIC SOCIAL TEACHING AND DEMOCRACY

Shift from Applying Abstract Universals and Philosophical Idealism to the Priority of Geopolitical Praxis with and for les damnés.

The "seeds of alienation have been sown among the colonized," Frantz Fanon wrote, by "Christianity and this should come to no surprise to anyone." He went on to say that the "Church in the colonies is the white man's Church, a foreigner's Church. It does not call the colonized to the ways of God, but to the ways of the white man, to the ways of the master, the ways of the oppressor."[102] In this context of the church's complicity in coloniality, prioritizing the call of historical struggle is most important for witness to the truth of the Gospel. As Gustavo Gutierrez has never tired of declaring:

---

[97] Mignolo, *Darker Side*, 79.
[98] Sylvia Wynter, "The Pope Must Have Been Drunk, The King of Castile a Madman: Culture as Actuality, and the Caribbean Rethinking Modernity," in *The Reordering of Culture: Latin America, the Caribbean, and Canada*, ed. Alvenia Ruprecht and Cecilia Taiana (Ottawa: Carleton University Press, 1995), 19.
[99] Wynter, "The Pope Must Have Been Drunk," 18–19.
[100] Wynter, "The Pope Must Have Been Drunk," 19.
[101] Copeland, "Anti-Blackness and White Supremacy," 7.
[102] Frantz Fanon, *The Wretched of the Earth*, trans. Richard Philcox (New York: Grove, 2004, first published in English in 1967), 7.

> The first stage of theological work is the lived faith that finds expression in prayer and commitment. To live the faith means to put into practice, in light of the demands of the reign of God, these fundamental elements of Christian existence. . . . The second act of theology, that of reflection in the proper sense of the term, has for its purpose to read this complex praxis in the light of God's word.[103]

M. Shawn Copeland extends Gutierrez's point by clarifying that our role as theologians means sinking deep roots into the ground of spirituality and practice where we "collaborate fundamentally in bringing about a different world in the here and now."[104] She elaborates that our ultimate commitment can never be to any "system or structure, person or group, church or university, but only to the God of Jesus Christ."[105] It is the witness of prophetic praxis "that demonstrates the risk and meaning of a life lived in prayerful hope."[106] For CST, that means Catholic social justice institutes and centers are not the starting point or core of living the Gospel. Theologians, ethicists, and activists engaged in decolonial movements need to unlearn how we have been malformed in the midst of imperial domains and humbly live in recognition of James Cone's insight that we can meet Jesus only in the "crucified bodies in our midst," where we may yet remember the real scandal of the cross.[107] Boaventura de Sousa Santos calls our attention to the ways Eurocentric knowledges tend to be "monuments" of written and archival knowledge. Decolonial praxis includes opening to diverse ways of knowing and being. CST, I contend, needs a "demonumentalizing intervention" to recognize that the written body of CST is not the purpose of our work; rather, becoming "open to other ways of knowing [that] may be able to show their possible contribution to a more diverse and profound understanding of the world and a more efficient and widely shared progressive social transformation."[108]

A decolonial prophetic praxis means joining in local struggles for global liberation, learning from these contexts, and learning how to

---

[103] Gutierrez, *A Theology of Liberation*, xxxiv. See Gustavo Gutierrez, *On Job: God-talk and the Suffering of the Innocent*, trans. Matthew O'Connell (Maryknoll, NY: Orbis Books, 1987), xiii.

[104] M. Shawn Copeland, "Racism and the Vocation of the Christian Theologian," *Spiritus* 2, no. 1 (Spring 2002): 26, doi.org/10.1353/scs.2002.0008.

[105] Copeland, "Racism and the Vocation of the Christian Theologian," 26.

[106] Copeland, "Racism and the Vocation of the Christian Theologian," 26.

[107] Alex Mikulich, "Authentically Catholic and Truly Black: On the Condition of the Possibility of a Just Peace Approach to Anti-Black Violence," in *A Just Peace Ethic Primer: Building Sustainable Peace and Breaking Cycles of Violence*, ed. Eli McCarthy (Washington, DC: Georgetown University Press, 2020), 121.

[108] Boaventura de Sousa Santos, *The End of Cognitive Empire: The Coming of Age of Epistemologies of the South* (Durham, NC: Duke University Press, 2018), 187.

become fully human with and for peoples re-existing on their own terms.[109] In decolonial terms, re-existing means epistemological and ethical disobedience to modernity/coloniality and its genres of the human, and re-linking with "legacies one wants to preserve in order to engage in modes of existence with which one wants to engage" to live and thrive.[110] For example, African *ubuntu*,[111] Andean *sumak kawsay* or *vivir bien*,[112] or the Abenaki common pot,[113] far from being idiosyncratic, "are constitutive of pluriversal polyphony, a polylectal, rather than idiolectal, conception of cultural and political imagination."[114] These are examples of the legacies with which diverse peoples are re-linking to re-exist. In this way, the *damnés* emerge as the primary agents of social transformation, "to affirm their own selves and to create a world *in which many worlds can fit*."[115] These are concrete ways CST needs to move from Western pluralism to relearn through pluriversal perspectives.[116]

Last, but not least, decolonial praxis is both an eschatological and historical reality. As Joseph Drexler-Dreis suggests, this does not necessarily mean changing the orientations of liberation theologies, but it does entail "investing in new forms of analysis and continuing to ground theological language more strongly in historical realities while doing so in light of the imagination and commitment to the sacred."[117] A decolonial moral imagination is fostered in the midst of praxis "toward social transformation in the direction of the Reign of God with its justice, equality, freedom, and peace. . . . Eschatological freedom demands that we work to change things now."[118] Eschatological freedom means taking responsibility for the roles we play in reifying white pathologies and violence. People on the colonial side of the abyssal line need to unlearn coloniality and relearn what it means to be human so others may thrive through their own ways of

---

[109] de Sousa Santos, *End of Cognitive Empire*, 220.
[110] Walter Mignolo, "Coloniality is Far from Over, and So Must Be Decoloniality," *Afterall* 43, (2017): 41, dx.doi.org/10.1086/692552.
[111] de Sousa Santos, *End of Cognitive Empire*, 9–12.
[112] Mignolo, *Darker Side*, 64 and 306–312.
[113] Lisa Brooks, *The Common Pot: The Recovery of Native Space in the Northeast* (Minneapolis: University of Minnesota Press, 2008), 4 and 253–254.
[114] de Sousa Santos, *End of Cognitive Empire*, 12.
[115] Nelson Maldonado-Torres, *Against War: Views from the Underside of Modernity* (Durham, NC: Duke University Press, 2008), 230.
[116] See, for example, Achille Mbembe and Felwine Sarr, eds., *To Write the Africa World* (Cambridge: Polity, 2023, originally published in French as *Écrire l'Afrique-monde* (Dakar: Jimsaan, 2017).
[117] Joseph Drexler-Dreis, *Decolonial Love: Salvation in Colonial Modernity* (New York: Fordham University Press, 2019), 161.
[118] Rayan, "Decolonization of Theology," 149 and 151.

knowing and being. Otherwise, eschatology easily becomes a spiritualized individualism.

Shift from Anthropocentrism to a Primary Focus on Land and Earth Democracy

"For a colonized people," wrote Frantz Fanon, "the most essential value, because it is the most meaningful, is first and foremost the land: the land, which must provide bread, and naturally dignity. But this dignity has nothing to do with 'human' dignity."[119] Land is at the heart of decolonization struggles in Canada, New Zealand, Australia, and the United States.[120] Decolonization requires repatriation of Indigenous land and life.[121] This is not to claim that repatriation of land is an easy process; given the history of stolen lands, it is difficult to foresee anything but conflict. The work requires repatriation and recovering how "living cultures based on recovery of the earth identity create potential for reintegrating human activities into the earth's ecological processes and limits."[122]

Earth democracy is fundamentally oriented to the earth's cycles, recognizing that all beings have the right to sustenance and security within local ecologies interconnected with all other fragile ecosystems that no humans have the right to own.[123] Economic systems in earth democracy protect ecosystems and their integrity, and they protect people's livelihoods and basic needs. Earth democracy means shifting from individual rights to acknowledging and protecting collective rights of Indigenous peoples and local ecosystems. In this way, a shift to earth democracy is really a return to the early church teaching of the Cappadocians—the goods of God's creation yield abundance for all, in which our shared responsibility is for all of our human and non-human kin. Private property ownership must be re-oriented to a decolonial earth ethic so that Black, LatinX, and Indigenous peoples can re-exist. Shiva reminds us that the "earth economy is a living economy. It is based on sustainable, diverse, pluralistic systems that protect nature and people, are chosen by the people, and work for the common good."[124]

---

[119] Fanon, *The Wretched*, 9.
[120] Jakeet Singh, "Decolonizing Radical Democracy," *Contemporary Political Theory* 18 (2019): 341, doi.org/10.1057/s41296-018-0277-5.
[121] Tuck and Yang, "Decolonization is Not a Metaphor," 21, 25, 31.
[122] Vandana Shiva, *Earth Democracy: Justice, Sustainability, and Peace* (Cambridge, MA: South End, 2005), 7.
[123] Shiva, *Earth Democracy*, 9.
[124] Shiva, *Earth Democracy*, 10.

Theologian Melissa Pagán suggests two concepts that assist in challenging extractivist approaches to bodies and lands.[125] Her first practice "privileges a hermeneutics of *el grito,* which can be translated as 'the cry.'"[126] She explains that "from a Puerto Rican perspective, a *hermeneutics of el grito* is rooted in *El Grito de Lares,* a rebellion against colonial rule and oppression that took place in 1868."[127] Pagán integrates Frantz Fanon's phenomenology of the cry, the eruption of grief and desire for recognition "within the space of colonial difference" with lament.[128] This is a way of "undermining the extractive view of persons and lands" to "facilitate growth of an integral ecology that authentically allows" an ecological approach to become a social approach that promotes hearing the cries of both the earth and the poor.[129] This organically leads to the second practice, that of *vincularidad. Vincularidad,* a core practice of the Amawtay Wasi, means co-relationality, but the Western translation misses its cosmological context as the center of all life-giving energies. In its Andean context *vincularidad* "is another way of expressing relationality and solidarity with the land and the cosmos *outside the one mode of knowledge and being.*"[130] It cultivates resistance to extractive zones and facilitates a decolonial way of people and non-human kin re-existing on their own terms.[131]

Shift from Exclusive Focus on Western Linear Time to Pluriversal Non-Linear Time

Too often, chronological Western time is taken as natural, neutral, and global. Walter Mignolo draws upon the work of Johannes Fabian to explain how Western time is a colonizing strategy, especially through the "denial of coevalness."[132] Fabian defines the "denial of coevalness" as a "persistent and systematic tendency to place the referent(s) of anthropology in a Time other than the present of the producer of anthropological discourse."[133] Fabian delineates an

---

[125] Melissa Pagán, "Cultivating a Decolonial Feminist Integral Ecology: Extractive Zones and the Nexus of Coloniality of Being/Coloniality of Gender," *Journal of Hispanic/Latino Theology* 22, no. (2020): 6, repository.usfca.edu/jhlt/vol22/iss1/6.
[126] Pagán, "Cultivating a Decolonial Feminist Integral Ecology," 20–21.
[127] Pagán, "Cultivating a Decolonial Feminist Integral Ecology," 21.
[128] Pagán, "Cultivating a Decolonial Feminist Integral Ecology," 21.
[129] Pagán, "Cultivating a Decolonial Feminist Integral Ecology," 23. Pagán cites *Laudato Si'*, no. 49.
[130] Pagán, "Cultivating a Decolonial Feminist Integral Ecology," 26.
[131] Pagán, "Cultivating a Decolonial Feminist Integral Ecology," 25.
[132] Mignolo, *Darker Side*, 152. He cites Johannes Fabian, *Time and the Other: How Anthropology Makes Its Object* (New York: Columbia University Press, reprint, 2014, [1983]), 1.
[133] Fabian, *Time and the Other*, 31.

intellectual history of anthropology's complicity in European colonialism rooted in both the Judeo-Christian Mediterranean conception of time and the Western notion of evolutionary time.[134]

The result is that the colonial matrix of power (CMP) locates "barbarians" and "primitives" as behind and subordinate to superior Western knowledge. "Barbarians" and "primitives" are categorically in a lower chronological scale that "naturally" drives toward Western civilization.[135] The construct of Western chronological time implies that barbarian, primitive, and pagan ways of knowing are all subordinate to European knowledge. Evolutionary time, Mignolo explains, becomes "the beginning of time, the secular version of the beginning of the world and human beings." Mignolo's point is that "time was naturalized as both the measure of human history (modernity) and the time-scale of human beings (primitives) in their distance [from] modernity."[136] The redefinition of time through the denial of coevalness "contributed to holding together the colonial matrix of power imaginary from its emergence as part of the Atlantic circuit (in the sixteenth century) to the current consolidation of the North Atlantic (the United States and the European Union)."[137]

Reexamining time is necessary because Western assumptions erase Indigenous knowledge. Consider feminist cultural critic Heather Davis's and Metis scholar Zoe Todd's reflection on the entanglements across time between other-than-human and human kin that herald Black and Indigenous ways of attending to mutually complex interrelationships between rocks, fish, and human kin.[138] They contemplate Christina Sharpe's *In the Wake: On Blackness and Being* where she invites readers to imagine the historical, hydrological wake of an Atlantic slave ship to co-sense the enslaved peoples deliberately drowned in the Middle Passage who endure through "residence time." The amount of time it takes a substance to enter the ocean and leave it is what scientists call "residence time." A colleague who is a marine geographer informs Sharpe that human blood is salty, and sodium has a residence time of 260 million years.[139]

Sharpe then asks: "What happens to the energy produced in the waters? It continues cycling like atoms in residence time. We, Black people, exist in the residence time of the wake, a time in which 'all is

---

[134] Fabian, *Time and the Other*, 2–21.
[135] Mignolo, *Darker Side*, 153.
[136] Mignolo, *Darker Side*, 153.
[137] Mignolo, *Darker Side*, 153–154.
[138] Heather Davis and Zoe Todd, "On the Importance of a Date, or Decolonizing the Anthropocene," *ACME* 16, no. 4 (2017): 761–780, acme-journal.org/index.php/acme/article/view/1539.
[139] Christina Sharpe, *In the Wake: On Blackness and Being* (Durham, NC: Duke University Press, 2016), 41.

now. It is all now.'"[140] Residence time offers the possibility of learning from Black and Indigenous ancestors whose bodies endure in landmass and oceans as "oxygen, hydrogen, and atoms."[141]

Returning to the opening of this essay, I contend that the Roman Catholic Church cannot adequately reckon with its complicity in the catastrophic transformation of power, knowledge, and being that began in the 15th century without decoloniality. Pluriversal ways of practicing decoloniality are available to local faith communities and the global church. Decolonizing Catholic social teaching is incommensurable with the feudal and orthodox social models because decolonization means returning stolen lands, healing wounds of genocide and slavery, ending racial capitalism, and providing reparations to local communities experiencing the oppressive legacies of the colonial matrix of power. Catholic social teaching needs pluriversal approaches to enflesh an integral ecology, remember how coloniality endures in time and space, and attend to the ways decolonization of time demands healing of colonial wounds. Decolonizing CST begins with geopolitical praxis with and for people below the abyssal line, shifting from anthropocentric philosophical arguments to the priority of land and earth democracy, and re-orienting conceptions of time and space that prioritize the full thriving of all our human and non-human kin. M

Alex Mikulich, PhD, is a Catholic social ethicist, award winning author, antiracism facilitator and activist. He is the author of *Unlearning White Supremacy: A Spirituality for Racial Liberation* (Orbis Books, 2022). He has served as an invited affiliate member of the Black Catholic Theological Symposium since 2008.

---

[140] Sharpe, *In the Wake*, 41. Sharpe quotes Toni Morrison, *Beloved* (New York: Plume, 1987), 198.
[141] David and Todd, "On the Importance of a Date."

Afterword

John T. McGreevy

Abstract: In 1941, Jacques Maritain mused about writing a variation on the Federalist papers, this time keyed not only to approval of the United States constitution but for the "entire world."[1] We could use such a document now, as democracies falter. Maritain, more than any other thinker, laid the groundwork for the Catholic Church's endorsement of democracy. The task today, therefore, is to remember and also improve upon what Maritain once taught us.

EXILED TO NEW YORK CITY AS THE WEHRMACHT OCCUPIED France, Jacques Maritain asked his friend Yves Simon, also a philosopher exiled from France to the United States, where he was teaching at the University of Notre Dame, for a favor. Could he run to the library and confirm that Thomas Aquinas understood "that consent of the people is required for the legitimacy of the state"?[2]

Simon supplied the citation. Bitterly. Both Simon and Maritain knew that Catholic intellectuals around the world during the 1930s had admired Austria's Engelbert Dolfuss, who had dissolved that country's Parliament in an effort to build a "Catholic" state. Others lauded Portugal's Antonio Salazar, a dictator and onetime Catholic youth leader, whose corporatist regime invoked *Rerum Novarum* while prohibiting independent trade unions or political parties. Salazar's influence extended from Portugal to Brazil and across Latin America. Most Catholics supported Francisco Franco during the Spanish Civil War, and photos of Spanish bishops blessing the generalissimo became a staple of the Catholic press. In France itself, after the German occupation of the country in 1940, many Catholics, and probably a majority of Catholic intellectuals, rallied to the banner of the authoritarian Vichy government.

---

[1] Jacques Maritain to Yves Simon, October 3, 1941, in *Jacques Maritain, Yves Simon Correspondance. Tome 2: Les années américaines*, ed. Florian Michel (Tours: CLD, 2008), 76–77.
[2] This afterword draws upon material in John T. McGreevy, *Catholicism: A Global History from the French Revolution to Pope Francis* (New York: W. W. Norton, 2022) and John T. McGreevy, "'Natural Enemies' No More: How Rome Finally Embraced Democracy," *Commonweal*, July/August 2022, www.commonwealmagazine.org/natural-enemies-no-more. Reproduced with permission.

When Simon scanned this Catholic political landscape in 1941, he despaired. As he told Maritain, talking of Catholic democracy in this context was "only trash." The antagonism of Catholics to democracy "is the problem we are asked to overcome."[3]

A generation later, the problem of Catholic democracy seemed not a problem at all. The final document at the Second Vatican Council, *Gaudium et Spes* (1965), urged recognition of the fact that all people "individually or collectively, can take an active part in the life and government of the state."[4] During the 1980s and 1990s, Catholics in Brazil, Poland, the Philippines, South Korea, and Spain led movements for democratic reform, often invoking documents of the Second Vatican Council as they did so.[5]

The sentence on democracy in *Gaudium et Spes* (1965) built upon decades of work by many hands, but perhaps the writings of Maritain most of all. In his 1936 masterpiece, *Integral Humanism*, Maritain had already outlined his Catholic and democratic vision. The flourishing of the human "person" required respect for her embeddedness in communities such as the family, professions, and churches. Catholics should not translate theological categories directly into politics and should instead welcome pluralism. Democratic governments with universal suffrage (for women as well as men) followed from this distinction between religious and political authority.

Maritain promoted his version of democratic personalism through ceaseless writing and traveling, from Germany to Canada, Poland, Argentina, Spain, and the United States. In Italy—where many Catholic intellectuals supported Mussolini into the late 1930s—Maritain's ideas thrilled a cadre of young activists disenchanted with Il Duce, including Fr. Giovanni Battista Montini, the future Pope Paul VI. Maritain also sailed to South America. In Rio de Janeiro and Buenos Aires, his lectures attracted the country's leading intellectuals. He persuaded the director of Brazil's most influential Catholic think tank to identify himself as an "open Catholic, democratic, and reformist."[6]

Exile in the United States from 1940 to 1944 deepened Maritain's convictions. In 1941, he defended democracy as a system of government superior to any alternative. "It is necessary to show," he

---

[3] Yves Simon to Jacques Maritain, July 16, 1941, in *Maritain-Simon Correspondence*, tome 2, 64–66.
[4] *Gaudium et Spes*, no. 75.
[5] Samuel P. Huntington, "Democracy's Third Wave," *Journal of Democracy* 2, no. 2 (1991): 12–34, doi.org/10.1353/jod.1991.0016.
[6] Michael Löwy and Jesús García-Ruiz, "Les sources françaises du christianisme de la libération au Brésil," *Archives de sciences sociales des religions* 42 (1997): 14–18, doi.org/10.3406/assr.1997.1120.

told Yves Simon, that "St. Thomas was a democrat, in this sense . . . the Gospel works in history in a democratic direction."[7]

Pope Pius XII himself almost certainly drew on Maritain's writings. In his 1944 Christmas address, after several caveats, the pope announced that "the democratic form of government" now appeared "to many as a postulate of nature imposed by reason itself." One of Maritain's friends, a distinguished Swiss theologian, archly noted "numerous coincidences" between the papal address and Maritain's prose.[8]

After the war, Maritain played an important role in the UNESCO committee that helped draft the 1948 Declaration of Human Rights. At the same time, Maritain's ideas underwrote one of the key achievements of twentieth century political history: Christian Democratic parties. After almost a century of doubting the efficacy of democracy, at least in Europe and Latin America, Catholics became its guarantors. For all or part of the period between 1945 and 1980, Christian Democratic parties held power in Italy, Germany, Switzerland, Belgium, the Netherlands, Austria, Brazil, Chile, Venezuela, Ecuador, El Salvador, Guatemala, and Costa Rica. Even parties not formally identified as Christian Democratic—such as the Mouvement Républicain Populaire in France, the Democratic Party in Uganda, the Indische Katholieke Partij in Indonesia, or the Fianna Fáil in Ireland—adopted parallel language as they pushed for family allowances, encouraged trade unions and urged Catholics to participate in democratic governance.

Not only Catholics belonged to Christian Democratic parties, and they were never controlled by the institutional church. Maritain himself never became active in a political party. But the lineage is direct. By 1960, the list of Catholic presidents and prime ministers influenced by Maritain was striking. It included Konrad Adenauer (West Germany) and Alcide de Gasperi (Italy), leaders of Europe's most prominent Christian Democratic parties. It included Robert Schuman (Prime Minister of France in 1947–1948 and later head of the European Parliamentary Commission), and Charles de Gaulle (France), who corresponded with Maritain while mobilizing Free French forces in London during the war and appointed Maritain as French ambassador to the Holy See in 1945. It included Presidents Léopold Senghor (Senegal), raised in the French empire, and Prime Minister Benedicto Kiwanuka (Uganda) raised in the British empire. By 1970 such a list would have included Eduardo Frei (Chile), Rafael

---

[7] Jacques Maritain to Yves Simon, June 15, 1941, in *Maritain-Simon Correspondance,* tome 2, 60–62.

[8] "Pope's Christmas Message, 1944," *Catholic Mind* 43 (1945), 68; Charles Journet to Jacques Maritain, April 5, 1945, in *Journet-Maritain Correspondance*, ed. Msgr. Pierre Magie and Georges Cottier, OP (Fribourg: Saint-Augustin, 1996), tome 3, 310.

Caldera (Venezuela), and Pierre Trudeau (Canada). It did not include John F. Kennedy (United States) whose intellectual formation was innocent of Catholic social thought, but it did include his brother-in-law, Sargent Shriver, the first director of the Peace Corps and the War on Poverty, and the Minnesota Senator Eugene McCarthy, famous for his opposition to the Vietnam War. It even included Joseph R. Biden, Sr., father of a future United States President. Maybe it is not true, as President Biden told journalist David Brooks, that his working-class father read Maritain in the 1950s. But President Biden's remembering, or even misremembering, remains significant.[9]

The decision of the editors of the *Journal of Moral Theology* to dedicate an issue to Maritain and democracy conveys our distance from this soothing narrative. The contemporary democratic crisis is now acutely felt. Catholic leaders in Poland edge toward authoritarianism, and voters in the heavily Catholic Philippines elect a dictator disdainful of civil liberties. Steven Levitsky and Daniel Ziblatt, in their superb *How Democracies Die,* identify markers of democratic decline. They observe how in the 1930s hierarchical Catholicism rested uneasily next to democratic politics. Some Catholic leaders—as in Belgium—actively resisted authoritarianism. Others—as in Austria, Portugal, Brazil, and Argentina—welcomed it.[10]

The fine essays in this special issue probe the question of democracy and Catholicism in multiple ways. I will not rehearse their many individual merits, but will note that the cumulative effect is to place democracy near the center of Catholic social thought. We should not take this for granted. For much of the twentieth century democracy was the dog that did not bark in Catholic social thought. The term did not appear in *Rerum Novarum* (1891) or *Quadragesimo Anno* (1931). Even in the 1970s, as noted in some of the essays in this volume, liberation theologians dismissed Maritain's focus on democracy and human rights as a form of complacency in societies marked by grave inequalities.

These criticisms of Maritain have rich roots in the French *nouvelle théologie*, and also reflect the particular situation of Latin America in the 1970s.[11] But in the current moment they seem less compelling than another project: connecting Catholic social thought to democratic

---

[9] David Brooks, "Has Biden Changed? He Tells Us," *New York Times*, May 20, 2021, www.nytimes.com/2021/05/20/opinion/joe-biden-david-brooks-interview.html.
[10] Steven Levitsky and Daniel Ziblatt, *How Democracies Die* (Cambridge, MA: Broadway, 2018), esp. 26–29.
[11] Sarah Shortall, *Soldiers of God in a Secular World: Catholic Theology and Twentieth-Century French Politics* (Cambridge, MA: Harvard University Press, 2021).

theory. The immediate challenge is not to narrow the distance between theology and politics, as Gustavo Gutiérrez and his disciples once desired, but to justify self-government in theological terms. The focus in the last generation of Catholic social thought on particular issues—most notably abortion—has obscured the importance of compromise, negotiation, and the acceptance of unpredictable outcomes. Too often the tone has been prophetic, not pragmatic, a difficult rhetorical stance in a pluralist society.

In 1941, Jacques Maritain mused about writing a variation on the Federalist papers, this time keyed not only to approval of the United States constitution but for the "entire world."[12] We could use such a document now, as democracies falter. The task is not only to remember, but to improve upon, what Maritain once taught us.

John T. McGreevy, PhD, is the Charles and Jill Fischer Provost and Francis A. McAnaney Professor of History at the University of Notre Dame. His scholarship focuses on both American and global religion and politics, and he has authored four books that explore the people and the impact of the Catholic Church including, most recently, *Catholicism: A Global History from the French Revolution to Pope Francis* (W. W. Norton, 2022).

---

[12] Jacques Maritain to Yves Simon, October 3, 1941, *Maritain-Simon Correspondance*, tome 2, 76–77.

www.ingramcontent.com/pod-product-compliance
Lightning Source LLC
Chambersburg PA
CBHW062023220426
43662CB00010B/1450